Culture, Health and Development in South Asia

This book carries a timely intervention into biomedical discourses about arsenicosis, billed as a long-standing national health disaster in Bangladesh. Relying on ethnographic work the author privileges patients' perspectives by documenting how the biomedical reality of arsenicosis has been vernacularized as *ghaa* in practice. The turn to alternative healing to manage *ghaa* suggests strongly both the therapeutic and cultural limits of biomedicine. The book carries insights about the need for community ownership and engagement in order to imagine sustainable and viable solutions to the problem of arsenic poisoning. I would unhesitatingly recommend this as a 'must read' book for medical anthropology students and scholars as well as health practitioners and policy makers.

Vineeta Sinha, *National University of Singapore, Singapore*

Recently, mass arsenic poisoning of groundwater has emerged as a disastrous public health concern in Bangladesh. Apart from hundreds of deaths that have already been reported, 85 million people are estimated to be at high risk of developing deadly arsenicosis symptoms. The severity and extent of arsenicosis have obliged the government of Bangladesh to declare it the "worst national disaster" the country has ever faced, and further to be deemed a "state of emergency." To fight this pervasive public health disaster, the Bangladesh government has collaborated with the international and national NGOs to implement development projects to provide arsenic-free water to rural villagers.

Drawing upon ethnographic research in rural Southwestern Bangladesh, this book discusses arsenic contamination and its resultant health impact from a medical anthropological and anthropology of development perspectives. It examines how the actual patients perceive, explain, manage and respond to this catastrophic public health outbreak, and goes on to analyse how such lay perceptions shape health-seeking behaviour of subjects in a medically plural context. To make the issue more holistic, this book further examines mitigation strategies and community participation in these projects.

Challenging approaches to development and development project management, the book is of interest to policy makers, practitioners and academics working in the field of development studies, South Asian studies, medical anthropology, anthropology and sociology of development.

M. Saiful Islam is an anthropologist and Associate Professor of Development Studies at the University of Dhaka, Bangladesh. His research interests include medical anthropology; cultural dimensions of health and illness; health, environment, and sustainable development. He is the author of *Pursuing alternative development: Indigenous people, ethnic organization and agency* (Palgrave Macmillan, 2015).

Routledge Contemporary South Asia Series

1. **Pakistan**
   Social and cultural transformations in a Muslim nation
   Mohammad A. Qadeer

2. **Labor, Democratization and Development in India and Pakistan**
   Christopher Candland

3. **China–India Relations**
   Contemporary dynamics
   Amardeep Athwal

4. **Madrasas in South Asia**
   Teaching terror?
   Jamal Malik

5. **Labor, Globalization and the State**
   Workers, women and migrants confront neoliberalism
   Edited by Debdas Banerjee and Michael Goldfield

6. **Indian Literature and Popular Cinema**
   Recasting classics
   Edited by Heidi R.M. Pauwels

7. **Islamist Militancy in Bangladesh**
   A complex web
   Ali Riaz

8. **Regionalism in South Asia**
   Negotiating cooperation, institutional structures
   Kishore C. Dash

9. **Federalism, Nationalism and Development**
   India and the Punjab economy
   Pritam Singh

10. **Human Development and Social Power**
    Perspectives from South Asia
    Ananya Mukherjee Reed

11. **The South Asian Diaspora**
    Transnational networks and changing identities
    Edited by Rajesh Rai and Peter Reeves

12. **Pakistan–Japan Relations**
    Continuity and change in economic relations and security interests
    Ahmad Rashid Malik

13. **Himalayan Frontiers of India**
    Historical, geo-political and strategic perspectives
    K. Warikoo

14. **India's Open-Economy Policy**
    Globalism, rivalry, continuity
    Jalal Alamgir

15 **The Separatist Conflict in Sri Lanka**
Terrorism, ethnicity, political economy
Asoka Bandarage

16 **India's Energy Security**
Edited by Ligia Noronha and Anant Sudarshan

17 **Globalization and the Middle Classes in India**
The social and cultural impact of neoliberal reforms
Ruchira Ganguly-Scrase and Timothy J. Scrase

18 **Water Policy Processes in India**
Discourses of power and resistance
Vandana Asthana

19 **Minority Governments in India**
The puzzle of elusive majorities
Csaba Nikolenyi

20 **The Maoist Insurgency in Nepal**
Revolution in the twenty-first century
Edited by Mahendra Lawoti and Anup K. Pahari

21 **Global Capital and Peripheral Labour**
The history and political economy of plantation workers in India
K. Ravi Raman

22 **Maoism in India**
Reincarnation of ultra-left wing extremism in the twenty-first century
Bidyut Chakrabarty and Rajat Kujur

23 **Economic and Human Development in Contemporary India**
Cronyism and fragility
Debdas Banerjee

24 **Culture and the Environment in the Himalaya**
Arjun Guneratne

25 **The Rise of Ethnic Politics in Nepal**
Democracy in the margins
Susan I. Hangen

26 **The Multiplex in India**
A cultural economy of urban leisure
Adrian Athique and Douglas Hill

27 **Tsunami Recovery in Sri Lanka**
Ethnic and regional dimensions
Dennis B. McGilvray and Michele R. Gamburd

28 **Development, Democracy and the State**
Critiquing the Kerala model of development
K. Ravi Raman

29 **Mohajir Militancy in Pakistan**
Violence and transformation in the Karachi conflict
Nichola Khan

30 **Nationbuilding, Gender and War Crimes in South Asia**
Bina D'Costa

31 **The State in India after Liberalization**
Interdisciplinary perspectives
Edited by Akhil Gupta and K. Sivaramakrishnan

32 **National Identities in Pakistan**
The 1971 war in contemporary Pakistani fiction
Cara Cilano

33 **Political Islam and Governance in Bangladesh**
Edited by Ali Riaz and C. Christine Fair

34 **Bengali Cinema**
'An other nation'
Sharmistha Gooptu

35 **NGOs in India**
The challenges of women's empowerment and accountability
Patrick Kilby

36 **The Labour Movement in the Global South**
Trade unions in Sri Lanka
S. Janaka Biyanwila

37 **Building Bangalore**
Architecture and urban transformation in India's Silicon Valley
John C. Stallmeyer

38 **Conflict and Peacebuilding in Sri Lanka**
Caught in the peace trap?
Edited by Jonathan Goodhand, Jonathan Spencer and Benedict Korf

39 **Microcredit and Women's Empowerment**
A case study of Bangladesh
Amunui Faraizi, Jim McAllister and Taskinur Rahman

40 **South Asia in the New World Order**
The role of regional cooperation
Shahid Javed Burki

41 **Explaining Pakistan's Foreign Policy**
Escaping India
Aparna Pande

42 **Development-induced Displacement, Rehabilitation and Resettlement in India**
Current issues and challenges
Edited by Sakarama Somayaji and Smrithi Talwar

43 **The Politics of Belonging in India**
Becoming Adivasi
Edited by Daniel J. Rycroft and Sangeeta Dasgupta

44 **Re-Orientalism and South Asian Identity Politics**
The oriental Other within
Edited by Lisa Lau and Ana Cristina Mendes

45 **Islamic Revival in Nepal**
Religion and a new nation
Megan Adamson Sijapati

46 **Education and Inequality in India**
A classroom view
Manabi Majumdar and Jos Mooij

47 **The Culturalization of Caste in India**
Identity and inequality in a multicultural age
Balmurli Natrajan

48 **Corporate Social Responsibility in India**
Bidyut Chakrabarty

49 **Pakistan's Stability Paradox**
Domestic, regional and international dimensions
Edited by Ashutosh Misra and Michael E. Clarke

50 **Transforming Urban Water Supplies in India**
The role of reform and partnerships in globalization
Govind Gopakumar

51 **South Asian Security**
Twenty-first century discourse
Sagarika Dutt and Alok Bansal

52 **Non-discrimination and Equality in India**
Contesting boundaries of social justice
Vidhu Verma

53 **Being Middle-class in India**
A way of life
Henrike Donner

54 **Kashmir's Right to Secede**
A critical examination of contemporary theories of secession
Matthew J. Webb

55 **Bollywood Travels**
Culture, diaspora and border crossings in popular Hindi cinema
Rajinder Dudrah

56 **Nation, Territory, and Globalization in Pakistan**
Traversing the margins
Chad Haines

57 **The Politics of Ethnicity in Pakistan**
The Baloch, Sindhi and Mohajir ethnic movements
Farhan Hanif Siddiqi

58 **Nationalism and Ethnic Conflict**
Identities and mobilization after 1990
Edited by Mahendra Lawoti and Susan Hangen

59 **Islam and Higher Education**
Concepts, challenges and opportunities
Marodsilton Muborakshoeva

60 **Religious Freedom in India**
Sovereignty and (anti) conversion
Goldie Osuri

61 **Everyday Ethnicity in Sri Lanka**
Up-country Tamil identity politics
Daniel Bass

62 **Ritual and Recovery in Post-Conflict Sri Lanka**
Eloquent bodies
Jane Derges

63 **Bollywood and Globalisation**
The global power of popular Hindi cinema
Edited by David J. Schaefer and Kavita Karan

64 **Regional Economic Integration in South Asia**
Trapped in conflict?
Amita Batra

65 **Architecture and Nationalism in Sri Lanka**
The trouser under the cloth
Anoma Pieris

66 **Civil Society and Democratization in India**
Institutions, ideologies and interests
Sarbeswar Sahoo

67 **Contemporary Pakistani Fiction in English**
Idea, nation, state
Cara N. Cilano

68 **Transitional Justice in South Asia**
A study of Afghanistan and Nepal
Tazreena Sajjad

69 **Displacement and Resettlement in India**
The human cost of development
Hari Mohan Mathur

70 **Water, Democracy and Neoliberalism in India**
The power to reform
Vicky Walters

71 **Capitalist Development in India's Informal Economy**
Elisabetta Basile

72 **Nation, Constitutionalism and Buddhism in Sri Lanka**
Roshan de Silva Wijeyeratne

73 **Counterinsurgency, Democracy, and the Politics of Identity in India**
From warfare to welfare?
Mona Bhan

74 **Enterprise Culture in Neoliberal India**
Studies in youth, class, work and media
Edited by Nandini Gooptu

75 **The Politics of Economic Restructuring in India**
Economic governance and state spatial rescaling
Loraine Kennedy

76 **The Other in South Asian Religion, Literature and Film**
Perspectives on Otherism and Otherness
Edited by Diana Dimitrova

77 **Being Bengali**
At home and in the world
Edited by Mridula Nath Chakraborty

78 **The Political Economy of Ethnic Conflict in Sri Lanka**
Nikolaos Biziouras

79 **Indian Arranged Marriages**
A social psychological perspective
Tulika Jaiswal

80 **Writing the City in British Asian Diasporas**
Edited by Seán McLoughlin, William Gould, Ananya Jahanara Kabir and Emma Tomalin

81 **Post-9/11 Espionage Fiction in the US and Pakistan**
Spies and 'terrorists'
Cara Cilano

82 **Left Radicalism in India**
Bidyut Chakrabarty

83 **"Nation-State" and Minority Rights in India**
Comparative perspectives on Muslim and Sikh identities
Tanweer Fazal

84 **Pakistan's Nuclear Policy**
A minimum credible deterrence
Zafar Khan

85 **Imagining Muslims in South Asia and the Diaspora**
Secularism, religion, representations
Claire Chambers and Caroline Herbert

86 **Indian Foreign Policy in Transition**
Relations with South Asia
Arijit Mazumdar

87 **Corporate Social Responsibility and Development in Pakistan**
Nadeem Malik

88 **Indian Capitalism in Development**
Barbara Harriss-White and Judith Heyer

89 **Bangladesh Cinema and National Identity**
In search of the modern?
Zakir Hossain Raju

90 **Suicide in Sri Lanka**
The anthropology of an epidemic
Tom Widger

91 **Epigraphy and Islamic Culture**
Inscriptions of the Early Muslim Rulers of Bengal (1205–1494)
Mohammad Yusuf Siddiq

92 **Reshaping City Governance**
London, Mumbai, Kolkata, Hyderabad
Nirmala Rao

93 **The Indian Partition in Literature and Films**
History, politics, and aesthetics
Rini Bhattacharya Mehta and Debali Mookerjea-Leonard

94 **Development, Poverty and Power in Pakistan**
The impact of state and donor interventions on farmers
Syed Mohammad Ali

95 **Ethnic Subnationalist Insurgencies in South Asia**
Identities, interests and challenges to state authority
Edited by Jugdep S. Chima

96 **International Migration and Development in South Asia**
Edited by Md Mizanur Rahman and Tan Tai Yong

97 **Twenty-first Century Bollywood**
Ajay Gehlawat

98 **Political Economy of Development in India**
Indigeneity in transition in the state of Kerala
Darley Kjosavik and Nadarajah Shanmugaratnam

99 **State and Nation-Building in Pakistan**
Beyond Islam and security
Edited by Roger D. Long, Gurharpal Singh, Yunas Samad, and Ian Talbot

100 **Subaltern Movements in India**
Gendered geographies of struggle against neoliberal development
Manisha Desai

101 **Islamic Banking in Pakistan**
Shariah-compliant finance and the quest to make Pakistan more Islamic
Feisal Khan

102 **The Bengal Diaspora**
Rethinking Muslim migration
Claire Alexander, Joya Chatterji, and Annu Jalais

103 **Mobilizing Religion and Gender in India**
The role of activism
Nandini Deo

104 **Social Movements and the Indian Diaspora**
Movindri Reddy

105 **Religion and Modernity in the Himalaya**
Edited by Megan Adamson Sijapati and Jessica Vantine Birkenholtz

106 **Devotional Islam in Contemporary South Asia**
Shrines, journeys and wanderers
Edited by Michel Boivin and Rémy Delage

107 **Women and Resistance in Contemporary Bengali Cinema**
A freedom incomplete
Srimati Mukherjee

108 **Islamic NGOs in Bangladesh**
Development, piety and neoliberal governmentality
Mohammad Musfequs Salehin

109 **Ethics in Governance in India**
Bidyut Chakrabarty

110 **Popular Hindi Cinema**
Aesthetic formations of the seen and unseen
Ronie Parciack

111 **Activist Documentary Film in Pakistan**
The emergence of a cinema of accountability
Rahat Imran

112 **Culture, Health and Development in South Asia**
Arsenic poisoning in Bangladesh
M. Saiful Islam

113 **India's Approach to Development Cooperation**
Edited by Sachin Chaturvedi and Anthea Mulakala

114 **Education and Society in Bhutan**
Tradition and modernisation
Chelsea M. Robles

Culture, Health and Development in South Asia
Arsenic poisoning in Bangladesh

M. Saiful Islam

LONDON AND NEW YORK

First published 2016
by Routledge
2 Park Square, Milton Park, Abingdon, Oxon OX14 4RN

and by Routledge
711 Third Avenue, New York, NY 10017

Routledge is an imprint of the Taylor & Francis Group, an informa business

© 2016 M. Saiful Islam

The right of M. Saiful Islam to be identified as author of this work has been asserted by him in accordance with sections 77 and 78 of the Copyright, Designs and Patents Act 1988.

All rights reserved. No part of this book may be reprinted or reproduced or utilised in any form or by any electronic, mechanical, or other means, now known or hereafter invented, including photocopying and recording, or in any information storage or retrieval system, without permission in writing from the publishers.

Trademark notice: Product or corporate names may be trademarks or registered trademarks, and are used only for identification and explanation without intent to infringe.

British Library Cataloguing in Publication Data
A catalogue record for this book is available from the British Library

Library of Congress Cataloging-in-Publication Data
Names: Islam, M. Saiful (Anthropologist), editor.
Title: Culture, health and development in South Asia : arsenic poisoning in Bangladesh / [edited by] M. Saiful Islam.
Other titles: Routledge contemporary South Asia series ; 112.
Description: Abingdon, Oxon ; New York, NY : Routledge, 2015. | Series: Routledge contemporary South Asia series ; 112 | Includes bibliographical references and index.
Identifiers: LCCN 2015044465 | ISBN 9781138654082 (hardback) | ISBN 9781315623436 (ebook)
Subjects: MESH: Arsenic Poisoning—ethnology—Bangladesh. | Arsenic Poisoning—prevention & control—Bangladesh.
Classification: LCC RA1231.A7 | NLM QV 294 | DDC 615.9/25715095492—dc23
LC record available at http://lccn.loc.gov/2015044465

ISBN: 978-1-138-65408-2 (hbk)
ISBN: 978-1-315-62343-6 (ebk)

Typeset in Times New Roman
by Apex CoVantage, LLC

Contents

	List of figures	xii
	List of tables	xiii
	Acknowledgements	xiv
	List of abbreviations	xvi
1	Introduction: the paradise poisoned	1
2	Arsenic poisoning: culture, health and development perspectives	14
3	Arsenic poisoning in Bangladesh: causes, health impacts and health care services	28
4	*Ghaa*: the social construction of arsenicosis	42
5	Arsenicosis as *ghaa* and health-seeking behaviour	67
6	Arsenic mitigation strategies: why do they fail?	94
7	Conclusion: the primacy of culture in health and development	121
	Bibliography	129
	Index	143

Figures

1.1	Field site in southwestern Bangladesh	6
6.1	BAMWSP project structure, stakeholders and their responsibilities	98
6.2	Abandoned dug-well	105
6.3	Unused pond-sand filter	108
6.4	Rejected water treatment plant	112

Tables

3.1 Global occurrences of arsenic poisoning   29
4.1 Local terms used to explain *ghaa*   57
6.1 Financing BAMWSP   96
6.2 The World Bank's evaluation of the project   101

Acknowledgements

The course of my PhD study at the National University of Singapore (NUS) and the fieldwork in Bangladesh that have culminated in this book have left me indebted to many individuals and organizations. First and foremost, I wish to extend my sincere thanks to the villagers of Rupnogor, who accepted and accommodated me and willingly shared their insights and experiences of their everyday lives. Without them, this study would not have been possible. Although I hesitate to name any individuals for fear of overlooking others, I must convey my special thanks to Mr. Altaf Hossain and his family members, who considered me their "brother" and introduced me to the community during the early days of my fieldwork. My fieldwork in this village may not have been possible without their help. Thanks are also due to Mr. Abdur Rouf, the headmaster of the village high school, who shared invaluable information with me. I would also like to convey my special gratitude to the arsenicosis patients, their family members, the village doctor, alternative healers and many other villagers who graciously sacrificed their time to share information with me. This research would only be successful if it is able to be of some help to these individuals who suffer from deadly arsenicosis, for which there is no cure.

I express my special thanks to officials in many organizations who provided invaluable information about arsenicosis and various development initiatives. I am thankful to the officials of the Bangladesh Arsenic Mitigation Water Supply Project, the Department of Public Health Engineering, the World Bank–Dhaka office, the UNICEF–Dhaka office and GlaxoSmithKline.

At NUS, I am especially indebted to Dr. Vineeta Sinha, Professor of Sociology and head of the South Asian Studies Program, who motivated me to think critically and to study arsenicosis anthropologically. This book would not have been in its present shape without her constant assistance, reassurance, careful reading of the earlier version of the manuscript and invaluable comments on it. I would like to honour the memory of Dr. Ananda Rajah, who passed away precipitously and unexpectedly, leaving the whole university in mourning. His comments on earlier version of this manuscript were immensely valuable. I would also like to thank Dr. Rachel Safman for her constructive comments on this manuscript. I am thankful to NUS for awarding me a Research Scholarship, a President's Graduate Fellowship and the Graduate Research Support Scheme, all of which enabled me to live in Singapore, conduct research in Bangladesh and prepare this manuscript.

I am also grateful to my friends in NUS who have sustained me throughout. I am happy to have friends like Seuty Sabur, Siddiqur Rahman, Sarada Prasanna Das, Sojin Shin, Masud Parvez Rana, Kelvin Low, Reiko Yamagishi, Yang Chengsheng, Cheong Kah Meng, Chen Baogang, Thomas Barker, Yang Wei and many others. Special thanks go out to Sarbeswar Sahoo, Lou Antolihao and Sim Hee Juat for their time, intellectual debate, "friendly hostility", lunch, dinner and what not.

In Bangladesh, I owe special thanks to the Department of Development Studies, University of Dhaka for granting me study leave, which allowed me to go abroad and conduct this study. I thank Shafiul Hassan Sumon for helping me out in drawing necessary maps for this study. Dr. A.K.M. Ahsan Ullah, Associate Professor and Deputy Dean at the Faculty of Arts and Social Sciences, University Brunei Darussalam (UBD), has been particularly insistent in motivating me to complete this manuscript. Inspiration from him is invaluable. At Routledge, I sincerely thank Dorothea Schaefter and Jillian Morrison for their outstanding support and utmost professionalism in making this book project successful. It was also a wonderful experience working with Chris Mathews and his team at Apex CoVantage who provided excellent support in producing this book.

My family has always been a source of my inspiration. I thank my parents, who not only taught me to dream, but also provided everything they could afford to make my dream possible. Despite weathering a financial crisis, they continued to support my tertiary education, and it is because of them that I am where I am today. My wife, Nila, has experienced a lot of difficulty with our two young kids, Adrita and Anisha. She took care of them to make me free so that I could concentrate on my manuscript. No word would suffice to express my thanks to her. My very young children missed their "baba" as I could not attend to them the way they wanted me to do. It is because of their sacrifices that I have been able to complete this book project. It is with deep affection that I dedicate this book to Nila, Adrita and Anisha.

Abbreviations

AAM	Association for Arsenic Mitigation
ASA	Association for Social Advancement
BAMWSP	Bangladesh Arsenic Mitigation Water Supply Project
BFD	Blackfoot Disease
BGS	British Geological Survey
BRAC	Bangladesh Rural Advancement Committee
CAP	Community Action Plan
CBO	Community-based organization
DCH	Dhaka Community Hospital
DFID	Department for International Development
DMSA	Dimercaptosuccinic acid
DPHE	Department of Public Health Engineering
EHS	Essential Healthcare Service
FWA	Female Welfare Assistant
GoB	Government of Bangladesh
GSK	GlaxoSmithKline
HA	Health assistants
IMF	International Monetary Fund
LGI	Local government institution
MATS	Medical Assistant Training School
MOU	Memorandum of Understanding
NAMIC	National Arsenic Mitigation Information Centre
NDP	National Drug Policy
NGO	Non-governmental organization
PC	*Palli-chikitshok*
PHC	Primary health care
SDC	Swiss Development Corporation
SOES	School of Environmental Studies
TBA	Traditional Birth Attendant
UHC	Upazilla Health Complex
UHFWC	Union Health and Family Welfare Center
UHO	Upazilla Health Officer
UNDP	United Nations Development Programme

UNICEF	United Nations Children's Fund
UP	*Union Parishad*
USAID	United States Agency for International Development
USEPA	United States Environmental Protection Agency
WAMWUG	Ward Arsenic Mitigation Water User's Group
WB	The World Bank
WHO	World Health Organization

1 Introduction
The paradise poisoned

Introduction

In November 1998, the *New York Times* reported that a "young mother, Pinjira Begum, found out that her own slow dying was nothing unusual, that tens of thousands of Bangladeshi villagers are suffering the same ghastly decay, their skin spotted like spoiled fruit and warts and sores covering their hands and feet" (cited in Cullen 2008: 354; Meharg 2005: 2). Pinjira Begum, a mother of three, had been abandoned by her husband due to arsenicosis, which she died from the following year. Her dying wish was: "please save my three children from the deadly arsenic" (Meharg 2005: 2). Pinjira Begum was one of the earliest known victims of arsenic poisoning in Bangladesh. Among many other health hazards, the levels of arsenic in the groundwater that Bangladesh is currently exposed to have led the poisoning to be declared the "worst national disaster Bangladesh has ever faced" and further deemed a "state of emergency". The mass poisoning of groundwater by arsenic is considered to be the "largest mass poisoning of a population in history" (Meharg 2005: 3; Smith, Lingas, and Rahman 2000: 1093). In terms of the scale of exposure to the population and the arsenic concentration levels in the groundwater, Bangladesh is considered to be among the most seriously contaminated countries in the world. The groundwater of fifty-nine (out of a total of sixty-four) districts in Bangladesh is tainted with high concentrations of arsenic (World Bank 2007). Apart from thousands of deaths having already been reported, about 85 million people are estimated to be at risk of developing arsenicosis symptoms, including symmetric hyperkeratosis of the palms and soles, skin cancer, cancer of the kidneys and lungs and diseases of the blood vessels (Meharg 2005).

To fight this pervasive public health disaster, the GoB has collaborated with the World Bank, WHO, UNICEF, the SDC and various other international and national NGOs, which have invested millions of dollars in providing arsenic-free water to rural villagers. A majority of these projects, however, are rejected by the communities in which they are implemented and have therefore "failed". These "failures", the continuing large scale of the problem and the tragedy of arsenicosis in Bangladesh have inspired the focus of this research and writing this book. This book is profoundly led by the question of why individuals who are suffering from deadly arsenicosis reject options that might provide them with arsenic-free water and save them from this fatal disease. It further examines why, despite the existence of high-profile, interventional, government-led initiatives, there is so little "success" in arsenic mitigation strategies in Bangladesh. Why do arsenic mitigation strategies fail? Why do arsenicosis patients seek alternative healing services far more readily than biomedical options that are conveniently available?

In an effort to address these questions from an anthropological point of view, it has been explored how different social actors, including biomedical doctors, development experts and villagers, understand the issue of arsenicosis. The focus is on how a rural community in southwestern Bangladesh perceives, experiences and responds to this disease, which has been medically and scientifically labeled as arsenicosis. It is important to examine the general health and illness beliefs and practices in rural Bangladesh and to observe how arsenicosis is understood and explained within such a framework. In addition, it is significant to explore how such popular understandings of arsenicosis depart from biomedical and official explanations, and to consider the general implications of such a departure on the health-seeking behaviour of subjects and their participation in mitigation strategies. This approach to the analysis of arsenicosis may help solve the puzzle of why highly essential arsenic mitigation strategies fail in rural Bangladesh. At this point, it may be argued that these mitigation strategies failed primarily because of differential and contradictory understandings of arsenicosis by different social actors involved in the process.

Before discussing this issue further, it is helpful to explicate a general understanding of the magnitude of arsenic poisoning in Bangladesh. This involves an examination of the patterns and histories of domestic water use in rural Bangladesh.

The tubewell revolution, a water miracle and arsenic poisoning

In the past, rural Bangladeshis had to depend on surface water from ponds, rivers and dug-wells for their household water consumption and irrigation purposes. These water sources, however, were highly contaminated with microorganisms and bacteria that cause various waterborne diseases, such as diarrhoea, cholera and other gastrointestinal problems, leading to very high infant and child mortality rates (Black and Talbot 2005; Meharg 2005; Ravenscroft, Brammer, and Richards 2009). During the 1970s, about 2.5 million people died every year due to the outbreak of such diseases (Meharg 2005: 6). Following independence in 1971, the GoB urged the international community to assist in fighting these waterborne epidemics. This call was met instantaneously with an international response. UNICEF came forward with a proposal to utilize groundwater, which was perceived to be free of contaminants. A specially designed hand-pump with a 1.5-inch PVC pipe was drilled into the ground to a depth of about 8–10 meters to tap into the groundwater. Rural communities liked that system, became accustomed to it, and by the year 2000, nearly 11 million tubewells had been drilled across rural Bangladesh (Cullen 2008: 350). The tubewell revolution created a "water miracle" by providing most rural households with the option of securing safe water. Owning a tubewell became a status symbol in rural Bangladesh, and the age-old tradition of using water from dug-wells and ponds was abandoned (Cullen 2008: 350). By 1997, UNICEF declared that it had surpassed its target of providing 80 percent of rural populations with access to safe drinking water (Smith, Lingas, and Rahman 2000: 1094).

The impact of this water miracle was dramatic, as there was a sharp reduction in waterborne diseases, which was reflected in a reduced infant mortality rate, from 151 per thousand in 1960 to 83 per thousand in 1996 (UNICEF 2006). The child mortality rate (among those under 5 years old) due to waterborne diseases also dropped, from 247 per thousand to 112 per thousand (Meharg 2005). Despite these successes, unfortunately and ironically, the water that once saved millions of lives now appears to be a major killer, since groundwater has been found to be contaminated with high concentrations of arsenic. Almost unknowingly, for at least four decades, the Bangladeshis have been exposed to high arsenic toxicity levels by drinking arsenic-contaminated groundwater. Neither the BGS nor UNICEF, which tested the water quality and promoted groundwater for mass consumption in rural Bangladesh, had paid any attention to the fact that water should be tested for arsenic contamination, simply because there was no recognition that groundwater could be contaminated by arsenic. This gross inattention to these details has placed the lives of millions of people under a serious health threat due to the emergence of arsenicosis.

Although arsenic contamination was first detected in Bangladesh in 1993, no initiative was taken at first to survey the extent of the problem. It was Dipankar Chakraborti, along with a team from DCH, who surveyed 294 tubewells in the Chapai Nawabgonj district of northeastern Bangladesh and found that 29 percent of the water samples had high concentrations of arsenic (Meharg 2005: 16). The same team conducted another survey in the Jessore district of southwestern Bangladesh and found that 90 percent of tubewells there contained arsenic at higher than permissible levels (Biswas et al. 1998). After examining 7,364 individuals, Chakraborti and his colleagues found that one-third of them suffered from arsenic-related skin lesions (Meharg 2005: 17). In 1998, the first extensive water survey was carried out by the BGS and Mott MacDonald Ltd. UK, under the project of Groundwater Studies for Arsenic Contamination in Bangladesh, which was financed by the Department for International Development, UK. After examining about 2,000 water samples from forty-one districts, 35 percent of the tubewells were found to contain arsenic beyond permissible levels (BGS 1999: 160).

The largest project that has been conducted to explore arsenic contamination in Bangladesh is the Bangladesh Arsenic Mitigation Water Supply Project, which was a US$44.4 million project jointly financed by the World Bank, SDC and the GoB. This project examined water samples from 3.04 million tubewells across Bangladesh and found that 29.19 percent of them were highly contaminated by arsenic (World Bank 2007). A total of 29,500 patients with arsenic-related skin lesions were identified, and about 35 million people were found to be exposed to high arsenic toxicity levels, to the extent that they might gradually develop arsenicosis symptoms in the near future. It is expected that if exposure to arsenic through drinking water continues, about 85 million people will be at risk, and the mortality rates due to arsenic poisoning are expected to increase substantially in the near future (Ahmad, Goldar, and Misra 2005; Paul 2004; World Bank 2007). Given the magnitude of the problem, it has been stated that casualties of arsenic contamination may exceed those of the gas poisoning in Bhopal, India in 1984, and Chernobyl, Ukraine in 1986 (Smith, Lingas, and Rahman 2000: 1093). The USEPA has predicted that one out of every 100 individuals in Bangladesh will develop bladder or lung cancer, resulting in an epidemic of cancer, in the next ten years (Meharg 2005: 17).

These staggering statistics reveal the extent of the crisis facing Bangladeshis in accessing safe drinking water. This human tragedy goes beyond issues of public health, and it is literally a matter of life and death for millions of ordinary Bangladeshis. Despite such a severe impending public health disaster, medical anthropological research in recent years has paid very cursory attention to the problem of arsenic contamination. We do not have enough information about how people, who are suffering from arsenicosis, make sense of this disease and how they live with and respond to this serious health crisis. Given the paucity of anthropological research in this area, this book examines how a lay community in rural southwestern Bangladesh understands, experiences and responds to arsenicosis. It also documents the various mitigation strategies that are offered by the state and national and international organizations as solutions to the problem of arsenicosis. Drawing upon primary ethnographic data, this book approaches arsenicosis as an illness and attempts to understand it within the general health and illness beliefs and practices of a rural community in southwestern Bangladesh.

In order to achieve a holistic understanding of arsenicosis and its implications, three broad areas have been identified for examination: (1) popular perceptions of arsenicosis, (2) health-seeking behaviour of arsenicosis patients and (3) community participation in arsenic mitigation strategies. A scrutiny of popular beliefs that are held, practices, social interactions and participation in mitigation strategies would generate significant empirical knowledge about how individuals on the ground understand and act upon arsenicosis. This book begins with the assumption that a complete narrative of arsenicosis cannot be understood without taking into account the presence of multiple social actors: arsenicosis patients, biomedical and alternative health service providers, the state and development agencies that plan mitigation strategies. Each of these social actors constructs different realities of arsenicosis. It is crucial to establish the particular labels, vocabularies, local taxonomies, etiologies and symptoms that each of those actors use to explain this illness. This has specifically led to the question of how arsenicosis, explained medically as a disease and denoted through the use of an English term, makes sense to a predominantly Bengali-speaking local community in rural Bangladesh. How is arsenicosis vernacularized in this local context? How do popular perceptions of arsenicosis depart from the biomedical constructions of it, which are adapted in official and developmental discourses? Responses to these questions via primary ethnographic data enable us to address another field of enquiry: the implications of such popular understandings of arsenicosis on health-seeking behaviour of subjects and their participation in mitigation efforts offered by the state and development organizations.

Another very crucial aspect of this study is to examine how arsenicosis patients make decisions and seek health care services within a plural medical context in rural Bangladesh. Why do patients extensively utilize alternative healing services rather than biomedicine, which is readily available to them? To answer this question, this book explores the therapeutic management of arsenicosis with particular reference to the ways in which this illness is understood, categorized and treated. Starting from rudimentary home-based treatment, this book delineates the other formal and informal medical systems utilized by patients in a medically plural rural Bangladesh. The focus is predominantly on the link between popular understandings of arsenicosis and the ways in which these shape health-seeking behaviour of the affected individuals. While exploring a comprehensive and in-depth understanding of health-seeking processes, this book heavily draws upon the perspectives of the affected individuals, their family members and health service providers. The vivid ethnographic narratives presented here enable readers to appreciate the syncretic nature of different medical systems in rural Bangladesh, which do not just coexist but are simultaneously used, evaluated and appreciated by actual users.

This study on arsenicosis would be incomplete without understanding the interactions between development organizations, their mitigation efforts and community participation. A critical question to examine is: why do villagers who are suffering from deadly arsenicosis reject mitigation options that might provide them with arsenic-safe water and could save them from this illness? Why do high-profile arsenic-safe water supply projects fail in rural Bangladesh? In addressing these queries, this book focuses on two development schemes, the BAMWSP water-supply and GSK water-treatment projects, which were aimed at providing arsenic-safe water to the community but have failed on all counts. A critical examination needs to be activated to evaluate how development organizations perceive the problem of arsenicosis and whether priorities and expectations of the villagers are reflected in these mitigation strategies. This book does not take "development" and its processes for granted; rather, it problematizes them, both conceptually and practically. Drawing on post-structuralist critique of development, particularly from the works of Escobar (1991, 1995) and Ferguson (1990), it is argued that development is inevitably a political and hegemonic effort that mostly ends up in failure and unintended consequences. By examining these arsenic mitigation water supply projects, this book reinforces the urgency that local cultural, political and ecological contexts must be taken into consideration for development planning, which are often neglected by policy planners, leading well-intentioned development projects into failure.

Although arsenicosis poses a major public health threat in Bangladesh, no systematic anthropological study has thus far been conducted on this issue. Most studies are on geological and water quality issues. Medical anthropological research on arsenicosis from the perspective of patients is inadequate. No substantial initiative has been taken up to document the perceptions, experiences and health-seeking behaviour of arsenicosis patients. This book thus attempts to address this dearth of knowledge and produce ethnographic narratives about the sociocultural aspects of arsenicosis that would be helpful for the government, NGOs, policy planners, development practitioners and others who are interested in understanding arsenic poisoning from health and development perspectives. From a practical point of view, the findings of this study would help further conceptualize the problem of arsenicosis in a way that would foster better health care services and sustainable development strategies for rural Bangladeshis. The overt objective of this book is not just to generate knowledge for its own sake but to provide feedback into mitigation strategies that would alleviate the appalling problem of arsenic poisoning.

Research methodology: collecting ethnographic data

This book is the outcome of anthropological fieldwork conducted in southwestern Bangladesh. Anthropological fieldwork requires the researcher to be in the study locale for a longer period of time to ensure establishment of adequate rapport to facilitate qualitative data collection. For this study, fieldwork was conducted at a village named Rupnogor[1] under Kalaroa Upazilla[2] of Satkhira District[3] (see Figure 1.1). The fieldwork was conducted in two phases, of which the first phase was during July 2007 and June 2008, followed by the second-phase visit in May 2009. Selecting an appropriate field site for this study was a significant methodological consideration. Since this research is about arsenic poisoning and its resultant health and development impacts, Rupnogor was found to be the most suitable field site for this research for a number of reasons. Firstly, it was one of the areas in Bangladesh worst affected by arsenic poisoning, with more than 99 percent of

Figure 1.1 Field site in southwestern Bangladesh

tubewells contaminated with high concentrations of arsenic (NAMIC 2006). A number of arsenicosis patients had been identified in this village, including one who died from this disease. Secondly, due to its geographical proximity to Kalaroa Upazilla headquarters, villagers of Rupnogor were expected to have access to plural medical systems, both in the village and in the Upazilla headquarters, which would enable me to examine health-seeking behaviour of arsenicosis patients from a holistic perspective. Thirdly, and most importantly, since this village was found to be a "hotbed" of arsenic poisoning, a number of state agencies, NGOs and international organizations were actively involved in fighting this calamity. Thus, this village was found to be well linked with the wider political economy, which allowed me to examine how villagers responded to it.

Although this ethnographic research was conducted in a village, the term "village" is found to be problematic. On the one hand, the village is officially identified through specific physical and geographical boundaries, whereas, in practice, these boundaries are often fluid rather than absolute. Because of the process of modernization and globalization, the village is no longer an isolated entity; rather, it is connected to the wider socio-economy and politics (Clammer 1984; Islam 2014; Palriwala 2005). This is especially evident in Rupnogor, where for the sake of seeking health care services and many other purposes, villagers routinely move back and forth between villages, towns and abroad. Through various development organizations and their projects, the village is well-connected with the wider political economy that invests thousands of dollars for implementing different projects. Thus the boundary of a village, as perceived and experienced by villagers, is not merely geographical; rather, it exists through interactions and relationships with the wider society (Palriwala 2005). For this study, the village is considered as a ground of the sociocultural system and an appropriate place to observe social actors by tracing their activities and networks (Barth 1993).

Unlike other villages in Bangladesh, Rupnogor is a relatively big village, with 551 households and the population is approximately 2,656 (4.8 people per household) at the time of this study. Most are nuclear households comprising two generations, husband and wife, with or without their unmarried children. Some households comprise three generations, since it is the cultural norm for the elder son to take care of his older parents. Muslims are the majority of this village, with about 35 Hindu households who live in one hamlet. Although the primary occupation of the majority of the villagers is agriculture, household income is often supplemented by many other economic tasks, including but not limited to running small shops in the village market, rearing poultry, working on agricultural lands as manual labourers and serving full time as school teachers, official clerks and NGO workers. Immense variations have been observed in income distribution among the villagers, as some well-off families had monthly incomes that far exceeded the average, while numerous other households were landless and lived a marginal existence.

Everyday activities of the villagers are centered around the village bazaar, which is known as Rupnogor bazaar. A wide range of retail shops provide goods which are necessary for everyday life. There are pharmacies, tea stalls, bicycle repair shops, a chamber of a homeopathic doctor and grocery shops in this village marketplace. The village doctor owns the allopathic pharmacy, which carries a wide range of medicines, from analgesics to antibiotics, on its shelves. This bazaar, however, is not only a place for providing goods for everyday necessities, but also a place for social interaction. Every afternoon, many villagers meet in the bazaar to gossip, exchange news and play football in the field. Any description of Rupnogor village would be incomplete without referring to its proximity to Kalaroa, the Upazilla headquarters, which is the nearest town from the village, just 5 kilometers away. Given the easy paved roads with Kalaroa, movement between the village and the Upazilla headquarters has become quite frequent for the villagers. Kalaroa has become the center of many facilities, including a hospital, colleges, markets and governmental offices. Besides a fifty-bed modern hospital, there are various health practitioners available in the town, including allopathic, homeopathic, Unani and herbal medicines. For their various needs, visiting Kalaroa has become an indispensable part of the everyday life of villagers.

During the initial stages of establishing rapport with the community, the villagers were not cooperative, as expected because of the suspicion that I might be an NGO agent. Such mistaken identities are not uncommon, since many fieldwork narratives have documented that the natives perceived anthropologists as missionaries, government officials, spies, tax collectors, military agents and journalists (Berreman 1972; Du Bois 1986; Forsey 2004; Horowitz 1996; Weidman 1986). In such cases of misconceived identities, anthropologists had to struggle to convince the informants that they were just researchers without any other motives or agendas (Tsuda 1998). As I achieved increased access to villagers, I shared my objectives with them and encouraged them to ask me any questions they had about myself and my research. Villagers used to ask me about how they would benefit from this research. Some others wanted to know how I would benefit from this study. As time passed and I became a familiar face in the village, I was fortunate enough to receive cooperation and assistance from the villagers. I sat at the local tea stall and shared tea with them, watched young people playing football in the afternoon, sat beside the hearth when women were cooking, accompanied them when they were travelling to Upazilla headquarters. Simply sitting beside the men when they fed their cattle allowed me to "break the ice" for informal conversations. Taking their photographs and giving them photos were other effective ways to establish rapport with the respondents. Thus, although I was initially denied entry into the village, they allowed me to take part in their everyday discussions, shared their free time with me and clarified many things relating to health, illness, arsenicosis and development issues. Most informants enthusiastically responded to my request to be interviewed, freely shared their ideas and talked incessantly. I obtained access to many villagers from whom I learnt a great deal about health, illness and arsenicosis issues and who provided the bulk of ethnographic data for this research.

Qualitative research methods have been adopted for collecting data for this study. Since the social construction of arsenicosis entails exploring subtleties and mundane and nuanced activities of everyday life, qualitative methods have been considered useful in flexibly and comprehensively addressing the research questions. A range of techniques such as surveys, participant observation and key informants were employed (Bernard 2002; Ellen 1984; Hammersley and Atkinson 1995; Pelto and Pelto 1978, 1990). Throughout the data collection process, an open-ended or semi-structured interview was preferred to allow respondents to share as much information as possible. Although my explicit aim was to examine arsenicosis, health-seeking behaviour and participation in mitigation strategies, respondents brought up many other issues, such as socio-economic, political, historical and ecological factors. I was open to document such diversities of information. Rather than being preloaded with my own ideas and research questions, I was open to learn what villagers understood, explained and experienced. I do not claim that I was able to grasp the "native's point of view", which is problematic (Geertz 1973; Marcus and Fischer 1986; Marcus 1998). Rather, my ethnographic research is an account of what I selected from what I understood of what my informants told me about being in a particular socio-economic and geopolitical setting (Sperber 1985).

Secondary sources were also an important data bank for this study, which consisted of many official documents (such as health policy and arsenic policy reports), reports from the NGOs, minutes of different NGO meetings, local, national and international newspaper reports, published academic articles and library archives (such as political and medical history of Bengal). These secondary data sources provided background information for making my points in Chapter 3. Additionally, the bulk of my ethnographic data was collected through primary, face-to-face and open-ended interviews, which are presented in Chapters 4, 5 and 6.

Since this research is about arsenicosis patients, their health-seeking behaviour, and participation in mitigation strategies, they were my primary set of informants. Using open-ended interviews, seventeen arsenicosis patients were interviewed. I usually asked them how they had gotten this disease, how this disease was different from other skin diseases and what they did to get rid of it. These set of questions provided me with ample insights into understanding local disease etiologies and the diagnosis and treatment process of arsenicosis. Besides arsenicosis patients, I also interviewed their family members, friends and neighbors to understand their views regarding health and illness in general and arsenicosis in particular. Some neighbors provided information about social stigma and stereotypes against arsenicosis patients, which patients themselves did not disclose. As part of my daily routine observation and informal meeting, I had spoken to many villagers, including but not limited to school teachers, students, farmers, housewives, shopkeepers, mosque imams, senior members of the village, political leaders, businessmen, trishaw pullers and tea-stall owners. I interviewed people in their homestead verandahs, the tea stalls, schools, village markets and playgrounds. During the peak agricultural season, when people were busy planting and harvesting rice and were not available at home most of the daytime, I followed them to their agricultural fields and interviewed them while they were working. This was especially helpful in maximizing my time, and I was careful not to bother respondents in the evening when they were tired and resting after day-long hard work.

Another category of informants I interviewed was health-service providers in both alternative and biomedical sectors. Within the group of alternative healers, I interviewed two village *kobiraj*,[4] one religious *hujur*[5] and two village homeopathic doctors who were actively involved in rendering health care services to arsenicosis patients. While interviewing them, I tried to understand how they perceived, explained and categorized this disease and their particular techniques used to alleviate the sufferings of arsenicosis symptoms. The information I collected helped me to understand the extent and nature of alternative healings and the ways in which such healing services were evaluated by actual patients in rural Bangladesh.

Any description of the rural Bangladeshi health care system would be incomplete without referring to "doctors without degrees", health service providers who practice Western biomedicine without any biomedical qualification. I interviewed such a village doctor, who ran his allopathic pharmacy cum private chamber in the village marketplace and treated many arsenicosis patients. His chamber was a crucial place for me to observe doctor–patient interactions and the ways in which he provided health care services to the patients. On many occasions, I informally spoke to him and came to know about his understandings and explanations about arsenicosis, its diagnosis, treatment and preventive measures. I interviewed many patients who visited this doctor to understand what motivated them to come for such health care services. I also interviewed two professional biomedical doctors who rendered health care services at the UHC.[6] Throughout the interview process, I was guided by the question of how arsenicosis was medically constructed, managed and treated. The information I collected from them allowed me to compare and contrast biomedical and lay understandings of arsenicosis.

Other significant categories of informants were officials of various state-affiliated agencies and NGOs who were involved in financing, designing, implementing and evaluating projects aimed at providing arsenic-free water in the rural areas. I interviewed the Upazilla public health officer at Kalaroa, officials of the DPHE in Dhaka and the BAMWSP project coordinator in the Dhaka office. I also interviewed the project coordinator for GSK who was assigned to take care of the arsenic-free water supply project in the rural areas. For them, I used semi-structured interviews to understand aims and objectives of these projects, the implementation process, interaction with the community people and achievements of these projects. I tried to understand how these project activities were planned and whether expectations, concerns and priorities of actual beneficiaries were taken into account. The information I collected allowed me to understand how different actors were incompatible in perceiving and explaining development projects and the ways in which knowledge and understandings of arsenicosis differ between lay people and the development experts. Such incompatibility and differential perceptions helped me to construct the argument of why development projects grossly failed in southwestern Bangladesh, which I discuss in Chapter 6.

Unlike my experience of conducting fieldwork in the village, interviewing the bureaucratic state officials was often frustrating and posed a number of challenges. Getting an appointment was particularly difficult, since most BAMWSP officials refused to be interviewed. I persistently followed them to their offices and sometimes waited outside their offices for hours before I was allowed to go in. Even though they agreed to be interviewed, many officials were not comfortable sharing information about the project, which was unsuccessful in achieving desired aims and objectives. Sometimes they were agitated and blamed villagers for not making development projects successful. Some other officials gave me specific appointments but cancelled at the last moment. I did not expect everything as I wished. I never despaired; rather, I was prepared for any kind of uncertainties and ready to find ways out of it. On some other occasions, I really enjoyed my fieldwork. I was thrilled when I obtained easy access to informants and got interesting information through many rewarding interviews, which did happen most of the time. I was welcomed in many offices and they shared their ideas in a friendlier environment. They were eager to know about me and my research project. I took that opportunity to establish friendship with them. Throughout the fieldwork, I always kept my patience and did not express anger or disappointment during difficult situations. I accepted and enjoyed the fieldwork process, which was exciting and rewarding most of the time and frustrating, dull and monotonous on other occasions.

Chapter outlines

This book consists of seven chapters. Chapter 1 provides an overview of the research, with particular reference to the research problems, the magnitude of the arsenic problem in Bangladesh and the objectives of this study. Methodological considerations have been outlined in this chapter to allow readers an understanding of the techniques followed for collecting qualitative data through ethnographic research. Readers are familiarized with the village in southwestern Bangladesh where primary fieldwork for this research was conducted.

Chapter 2 outlines theoretical and conceptual perspectives that are relevant to this study. It is argued that a holistic understanding of arsenicosis requires theoretical openness and flexibility. Arsenicosis is not just a "disease" that is experienced by individuals, but a microcosm of many cultural, political and global forces that shape its processes. Therefore, a single theoretical lens would not be sufficient to capture its multidimensional facets. At least two theoretical frameworks would be necessary to understand the interplay between arsenicosis, health and the development discourse: (1) social constructionism (Berger and Luckmann 1966; Schutz 1962; Schutz and Luckmann 1973) and (2) a post-structuralist critique of development (Escobar 1995; Ferguson 1990). Apart from these, other concepts, such as "medical pluralism" and "health-seeking behaviour", are invoked, given their relevance to understanding the findings of this research.

Chapter 3 details the politico-historical evolution of Bangladesh and examines how different medical systems have evolved in line with the political developments in Bangladesh that subsequently shape the health-seeking behaviour of the people. It is argued that a number of discrete medical systems have defined the medical landscape through the ancient, colonial and contemporary periods and contribute to the current pluralistic medical system in Bangladesh. Any study on health-seeking behaviour in rural Bangladesh must take into consideration the nature and constraints of public health care systems and how such constraints create ample space for burgeoning alternative health care services. This chapter then focuses on the general background information about arsenic, with particular reference to the global presence of arsenic contamination, its causes and health consequences. It is argued that biomedical and scientific explanations of arsenicosis are the norms, rather than exceptions, which only highlight the anatomical, physiological and clinical aspects of it, ignoring many cultural, politico-religious and ecological dynamics of everyday life through which lay individuals understand, explain and respond to arsenicosis.

Chapter 4 presents cultural understandings of arsenicosis as explained and experienced by lay villagers in southwestern Bangladesh. Arsenicosis has been conceptualized within the general health and illness beliefs and practices of rural Bangladesh. By examining the particular vocabularies, labels, etiologies and categories that villagers use to talk about this disease, this chapter demonstrates how a biomedical category of arsenicosis has been vernacularized as *ghaa*[7] in practice. It is argued that such a social construction of *ghaa* is particularly important, as it significantly shapes subsequent health-seeking behaviour of the subjects and their participation in mitigation strategies.

Chapter 5 illustrates the health-seeking behaviour of arsenicosis patients in a medically plural rural Bangladesh with particular reference to the ways in which arsenicosis is diagnosed, managed and treated by the actual affected individuals. Highlighting the various health care services that are available to them, this chapter analyzes the question of why arsenicosis patients use alternative healing services more extensively than allopathic medicine. One significant piece of evidence could be the link between the social construction of *ghaa* and the ways in which it shapes the health-seeking behaviour of subjects. It is argued that lay understandings of *ghaa* guide individuals to seek alternative healing services, which is believed to be highly, if not more, efficacious than biomedicine. It is further argued that both patients and alternative healers share similar cultural knowledge and disease etiologies of arsenicosis as *ghaa*, which places both actors on the same platform and allows them to easily share, communicate and reassure on healing efficacies. Such shared understandings about arsenicosis produce a strong basis for the prevalence of alternative healing services in rural Bangladesh.

Chapter 6 reveals mitigation strategies of arsenicosis by focusing on two development projects, the BAMWSP and GSK, which were aimed at providing arsenic-free water but were rejected by the communities in which they were implemented, and therefore "failed" to achieve their goals and objectives. A critical reexamination of these two projects through an anthropological perspective reveals that the failure of these projects was primarily due to the "mismatch" in understanding arsenicosis by the community people and development experts. The ways in which development experts perceive arsenicosis and prioritize solutions to the problem do not make cultural sense on the ground. It is demonstrated that development planners grossly failed to realize local perceptions and priorities about arsenicosis and ignored many cultural, political and technical aspects under which these projects were to be implemented, leading to the failure of these high-profile and essential water supply projects.

Finally, Chapter 7 summarizes the main arguments and findings of this book. It is argued that biomedical constructions limit our understandings of arsenicosis to the realms of physiological and clinical manifestations, which are valuable but discount many sociocultural and politico-ecological dynamics of everyday life through which arsenicosis is understood, explained and responded to by lay individuals. It is further argued that social construction of *ghaa* is crucial in determining subsequent health-seeking behaviour of subjects and their participation in mitigation strategies. The extensive prevalence and use of alternative healing services and the failure of arsenic mitigation strategies are mostly due to differential perceptions of arsenicosis by various social actors such as biomedical professionals, development experts and lay villagers. Development plans that are uninformed of the local sociocultural and politico-ecological priorities, under which these projects are to be implemented, are doomed to failure. To ensure optimum success and sustainability of development projects, anthropological findings of this book suggest that development planners should understand, address and accommodate lay expectations and priorities by appreciating the ways in which actual beneficiaries assess their problems. By recognizing local knowledge and priorities, both development planners and health service providers would have a deeper cultural understanding of the problem, which would allow them to formulate development projects and health delivery services in a way that would contribute to the greater success, sustainability and well-being of the wider community.

Notes

1 Pseudonyms have been used to protect the identities of the informants. The name of the village is also a pseudonym.
2 Upazilla is a Bengali word which can be literally translated as "subdistrict" in English, which is the second tier of administrative unit between the district and Union Parishad, and roughly equates to a US county.
3 District is the third tier of government administrative units, which comprises some Upazillas. The size and population of a district vary. Currently there are a total of sixty-four districts in Bangladesh, administered by the District Commissioner, who is a civil servant appointed by the government.
4 *Kobiraj* refers to a particular group of healers without any formal training who mostly use chanting and religious and herbal medications for curing different types of illnesses.
5 *Hujur* particularly refers to a religious guru or, at the village level, someone who conducts prayer at the village mosque. Besides his job of performing religious activities, a *hujur* routinely offers religious medicine, mostly in the form of chanting and amulets.
6 The Upazilla Health Complex is the lowest government referral hospital located at the subdistrict level in Bangladesh. This is usually a 50–100 bed hospital with ambulatory, inpatient and outpatient health care services. All doctors are public servants with a minimum MBBS degree.
7 *Ghaa* is a local Bengali word which literally refers to varieties of skin diseases. Villagers locally use the term *ghaa* to refer to the symptoms that are medically labeled as arsenicosis. The ethnography of *ghaa*, its cultural categorizations, causations and association with arsenicosis are detailed in Chapter 4.

2 Arsenic poisoning

Culture, health and development perspectives

Introduction

Theoretically, tasks and priorities of contemporary medical anthropology are not merely to engage in a conventional village or community-based health care system or health-seeking behaviour in isolated modes; rather, recent trends and shifts in medical anthropology incorporate wider political-economic factors that inevitably shape health, illness and health-seeking processes of subjects (Scheper-Hughes 1990; Singer and Baer 1995; Turner 1995). In this study, understanding of arsenicosis is not just restricted to its being merely a disease manifested in physiological and clinical conditions; rather, it is considered as an illness as understood, experienced and responded to by lay individuals who live in dynamic socio-historical, political-economic, ecological and developmental interventionist contexts. I agree with Turner (1995: 14), who notes that:

> given the complexity of health and illness in contemporary societies, various theories and methodologies will be necessary for medical sociology to develop an adequate perspective on medical phenomena. Illness, rather like crime, will not be explained satisfactorily in sociology by a narrow, unidimensional approach. Given the social character of chronic illness in advanced societies, a broad, multidisciplinary approach is necessary.

It is thus argued that theoretical openness is essential for a holistic understanding of health and illness in general, and arsenicosis in particular which will incorporate the complex intersections of individual, social, political and ecological factors. To illuminate such interconnectedness of these processes, at least two theoretical frameworks would be helpful: social constructionism (Berger and Luckmann 1966; Schutz 1962, 1967; Schutz and Luckmann 1973) and a post-structuralist critique of development (Escobar 1991, 1995; Ferguson 1990; Friedman 2006; Mohan 1997; Rahnema and Bawtree 1997). Apart from these theories, some other concepts, such as medical pluralism and health-seeking behaviour, need to be reconceptualized to adequately understand arsenicosis and its resultant health and development impacts. The following discussion presents elements of each of these theoretical and conceptual ideas which frame the theorizing offered in this study.

Arsenicosis as socially constructed

In this study, social constructionism has been used as a powerful analytical tool to understand the ways in which sociocultural factors shape "the knowledge base which produces our assumption about the prevalence, incidence, treatment and meaning of disease" (Brown 1995: 34). Although Alfred Schutz is considered to be the pioneer in the field of social constructionism through his influential books *The Phenomenology of the Social World* (1967) and *The Structures of the Life-World* (1973), Peter L. Berger and Thomas Luckmann fully developed the idea of social constructionism in their book entitled *The Social Construction of Reality* (1966). From these foundational works, two distinctive but overlapping concepts – "reality" and "knowledge" – have been identified to demonstrate the ways in which they provide insights to understand arsenicosis in rural Bangladesh.

"Reality", as Berger and Luckmann define it, is socially constructed, and "knowledge" refers to the "certainty that phenomena are real and they possess specific characteristics" (Berger and Luckmann 1966: 1). Reality is produced in everyday life, which is taken for granted and shared by members who actively participate in it through the "subjectively meaningful conduct of their lives" (Berger and Luckmann 1966: 20). Reality, thus, originates in the thoughts and actions of individuals in the social processes, which, in the "natural attitude", are considered "taken for granted and self-evidently real" (Schutz and Luckmann 1973: 4). Another crucial characteristic of reality is that it is ordered and patterned in a way that appears independent of individuals' apprehension or already objectified in an orderly manner "that [has] been designated [in terms of] objects before my appearance on the scene" (Berger and Luckmann 1966: 22). Here, language appears as an essential tool that continuously provides individuals with necessary meaning, ordering and objectification of everyday life. Using language, individuals communicate with others to create a meaningful and commonsense order of everyday life.

Reality is thus constructed intersubjectively. Individuals are not alone in their everyday lives but are part of a larger web of social relationships that are shared with others, "my life-world is not my private world but, rather, is intersubjective; the fundamental structure of its reality is that it is shared by us" (Schutz and Luckmann 1973: 4). This sharing is made possible through constant interaction and communication with fellow members of the society. Reality is, therefore, constructed through reciprocity and experiencing the world in the same way as do others. It is an ongoing process of negotiation and correspondence between "my meanings" and "their meanings" through which a commonsense reality is established (Berger and Luckmann 1966: 23). The production of knowledge and reality are inherently intersubjective, as they are "developed, transmitted and maintained in social situations" (Berger and Luckmann 1966: 3). In a constructionist framework, the process of knowledge production is neither automatic nor natural, but is a result of the dynamic, interactive and mutual enterprise of individuals in a web of social relationships.

This study on arsenicosis fits into the broader framework of social constructionism to explore the ways in which commonsense knowledge about arsenicosis is constructed, negotiated and (re)produced in a particular sociocultural setting of southwestern Bangladesh. Arsenicosis patients are not isolated individuals but are part of larger societal settings. They are interactively, pragmatically and consciously engaged with other members of the society within the family, village and beyond. Their life-world is shared with significant others, such as family members, relatives, friends, health service providers and NGO activists. These significant others, in conjunction with arsenicosis patients, produce a vast stock of knowledge about arsenicosis, which is anthropologically interesting to explore. Thus, any meaningful study related to the social construction of arsenicosis must take into account these larger social processes within which knowledge is produced, shared and negotiated.

It is specifically important to explore the everyday life of arsenicosis patients to understand the ways in which they produce "first-order" knowledge of this illness. To do this, it is crucial to explore the specific vocabularies, disease etiologies, signs and symptoms that patients use to explain this disease. To understand such first-order constructions of arsenicosis, it is important to explore the everyday beliefs and practices of the patients. Medical anthropologists interested in studying any illness must take into account the processes through which patients experience their lives and share their life-world with other members of the society. By illuminating such social processes and shared worldviews, medical anthropologists would be in a better position to construct second-order ethnographic knowledge.

A social constructionist framework continues to be useful in illustrating doctor–patient interaction in negotiating meanings of health and illness (Turner 2000). Jeffery and Jeffery (1993) illustrate the social organization of childbirth in Bijnor in North India and argue that "the practice of midwifery in any one place is conditioned by a wide set of social, economic, and symbolic considerations that give it particular shape and meaning" (p. 9). It is argued that the traditional knowledge of midwives is acquired over centuries of observation and experience (Ehrenreich and English 1978: 33). Popular knowledge of childbirth thus departs from Western biomedical knowledge. In another example, Kaufert and O'Neil (1993) examined the perception of risk in childbirth held by clinicians, epidemiologists and Inuit women to illustrate how biomedical construction departs from the local social construction of knowledge and experience. They argue that the risk of childbirth is medically perceived as "objective, scientific and expressible in numbers", whereas Inuit women's perception of risk is subjective, cultural and acquired through everyday experience over generations (Kaufert and O'Neil 1993: 50). Biomedical constructions are thus challenged by the everyday cultural knowledge of the lay individuals, and the biomedical authority is "variously taken up, negotiated, or transformed by members of the lay population in their quest to maximize their health status and avoid physical distress and pain" (Lupton 1997: 94–95).

It is pertinent here to explore how arsenicosis is variously perceived and explained by different social actors such as arsenicosis patients, biomedical doctors and development professionals. My argument here links up with a particular aspect of social constructionism that Berger and Luckmann identify as "multiple realities" to demonstrate that "different objects present themselves to consciousness as constituents of different spheres of reality" (Berger and Luckmann 1966: 21).

Clearly, arsenicosis patients are just one group of social actors amongst many others. In a societal setting, they encounter many other actors in their everyday lives, such as friends, relatives, alternative medical practitioners, biomedical doctors and development activists. Each of these actors produces a quite different reality about arsenicosis. The reality of arsenicosis constructed by patients is different from realities held by others, say, biomedical doctors and development planners. It is thus interesting to examine how different realities of arsenicosis are constructed, how they depart from each other and the implications of such departure for health-seeking behaviour of subjects and their participation in mitigation strategies. Berger and Luckmann (1966: 21) argue that the transition from one reality to the other is often experienced as shocking. It might be true that arsenicosis patients may not conform to the biomedical and developmental explanations of arsenicosis; rather, they may have their own cultural explanations of it through handling the illness in their everyday lives.

Thus far, it has been demonstrated how social constructionism can be a useful theoretical framework that would allow exploration of how a biomedical reality of arsenicosis is vernacularized in everyday life. It is argued that a meticulous phenomenological analysis may be useful to explore the various layers of experiences and different structures of meaning that contribute to socially construct arsenicosis as a reality (Berger and Luckmann 1966: 21). Many recent medical anthropological works find social constructionism helpful in examining the human experiences of illness, its symptoms and sufferings (Kleinman 1978, 1980, 1986, 1988; Lindenbaum and Lock 1993; Mattingly and Garro 2000).

A word of caution here is that although social constructionism is useful in this study, its use in social science research is not without limitations. Several criticisms of this approach have been identified. It is argued that this perspective is narrow and limited and does not comprehensively illustrate the complex and multidimensional contexts of health, illness and health care systems (Bury 1991; Weinberg 2009). According to Brown, social constructionism "refuses to accept any elements of a structural perspective, in particular the notion that fundamental social structure of society play key roles in health and illness" (Brown 1995: 35). Bury (1986) has identified at least four inherent limitations of social constructionism: (1) the problem of incoherence, (2) the problem of pragmatism, (3) the lack of reflexivity and (4) the problem of relativism. Bury (1986: 152–53) argues that if we consider all forms of knowledge as "discourses", then there is no room for constructionism, and if all forms of knowledge are socially constructed, then social construction itself must be socially constructed, as he notes:

> In fact, if knowledge and methods of enquiry are held to construct rather than disclose reality we are bound (as Foucault recognizes) to include human sciences, including critical thought in the process as well. This places us in a circle from which there appears to be no escape. If rationality cannot be treated as external to social forms, as a means of understanding reality or adjudicating accounts, what methods are available to evaluate the books, articles and arguments which put this view forward.

Despite these limitations, social constructionism appears to be a helpful theoretical framework in this research in uncovering particular vocabularies, labels and etiologies that individuals use to denote this illness. To illuminate the processes through which lay knowledge of arsenicosis is produced, I agree with Berger and Luckmann that "the method we consider best suited to clarify the foundations of knowledge in everyday life is that of phenomenological analysis, a purely descriptive method and, as such, 'empirical' but not 'scientific' " (Berger and Luckmann 1966: 20).

Why do arsenic mitigation strategies fail? A post-structuralist analysis

To better understand why high-profile and essential arsenic mitigation strategies fail, a post-structuralist development discourse provides powerful insights. Rather than taking development and its processes for granted, they are problematized to argue that development is "Eurocentric, patriarchal and disciplining" (Mohan 1997), it is an imposition of science as power (Nandy 1988), it does not work (Kothari 1988) and it ends up in "failure", "underdevelopment", "poverty" and "unintended consequences" (Escobar 1988, 1991, 1995, 2000, 2004; Esteva 1992; Ferguson 1990; Mohan 1997; Nederveen-pieterse 2000; Nustad 2001; Rahnema and Bawtree 1997). The impulse of post-structuralist development mostly draws upon the notions of discourse and deconstruction to refer to the ways in which language and power play an instrumental role in (de)constructing knowledge, meaning and identity (Foucault 1972). As far as development is concerned, discourse analysis is decisive in making sense of the "often fragile means by which knowledge about development or other societies are produced and circulated" (Corbridge 1995: xiii).

A post-structuralist analysis in this study is influenced by the contribution of Arturo Escobar, who argues that development is hegemonic, through which Western countries dominate, control and exploit the so-called Third World countries (Escobar 1995). The establishment of the IMF, the World Bank and many other international financial institutions ensure that these Third World countries are equipped with "the material and organizational factors required to pave the way for rapid access to the forms of life created by industrial civilization" (Escobar 1988: 429). Thus, development establishes "a system that brought together all of those elements, institutions, and practices creating among them a set of relations which endured their continued existence" (Escobar 1988: 430). With the establishment of these multilateral financial institutions, the "poor" and "Third World" countries "became the target of an endless number of programs and interventions that seemed to be inescapable and that ensured their control" (Escobar 1988: 430). The Third World is constructed in such ways that would allow "experts" of these institutions to prescribe appropriate courses of action for promoting development. Despite long periods of intervention, however, poverty and underdevelopment persist. These development projects, Escobar argues, do not only merely fail but culminate in a destructive force to produce "massive underdevelopment and impoverishment, untold exploitation and oppression . . . [such as] the debt crisis, the Sahelian famine, increasing poverty, malnutrition, and violence" (Escobar 1995: 4).

Escobar's argument as demonstrated above is relevant in this study to demonstrate the processes by which the World Bank, UNICEF, and SDC construct Bangladesh as a suitable object of intervention through the BAMWSP and the GSK water supply projects. Post-structuralist discourse unveils the power relationships in development projects in order to demonstrate the ways in which agendas are set and priorities are ranked. On the ground, it would be interesting to explore how international development initiatives are negotiated, evaluated and even resisted. Even more interesting anthropologically is to understand how international development projects have been variously taken up, understood, explained and experienced by different social actors on the ground. Are the rural Bangladeshis just passive recipients of international development projects? Do they actively take part in these processes? How do they evaluate these development projects? Why do individuals, who are suffering from deadly arsenicosis, reject options that might provide them arsenic-safe water? These are interesting questions to be explored in this study. There are different social actors involved in these water supply projects disguised by different ideologies and interests. At the macro level, international development organizations finance and plan development projects, while at the intermediary level, state agencies and national and local NGOs implement development projects; whereas at the micro level, locally elected representatives, village elites and lay villagers play an active role as beneficiaries of these development projects. Each stratum has specific political and ideological disguises. It is crucial to examine how different social actors are involved in power and politics while participating in these development projects.

In his book *The Anti-Politics Machine*, James Ferguson argues that development fails "astonishingly regularly", and it not only fails but also produces many unintended consequences (Ferguson 1990; 1997). Ferguson defines "failure" as the "outcomes of planned social interventions [that] can end up coming together into powerful constellations of control that were never intended and in some cases never even recognized" (Ferguson 1990: 19). Thus, for Ferguson, failure refers to the unintended consequences of planned development projects. Such unintended consequences may range from the failure of achieving aims and objectives and intrusion of capitalism and state bureaucratic control to socio-economic and environmental disasters. The planned intention and expected outcomes of the projects may not always be positive; rather, it may produce entirely unexpected outcomes. As Ferguson (1990: 20) argues:

> The most important political effects of a planned intervention may occur unconsciously, behind the backs or against the wills of the "planners" who may seem to be running the show ... intentional plans are always important, but never quite the way the planners imagined.

This study closely links up with the argument of Ferguson (1990) that the failure of development projects often leads to unforeseen consequences, which were not originally intended during project planning. By studying the Thaba-Tseka project, Ferguson argues that although the development apparatus in Lesotho claims to be an "anti-politics machine", in reality, development activities evolve in a preeminently political operation by strengthening the state presence at the local level (Ferguson 1990). Thus, for Ferguson, development is ultimately a political phenomenon. Yet, other scholars explain failure as an outcome of development planners' lack of meticulous planning and ignorance of local priorities. As Hobart (1993: 2) argues:

> What is signally absent in most public discussion of development are the ways in which the knowledges of peoples being developed are ignored or treated as mere obstacles to rational progress. In order for them to be able to progress, these peoples have first to be constituted as "underdeveloped and ignorant".

Thus, this study considers failure in two ways: firstly, failure in achieving goals and objectives of the project, which were originally expected, and secondly, the unintended consequences brought about by the failed development projects. Examples of such unintended consequences of failed development projects are many. In India, the Narmada Bachao Andolan is probably one of the biggest protests against the Narmada Valley Project, which received global attention because of its unprecedented consequences on the lives of people under this project. The project aimed at establishing 30 large, 135 medium, and 3,000 minor dams, uprooting nearly one million people, destroying 5 million hectares of agricultural lands due to water logging and salinity and leading to an extraordinary escalation of waterborne diseases in the project areas (Khagram 2004; Kothari and Bhartari 1984; Patkar 1998; Sangvai 2002). In Sri Lanka, the Mahaväli Development Program or "colonization schemes", which was envisaged as providing systematic irrigation for increasing rice production, had resulted in various unintended consequences, such as indebtedness of the local people, land fragmentation, massive sharecropping and high rates of suicide because of human misery and resettlement (Pfaffenberger 1990; Tennekoon 1988). In Nigeria, Jike (2004) reports that warped development projects resulted in massive environmental degradation and increased unemployment rates, leading to social disequilibrium, a rise of social miscreants, juvenile delinquents and other deviant behaviour. In Indonesia, mining activities drastically altered the environment through soil erosion and water and air pollution, creating conflict between the mining company and the local villagers (Robinson 1986).

Examples of unintended consequences of development projects are also abundant in Bangladesh. The Kaptai Hydro-electric Project in the Chittagong hill tracts is one example of how dams installed for producing hydro-electricity resulted in massive uprooting of indigenous peoples, destruction of forests, degradation of the environment and the transformation of the swidden cultivation into market-oriented commercial products. Rather than alleviating poverty, these projects resulted in a poverty-generating mechanism and extended state and market control over these indigenous people (Adnan 2004). Karim (2008) demonstrates how the microcredit program has inadvertently endangered women's position in the family as "Bangladeshi rural women's honor and shame are instrumentally appropriated by NGOs in the welfare of their capitalist interests" (Karim 2008: 6). Thus, rural Bangladeshi women have been exposed to capitalist projects and neoliberal ideologies through "grassroots globalization", which "weakens the sovereignty of the patriarchal-home family, and replaces it with the sovereignty of the market through NGOs" – an entirely new outcome which was unimagined during microcredit project planning (Karim 2008: 6).

My ethnographic analysis of two arsenic-safe water supply projects in rural Bangladesh corroborates the above findings that these mitigation strategies in rural Bangladesh not only failed to achieve goals and objectives of providing arsenic-safe water, but also produced unforeseen consequences, such as increased hostility and deterioration of relationships among different stakeholders, which project planners did not anticipate during the project planning. I do not say that these development projects were ill-planned or grounded in bad intentions, but the meticulous planning and careful implementation required for these projects to be successful were glaringly inadequate. The project planners failed to take into account the many political, cultural and environmental considerations within which these projects were to be implemented, leading these potentially useful projects into failure.

The post-structuralist critique of development further questions the concepts of "community participation", "community involvement" and "participatory development". It has been argued that participation is heavily guided by political motivations, power relations and differential interests (Jewkes and Murcott 1998; Morgan 1993). The concept of "the community" is also problematic, as it dissolves the local heterogeneity under the mask of the community as if there were no divergence in age, sex, gender roles, class and interest groups (Gardner and Lewis 1996: 112). For this study, community participation is considered as a "social process whereby specific groups with shared needs living in a defined geographic area actively pursue identification of their needs, take decisions and establish mechanisms to meet these needs" (Rifkin, Muller, and Bichmann 1988: 933).

Historically, community participation became an integral part of development agenda in the 1970s, when international development institutions such as WHO, UNICEF, the World Bank and USAID packaged and promoted community participation as a "one size fits all" development solution, which was believed to be applicable across the world. As far as the health sector is concerned, the failure of developmental states to ensure health care services for all obligated international organizations to revisit their policy by adopting the Alma Ata Declaration in 1978, with its focus on a PHC approach emphasizing the community participation in the process. It was envisaged that community members would not be passive recipients of health care interventions; rather, they would actively participate in the process and be responsible for their own health. As the declaration illustrates (WHO 1979: 17):

> Measures have to be taken to ensure free and enlightened community participation, so that notwithstanding the overall responsibility of governments

for the health of their people, individuals, families and communities assume greater responsibility for their own health and welfare, including self-care. This participation is not only desirable; it is a social, economic and technical necessity.

Many countries, as signatories of the declaration, enthusiastically incorporated community participation into their PHC approach and implemented these through their respective ministries of health. Soon after the initiation, however, community participation appeared as an illusion, as many governments realized that "participation could not be easily controlled or confined to the realm of health" and became skeptical about the viability of participation as a development strategy (Morgan 1993: 13). Although the Alma Ata Declaration assumed community participation as an apolitical strategy, an inherently political agenda was implicit in the declaration. The declaration assumed that the state, under the guardianship of international agencies, would be the right apparatus to define, label and manage participation. It was also assumed that the community members would comply with what the central government had planned for them. Such a policy automatically ruled out any spontaneous participation, social movement and participation from the grassroots (Morgan 1993: 13). It soon became obvious that participation was a politico-ideological persuasion guided by partisanship, the whims of the state and donor agencies and the interests of the intermediary groups (Madan 1987; Morgan 1993). It is alleged that in the name of community participation, the state and international development organizations legitimize their controversial policies and promote low-quality PHC services to the villagers (Ugalde 1985: 42).

Participatory governance and project management can also provide powerful insights into an examination of the failure of the arsenic mitigation water supply projects. Participatory governance has become influential in development discourse since the 1980s, as most donors and NGOs preferred this approach to ensure sustainable development outcomes. As a mechanism, participatory governance can be broadly defined as a kind of institutional arrangement that facilitates "the participation of ordinary citizens in the public policy process" (Andersson and van Laerhoven 2007: 1090). A number of key positive factors of participatory governance can be identified, such as: (1) it promotes accountability and responsiveness of the local government (Blair 2000; Crook and Manor 1998); (2) it ensures state decisions are more transparent and equitable (Bishop and Davis 2002; Weeks 2000; World Bank 2003); (3) it empowers the common citizens and enables them to influence the design and implementation of public services (Andersson, Gibson, and Lehoucq 2006; Gaventa 2004; Sen 1999). Despite its potential contribution to attaining sustainable development, participatory governance may not always be ensured. Corruption, lack of accountability, rigid bureaucratic attitudes of the state authorities and unwillingness of the public officials to consult with the community are some of the constraints (Bräutigam 2004; Shatkin 2000; Francis and James 2003).

My ethnographic evidence regarding the failure of arsenic mitigation strategies suggests that there were a number of reasons behind the underperformance and poor implementation of the project, including but not limited to conflicts among top managers of the project; lack of coordination among different stakeholders such as the World Bank, BAMWSP, and DPHE; corruption; appointment of a weak and incompetent person as project director; and reluctance on the part of the government to get involved and undertake such projects. Although people's participation was a key component of both projects, project officials failed to ensure minimum involvement of the community. An LGI, particularly UP's involvement as representative of the local people, was inadequate in these projects. Project designers also failed to anticipate the probable risks and standby measures to mitigate such consequences. These are essentially governance and management related constraints of these projects, which need to be examined through a perspective of participatory governance.

This study closely links up with these arguments that in the name of participation, an induced water-supply project has been implemented in the village. Rather than creating awareness and supporting spontaneous participation, these projects were imposed on the villagers from the top. In the process, a number of political, cultural and technical aspects were ignored by the project planners. For example, no initiatives were taken to understand how villagers perceived arsenicosis or prioritized solutions for this or whether villagers really supported these projects. Local knowledge and priorities were not taken into account in planning and executing development activities, which was partially responsible for the projects' failure. My point here supports Nichter (1984), who argues that a poor understanding of lay health knowledge and behaviour as well as the inability to negotiate meaning within the popular health cultures hinder health communication, which may ultimately contribute to the failure of any health project (Nichter 1984: 248).

Medical pluralism: a relevant concept?

Besides these theoretical frameworks just outlined, I hold that we need to rethink the concept of "medical pluralism" to understand the health context of rural Bangladesh. Although this concept has been very popular among social scientists, it has not been addressed adequately, as Minocha rightly notes, "What one finds is a plethora of assumptions, presuppositions, and generalizations having little or no relation to the real complexities of the situation" (Minocha 1980: 217). Thus, this study does not take medical pluralism for granted; rather, it problematizes it to address the inadequacies associated with it so that it becomes more relevant to the rural Bangladeshi context.

The first problem highlighted is the definition of medical systems. The most crucial questions are: What constitutes a medical system? Should supernatural healings be constitutive of a medical system? Should the village "quack" who prescribes biomedicine be called a medical practitioner and a doctor? What about those practitioners who dispense both biomedicine and alternative medicine? A number of scholars have already attended to these issues. For example, Dunn (1976: 125) defines medical systems as those social institutions and cultural traditions that people utilize to enhance health. Fabrega and Manning (1979: 41), on the other hand, prefer to use the term "medical care system" to incorporate different beliefs, practices, knowledge and personnel who are involved in providing health care services to cure illnesses. At a more general level, there is a straightforward definition of medical systems: "a patterned set of ideas and practices having to do with illness" (Glick 1977: 59). To be more precise, Press (1980) focuses on interrelated beliefs and practices which incorporate "meaning, identification, prevention, and treatment of sickness" (Press 1980: 47).

The second problem associated with medical pluralism is the usage of different labels to distinguish between biomedicine and non-biomedical systems. The term biomedicine has been variously referred to as "Western", "cosmopolitan", "scientific" and "modern", as opposed to alternative medical systems, which are labeled "traditional", "folk", "non-Western", "indigenous" and "primitive". Such a labeling of alternative medical systems might provoke serious political and ethical implications. The representation of biomedicine as "Western" and "modern" implicitly imposes a Western disposition where "all sorts of seemingly irrelevant, contradictory, and paradoxical observations intrude" (Glick 1977: 59). Thus, Western scientific medicine has been considered as a standard against which other medical systems are assessed. The terms "indigenous" and "native" may stimulate a "political" or "ethnic" connotation, as if non-Western medical systems are uninfluenced by non-indigenous elements (Janes 1999). Given such a problematic nature of labeling, Press prefers to abandon the whole epistemology of "ethnomedicine" and suggests that we use "ethnomedical" as a term to refer to "a type of study (rather than type of systems) that focuses upon the ideological and cultural bases of any medical system, including the official sector of Western biomedicine" (Press 1980: 45).

A third problem is associated with the fact that medical pluralism does not necessarily refer to the coexistence of different medical systems which remain isolated. Rather, different medical practitioners cross boundaries to incorporate therapeutic modalities from other medical systems. We have impressive ethnographic accounts from Asia which illustrate the prevalence of syncretic therapeutic practices. Nichter (1980) and Minocha (1980) report that Ayurvedic practitioners in India make extensive use of Western biomedicine, including antibiotics and instruments such as stethoscopes, injections, blood pressure monitoring machines, catheters and minor surgical equipment. In Malaysia, Heggenhougen (1980) demonstrates that biomedicine is perceived to be an incomplete medical system, and thus general physicians, both Western and traditional, prescribe medication from other systems to fulfill expectations of the patient. Such syncretic practices have also been documented in Sri Lanka (Nordstrom 1988; Waxler-Morrison and Nancy 1988; Wolffers 1989), in Japan (Lock 1980; Stoner 1986), in Guatemala (Cosminsky and Scrimshaw 1980) and in Thailand (Golomb 1988; Weisberg 1984), where traditional medical practitioners widen their practice by incorporating healing techniques beyond their therapeutic jurisdiction to "maximize their case loads and endeavor to curb the loss of traditional clientele to modern health facilities" (Golomb 1988: 766).

Having discussed all these characteristics, this study conceptualizes medical systems as: firstly, a total organization of cultural and social practices, including behavioural and technical aspects, which are aimed at achieving health and preventing illness. Secondly, pluralism may not merely mean coexistence of different medical practices and structures; rather, it may incorporate pluralistic characteristics within a particular medical system. Thirdly, medical pluralism further incorporates syncretic practices and "crossing boundaries", whereby practitioners borrow healing modalities from other medical systems. And last but not least, an extended meaning may incorporate pluralism in: (a) social actors' perception about health and illness, (b) their decision-making process in health-seeking behaviour, and (c) their pluralistic responses to different healing resorts. Thus, a simple definition of medical pluralism as "the coexistence of different medical systems" limits the reality by discounting many dynamic characteristics within it. Medical pluralism and its processes need to be reconceptualized to demonstrate the ways in which actual social actors pragmatically compartmentalize and integrate various medical systems in practice to constitute a functional and integrated medical system.

My ethnographic evidence corroborates such syncretic medical practices whereby village doctors dispense both allopathic and herbal medications for treating arsenicosis. The village *kobiraj* and religious healers, besides their own spiritual and religious healing techniques, use herbal medicines to cure arsenicosis. For achieving quick results and thereby maintaining their reputations, these practitioners incorporate many healing techniques available to them, including biomedicine, herbal medicine, homeopathy and religious modalities. Arsenicosis patients also follow such syncretic practices in their health-seeking behaviours by simultaneously or consecutively utilizing different healing resorts to achieve a quick relief of the symptoms.

Health-seeking behaviour in a medically plural setting

Another central theme in medical anthropology is to examine how lay individuals decide which health care services are to be sought in a medically plural setting. Janzen's (1978) classical work in Zaire shows that it is the "therapy managing group", a group of relatives, kinsmen, advocates and friends, who play a crucial role in managing illness and therapy (Janzen 1978: 4). Such a therapy managing group or "lay referral system" provides various emotional, financial and decision-making services during the course of illness. This group of people also provide information on where to get appropriate therapeutic consultation, how to arrange appointments and even how much is to be paid for the services. The therapy managing group thus plays a crucial role of "brokerage function between the sufferer and the specialist" (Janzen 1978: 4). Boswell (1969) has also recognized the mobilization of social networks, relatives and kinsmen in the course of personal crisis management in Zambia. Nichter (2002) argues that the concept of a therapy management group needs to be reconceptualized, since it is far more dynamic, extended and complex than what Janzen initially proposed, as Nichter (2002: 82) notes:

> It is important to investigate the social dynamics of households, extended kin groups and larger social networks as they influence one another and are influenced by political, economic and globalization processes.

In a globalized world, a therapy management group is no longer concentrated within the immediate geographical boundary. Rather, the extended kin-groups, such as overseas friends and relatives, also contribute in decision making for global health care services. The boundary of a therapy management group is crucial, which Janzen did not adequately address in his initial formulation. My data also corroborate such an extended therapy management group whereby arsenicosis patients, with the assistance of overseas relatives in Kolkata, visit India to seek health care services. In this sense, not only arsenicosis patients are affected by their illness, but also their overseas relatives who are concerned and actively take part in the health-seeking processes.

Medical anthropologists are also interested in examining the complex processes vis-à-vis health-seeking behaviour and why patients concurrently use different medical therapies. Quah, for example, demonstrates that the use of multiple therapies is shaped by two factors: firstly, patients are guided by "pragmatic acculturation" for selecting healing techniques which may solve their health problem, and secondly, lay individuals pragmatically choose medical services based on respective cost-benefit analyses (Quah 1989, 2003). Press (1980) argues that social actors are quite aware of the paradigmatic and methodological differences between medical systems, and they "shop around" until they find an appropriate and effective cure to illness. In another study, Young reports that health-seeking behaviour is shaped by a number of other variables, like age, sex, education, socio-economic status, religion and marital status (Young 2004).

A strong correlation is documented between perceptions of disease etiology and subsequent health-seeking behaviour. It is believed that Western biomedicine is effective for treating diseases, whereas alternative medicine is perceived to be useful in treating illnesses (Ashraf, Chowdhury, and Streefland 1982; Feldman 1983; Paul 1983). Kleinman (1978), for example, demonstrates that people integrate both naturalistic and personalistic etiologies and then take a pragmatic strategy for the management of specific illnesses. In this case, conceptual contradictions among different medical systems appear less significant than seeking instrumental and symbolic efficacy (Kleinman 1978: 663). Young (1983: 1207) points out that health-seeking behaviour is a complex process and very much depends on: (a) the perceived seriousness and prognosis of the sickness for the patient, (b) the perceived efficacy of the medical tradition and the practitioner for a particular patient and sickness, (c) the economic and geographic accessibility of different sectors of the medical system, (d) a cost-benefit analysis and (e) the sociocultural appropriateness of the treatment for a particular person.

This study links up with these arguments that arsenicosis patients, in the context of a medically plural rural Bangladesh, continue to use different medical systems based on their pragmatic calculation and the perception of what is advantageous and/or efficacious in alleviating their symptoms. In this context, the extensive use of alternative healing services can be explained by the fact that individuals perceive arsenicosis as *ghaa*, an illness which is believed to be treated better by alternative healers than biomedical practitioners. Thus, the social construction of an illness is important in shaping subsequent health-seeking behaviour of the person. My argument goes in line with Connor's that "users of mixed therapy regimens regard the felt effectiveness of therapies to be more important than legitimacy deriving from a professionalized scientific knowledge system" (Connor 2004: 1695).

Conclusion

Thus far, it has been argued that a holistic perspective is required to study arsenicosis and its resultant health and development impacts. A combination of social constructionism and post-structuralist critique of development would be helpful in providing a comprehensive understanding of the problem at question. A social constructionist framework is helpful in examining subjective perceptions, experiences and response to arsenicosis, whereas a post-structuralist development discourse provides insight to understand how local villagers in rural Bangladesh are incorporated into the global political economy through various development projects. This approach is also useful in reexamining development and its processes to demonstrate why arsenic mitigation strategies fail in rural Bangladesh. Thus, in this study, social constructionist and post-structuralist approaches are used synergistically, since they offer different insights into a holistic understanding of arsenicosis. Besides these theoretical frameworks, some other concepts, such as medical pluralism, health-seeking behaviour and participatory governance, need to be incorporated given the complex structure and plethora of syncretic medical practices associated with arsenicosis in rural Bangladesh.

3 Arsenic poisoning in Bangladesh
Causes, health impacts and health care services

Introduction

This chapter focuses on three intertwined aspects of arsenic poisoning: its causes, health consequences and health care systems in Bangladesh within which arsenic-affected individuals seek health care services. First of all, the crisis of arsenic contamination in Bangladesh is described with particular reference to its prevalence, causes and health consequences. It is argued that both natural and human factors are involved in the widespread occurrence of arsenic contamination that results in a major public health crisis in Bangladesh. The discussion then shifts to the historical narrative of medical systems in Bangladesh and shows how different medical systems emerged and interacted in Bangladeshi society. By illustrating the historical coexistence, transformation and syncretization of different medical beliefs and practices, it is demonstrated how this has led to the emergence of a medically plural Bangladesh, which shapes health-seeking behaviour of the Bangladeshis. The different health care options, both biomedicine and alternative, that exist in rural Bangladesh provide a plethora of choices for the Bangladeshis who are affected by arsenic poisoning. The burgeoning alternative health care services are considered privileges in the context of rural Bangladesh, where public health care services are constrained by numerous limitations and mismanagement.

Arsenic poisoning: how did it happen?

Arsenic, known as the "king of poisons", is a ubiquitous element in the environment, existing in either an inorganic form such as arsenite (AsO_3^{2-}) and arsenate (AsO_4^{3-}) or an organic form such as methyl arsenic acid [$CH_3AsO(OH)_2$] and dimethyl arsenic acid [$(CH_3)_2As(OH)$] (Hossain 2006; Ravenscroft, Brammer, and Richards 2009). Although arsenic is an omnipresent element in the environment, the problem arises when its amount is elevated beyond the permissible levels, which then poses a particular threat to human health. Despite considerable disagreement on the permissible amount of arsenic intake for human health, the WHO sets a standard of 0.01 mg/L as the tolerable limit of arsenic ingestion (WHO 2006b). Germany and the European Union adopt 0.01 mg/L, whereas Australia sets 0.007 mg/L as its national standard (Ravenscroft, Brammer, and Richards 2009: 165). The governments of India and Bangladesh set 0.05 mg/L of arsenic as the national standard for drinking water (Chowdhury et al. 1999; Paul 2004). A recent survey on the water quality of Bangladesh reveals that the average range of arsenic concentrations in drinking water is far higher than the permissible standard, which is between 0.25 mg/L and as high as 1670 mg/L (Kinniburgh et al. 2003).

Bangladesh is not alone with this problem, as arsenic poisoning has become a global concern. Almost all continents have some degrees of exposure to arsenic contamination in the groundwater. Although arsenic was first reported in Argentina and Taiwan in the 1920s and 1960s respectively, it received global attention only after its widespread detection in the groundwater in India and Bangladesh. Most Asian countries, such as Bangladesh, India, Taiwan, Vietnam, China, Cambodia, Mongolia and Pakistan, and many other South American countries (e.g., Chile, Mexico, even some states of the USA) are affected by elevated concentrations of arsenic in the groundwater (Smedley and Kinniburgh 2002). Blackfoot Disease, a unique peripheral vascular disease, is one of the precarious consequences of arsenic ingestion found in southwestern Taiwan (Chen et al. 2003; Lamm et al. 2006; Ravenscroft, Brammer, and Richards 2009). As a consequence of drinking arsenic-contaminated water, a specific skin cancer known as Bel Ville is found in Cordobá, Argentina. It has been estimated that about 100 million people across the globe are at risk of developing detrimental health effects due to prolonged exposure to arsenic (Mukherjee, Fryar, and O'Shea 2009: 313). Table 3.1 (Ravenscroft, Brammer, and Richards 2009) illustrates the major global occurrences of arsenic poisoning.

Table 3.1 Global occurrences of arsenic poisoning

Year	Country	Occurrences
1898	Poland	One of the earliest known cases of arsenic poisoning from well water that caused skin cancer
1920s	Cordobá, Argentina	Bel Ville disease was identified due to the drinking of arsenic-contaminated water
1935	Ontario, Canada	Groundwater was first identified containing arsenic. Report of death due to arsenic ingestion had been reported
1960	Taiwan	Identification of BFD due to drinking arsenic-contaminated water. Hyperpigmentation, keratosis and skin cancers were also identified as results of arsenic contamination
1960s	Antofagasta, Chile	Arsenic was found in the municipal water supply, which caused widespread arsenicosis
1975	India	First detection of arsenic poisoning in the drinking water
1980	Xinjiang, China	Detection of widespread arsenicosis in Xinjiang province in northwestern China followed by other eighteen provinces
1983	West Bengal, India	First arsenicosis patient detected, leading to widespread concern of groundwater poisoning in adjoining areas of Bangladesh and Nepal
2001	Vietnam	Arsenic contamination was found in the Red River Delta, Mekong Delta and bordering areas of Cambodia
2004	Bangladesh	Pervasive arsenic contamination of groundwater was established, with hundreds of deaths and thousands of arsenicosis patients, declared the worst disaster Bangladesh has ever faced

Causes of arsenic poisoning

The issue that puzzles scientists is the underlying causes that lead to arsenic poisoning in the groundwater. Although the causes have yet to be established conclusively, there are some important leads. Two particular assumptions are pertinent here: some geologists believe that arsenic poisoning is a natural occurrence because of particular geological formations of the alluvial sediments of the deltas. This natural occurrence is often explained with two accompanying hypotheses, which will be highlighted next: the pyrite oxidation hypothesis and the iron oxide reduction hypothesis. Some other scientists believe that arsenic poisoning is induced by humans because of excessive extraction of groundwater, disproportionate use of chemical fertilizers for agriculture and excessive mining activities.

The pyrite oxidation hypothesis is one of the earliest explanations of arsenic contamination. It explains that a particular geological and mineralogical composition of the hydrology triggers elevation of arsenic in the groundwater (Acharyya et al. 1999). The Gangetic Delta in West Bengal, India and Bangladesh, which comprises thick sediments deposited by the Ganga-Brahmaputra-Meghna river systems, is particularly prone to release arsenic into the groundwater. The mineralogical and sedimentological characteristics of the Gangetic Delta and Bengal Basin suggest that the sand, silt and clays of the Quaternary age contain pyrites and iron oxyhydroxides, which are rich in arsenic (Meharg 2005: 31). These pyrites, which are rich in sulphide minerals, react with oxygen through a chemical process, thus the insoluble sulphide turns into soluble sulphate to release arsenic into the groundwater (Meharg 2005: 31). In one study, Das and his team assumed that excessive extraction of groundwater lowers the water table, which causes the aquifer to fill with oxygen, leading to a chemical change in the aquifer to release arsenic (Das et al. 1996).

Some other scientists have argued that arsenic in the Gangetic Delta and Bengal Basin is transported by the river systems, which originated in the uplands of Chotanagpur, the Rajmahal highlands in Eastern Bihar and the Himalayas (Das et al. 1996; Kinniburgh et al. 2003). These rivers flow through the copper belt of Bihar, the coal basins of the Damodar Valley and Gondwana coal seams in the Rajmahal Basin to drain arsenic-rich minerals to be deposited in the Bengal Basin (Acharyya et al. 1999; Meharg 2005). It is assumed that the drainage of these sediments, rich in arsenopyrites, into the lower Bengal Basin is the main source of arsenic contamination in West Bengal, India and Bangladesh.

The iron oxide reduction hypothesis, on the other hand, explains that arsenic contamination is the result of a complex geochemical reaction between arsenic and iron concentrations in alluvial sediments (Bhattacharya, Chatterjee, and Jacks 1997; Nickson et al. 1998). Arsenic derives in the particular depth of groundwater because of "reductive dissolution of arsenic-rich iron oxyhydroxides, which in turn is derived from weathering of base-metal sulphides" (Nickson et al. 1998: 338). Since concentrations of arsenic, dissolved iron and bicarbonate increase with the depth of the aquifer, Nickson and his team inferred that iron oxyhydroxides which are rich in arsenic are reduced in the deep groundwater (Nickson et al. 1998: 1998).

A strong correlation between high extractable iron and the releasing of arsenic is established in the Bengal Basin (Harvey et al. 2005; Hossain 2006). Thus, according to the iron oxide reduction hypothesis, arsenic contamination is of natural rather than human origin (Paul 2004).

Besides natural causes, human factors are also believed to be involved in spreading arsenic in the groundwater. Use of agricultural pesticides, chemical fertilizers, excessive extraction of groundwater and mining activities induce modification of the geochemical process in the aquifer, which has led to the release of arsenic into groundwater. Among many other human-induced factors, the indiscriminate use of chemical fertilizers was highlighted first. During the early 1950s, a number of first-generation pesticides and fertilizers, such as Paris green, MMA and cacodylic acid, were introduced to increase productivity of the soil and protect agricultural products from insects. Later on, different organochlorine pesticides such as DDT and HCH were incorporated into this list. Furthermore, different chemical fertilizers such as nitrogen-rich urea and calcium phosphate–rich rock phosphate, which contain high arsenic properties, were also widely used (Meharg 2005; Yu 2001). Thus, indiscriminate and widespread use of such chemicals are believed to trigger microbiological and chemical processes of the shallow aquifer to further facilitate desorption of arsenic from alluvial sediments (Acharyya et al. 1999).

Besides such chemical stimulations, there is a strong correlation between occurrences of arsenic contamination and the excessive extraction of groundwater (Bhattacharya, Chatterjee, and Jacks 1997). The introduction of high-yielding varieties of rice cultivation requires an intensive irrigation facility. In West Bengal, India groundwater has been excessively extracted for irrigation purposes by sinking nearly 0.5 million tubewells, 0.1 million shallow tubewells, and 3,000 deep tubewells (Acharyya et al. 1999; Chakraborti et al. 2002; Das et al. 1996). In Bangladesh, the use of groundwater for irrigation purposes increased from 41 percent in 1982–1983 to 71 percent in 1996–1997 (Hossain 2006: 4). Although exact numbers are still unavailable, it is estimated that 8 to 12 million tubewells are now in operation in rural Bangladesh for extracting groundwater to meet the demand for drinking water for 97 percent of the rural populations (Ahmad et al. 2006; Caldwell et al. 2003; Hossain 2006; Kinniburgh et al. 2003). Such an increased extraction of groundwater has lowered the water table, which is believed to be one of the reasons that arsenic is released into the groundwater (Hossain 2006; Paul 2004).

The problem has further been exacerbated by the massive expansion of industries in Dhaka, Kolkata and other major cities in Bangladesh and India. The noxious wastes from these industrial sources trickle down directly into the shallow aquifer to transform the geochemical processes of hydrology (Meharg 2005). Mining activities also greatly affected the chemistry and oxidizing process of the aquifer by exposing the underlying sulphides to air and aerated water (Henke 2009; Meharg 2005). Arsenopyrite is one of the main arsenic-bearing minerals found in coal and ore mines and can be exposed to aquifer during the coal mining, ore processing and coal combustion processes (Henke 2009: 115). Geologists assume that the mining activities at the Gondwana coal seams in the Rajmahal Basin, the copper belt of Bihar and the coal basins of the Damodar Valley might have triggered the oxidizing process of the sulphide minerals in the aquifer, leading to leaching of arsenic into the groundwater (Acharyya et al. 1999).

Among other human-induced causes is the construction of dams and barrages on the waterways, which divert water from its original course. The construction of the controversial Farakka Barrage[1] is particularly mentioned as a factor for lowering the water table in the Bengal Basin and Gangetic Delta (Paul 2004: 1743). The drying up of the River Padma has created a particular problem to the geochemical and ecological processes of this region. The falling water table resulting from such man-made hazards triggers oxidization processes to contaminate the groundwater.

Clearly, both natural and human-induced causes trigger arsenic contamination in the groundwater. The pervasiveness of arsenic poisoning has put millions of people under the threat of developing arsenicosis disease. The following section describes the ways in which ingestion of arsenic-poisoned water impacts on human health.

Arsenic toxicity: impact on human health

According to the USEPA, arsenic is identified as a human carcinogen and categorized in a Group A classification – based on toxicity, next to mercury, thallium, beryllium, cadmium and many other toxic elements (Brammer and Ravenscroft 2009; Cullen 2008; Nguyen et al. 2009). Ingestion of a few milligrams of arsenic would be enough to induce serious health implications for human beings, whereas a dose of 100 to 200 mg would be fatal (Cullen 2008; Khan et al. 1997). The degree of arsenic toxicity in the human body depends on various factors, such as the chemical and physical compound of arsenic, the route through which the body is exposed to it, nutritional level and the age of the affected individuals (Khan et al. 1997; Ravenscroft, Brammer, and Richards 2009). Depending on the amount of ingestion, the acute toxic effect of arsenic can be observed within thirty minutes to several hours. However, the chronic implications of arsenic toxicity would only be revealed after ten to fifteen years, if not earlier (Cullen 2008; Tondel et al. 1999). Thus, arsenic is called the "silent killer", and many individuals are unaware of it until they get skin lesions.

The clinical manifestations of arsenic exposure can either be acute or chronic. Acute arsenic poisoning may take two forms: firstly, acute paralytic syndrome, such as collapse of cardiovascular systems and the failure of the central nervous system; and secondly, acute gastrointestinal syndrome, including abdominal cramps, vomiting, bloody or watery diarrhoea, throat constriction and skin rashes followed by death between twenty-four hours and two to four days, depending on the amount of exposure (Cullen 2008: 34; Ravenscroft, Brammer, and Richards 2009: 176). Chronic exposure to arsenic may result in the form of a simple everyday malaise, weight loss and general weakness, leading to many serious health hazards in the long run such as cardiovascular diseases, kidney failure, gangrene and cancer (Cullen 2008).

From a medical point of view, the impact of chronic arsenic poisoning on human health can be divided into three categories: dermatological, carcinogenic and non-carcinogenic manifestations (Ravenscroft, Brammer, and Richards 2009: 157).

The earliest symptoms of arsenic exposure are revealed through dermatological manifestations, which are often referred to as arsenicosis. There are three different clinical stages of dermatological implications. The first stage is manifested by such characteristics as melanosis and keratosis, which can be identified through black spots, rain drop signs and pigmentation on the skin. The second stage is attributed to hyperkeratosis (rough and thickening of the palms and soles, warts, corns or plaque-like elevation on the skin), peripheral neuropathy (disorder of nerves) and edema (swelling of the legs). The third stage is associated with precancerous skin lesions such as gangrene, cancer of the extremities, hepatopathy and nephropathy (late-stage kidney disease). Most arsenicosis patients identified in Bangladesh are between the melanosis, keratosis and hyperkeratosis stages.

The most worrying consequence of chronic arsenic poisoning is cancer. Carcinogenic effects of long-term arsenic exposure have been well documented in biomedical research. Three types of cancers are particularly associated with chronic arsenic poisoning: Bowen's disease, basal cell carcinoma and squamous cell carcinoma, which are clinical manifestations of late-stage keratosis (Khan et al. 1997). Almost all vital internal organs can be affected by arsenic poisoning, including the liver, heart, urinary bladder, prostate and haemopoietic and lymphatic tissues (Smith et al. 1994). Evidence from Argentina, Chile and Japan reveals a strong correlation between exposure to arsenic and the development of lung cancer (Ferreccio et al. 2000). In Taiwan, one epidemiological study suggests a strong association between long-term arsenic exposure and development of lung and bladder cancers. The later stage of BFD has resulted in gangrene and cancer (Chen and Wang 1990). In Argentina, a significant correlation has been found between exposure to arsenic and high mortality rates due to bladder, lung and kidney cancers (Hopenhayn-Rich et al. 1996, 2000).

Arsenic is also considered to be a major risk factor for developing cardiovascular and peripheral artery diseases. Clinical studies have established that long-term exposure to arsenic is responsible for hardening blood vessels of the heart due to plaque formation, leading to atherosclerosis and related cardiovascular diseases such as hypertension and high blood pressure (Engel et al. 1994). The atherosclerotic process further leads to ischemic heart disease and cerebral infarction at a later stage (Chen et al. 1994). Besides external manifestations of arsenic lesions on the skin, different internal organs such as the gastrointestinal tract, liver and pancreas are affected by arsenic poisoning (Ferreccio and Sancha 2006). In Taiwan, Chen and his team found a significant correlation between arsenic exposure and electrocardiogram-based ischemic heart disease, hypertension and diabetes mellitus (Chen et al. 1994). One crucial fact about arsenicosis is that many people drink arsenic-contaminated water from the same water sources, but not all are affected by arsenicosis at the same time. Thus, one most unsettling matter in biomedicine is to answer the question of who gets affected by arsenic poisoning, when and why. Although the answer has yet to be established conclusively, biomedical research demonstrates that the nutritional level of an individual and the body's natural immune system to resist diseases are important factors in determining who gets this disease (Khan et al. 1997). Thus, malnourished children, pregnant women and older individuals who lack sufficient nutrition are most susceptible to arsenicosis.

Another most disturbing factor for the management of arsenicosis is that there is no specific medical treatment for the chronic form. Stopping the intake of arsenic-contaminated water is considered to be the only preventive measure for improving the condition and restricting further infection (Cullen 2008; Khan et al. 1997). Depending on individual cases, medical doctors may recommend consumption of protein and vitamin-rich foods, such as beans, peas, pulse, lentils and leafy and green vegetables so that the body's general resistance against diseases can be improved. In case of the primary stages of arsenicosis, drinking arsenic-safe water in conjunction with taking vitamins A, E and C supplements may improve the condition. The later stages of keratosis, however, require advanced medical management, including topical application of ointment containing urea and salicylic acid (Khan et al. 1997). Recently, doctors have found chelation therapy, an alternative treatment using chelating agents such as penicillamine, dimercaptopropanesulfonic acid and DMSA, useful in removing toxic elements like arsenic from the body. Others, however, consider chelation therapy ineffective and simply a waste of money (Cullen 2008: 43). In the case of advanced stages like cancer and gangrene, surgery and amputation of the affected organs are the only medical procedures to be followed (Ravenscroft, Brammer, and Richards 2009: 158).

Having discussed the prevalence, causes and health consequences of arsenic poisoning, it is now necessary to describe the medical marketplace in rural Bangladesh, which invariably shapes the health-seeking behaviour of individuals affected by arsenic poisoning. The following discussion will allow readers to understand how a plural medical system in Bangladesh has emerged in line with the political transitions in ancient, colonial and postcolonial Bangladesh. Historically the Bangladeshis have been exposed to different health care services, and their healing choices are thus guided by various options that are readily available to them.

Medical systems in Bangladesh

From a historical point of view, different dynasties in ancient Bengal not only introduced new politico-religious traditions, but also injected new medical practices. It was the Aryans who contributed to the establishment of Vedic medicine in Bengal based on philological and religious contents. The earliest Vedic healers used magico-religious chants to defy demons, and herbs for setting bones (Islam 2005). The proliferation of Vedic medical knowledge was evident by the emergence of different medical specialists, such as the surgeons (*shalya vaidyas*), the general physicians (*bhisaks*) and the magic doctors, or *bhisak atharvans* (Bala 2007: 14). The practice of Ayurvedic medicine continued during the subsequent Mauryan and Gupta dynasties. Ashoka, the great Mauryan emperor, established Nalanda University in Patna, where medicine was first institutionally taught as a separate discipline. Two particular schools of Ayurvedic thought flourished at that time: the Caraka tradition was based on herbal pharmacopeia, while the Susruta school excelled in surgical procedures (Bala 2007: 37; Zysk 1991: 47). The practitioners of Ayurvedic medicine enjoyed full patronage from the royal courts and achieved high social prestige. The Vedic period contributed flourishing medical verses and incantations, writing on medicine, codification and proliferation of Ayurvedic medical knowledge.

Subsequently, the Muslim rulers not only brought Islamic philosophical traditions, but also introduced new medical knowledge and practice called Unani, based on Greek humoral philosophy. The arrival of a new medical system, however, did not threaten the already prevailing Ayurvedic medical system and other indigenous healing practices; rather, a peaceful coexistence of different medical systems was observed (Bala 2007). The presence in the royal courts of both *vaids*, those specializing in Ayurvedic medicine, and *hakims*, those specializing in Unani medicine, reflected equal treatment and royal support from the Mughal emperors. Another reason why both medical systems harmoniously coexisted was because of their internal similarities in that both systems were guided by the humoral philosophy, which brought both *vaids* and *hakims* closer to each other in practicing and sharing their therapeutic knowledge. On the ground, the common citizenry accepted Unani as one more healing option, thereby contributing towards a more pluralistic medical field in Bengal.

During the colonial period, medical systems in Bengal underwent tremendous changes, and a new scientific biomedicine was introduced in Bengal. The preexisting Ayurvedic and Unani medical systems lost support and dignity in the eyes of the colonial rulers and fell from the grace. The predicament of native medical systems started during the rule of Lord William Bentinck, who shifted Imperial policy from supporting indigenous medical systems to prioritizing the teaching and practice of biomedicine. Throughout the nineteenth century, the teaching and training of Western biomedicine was enormous under the direct patronage of the British empire, which paved the way for the future development of biomedicine in Bengal. This transformation mostly took place by suppressing and de-patronizing the native medical systems by the colonial rulers.

Under colonial rule, native medical systems were criticized as "unsystematic, incoherent and unreliable" and thus "rigid" and "closed", owing to their association with religion (Buckingham 2002: 70). The mythological characteristics of native medicine were perceived to be "unscientific" and were considered inferior to the newly established scientific biomedicine. The native medical practitioners were discouraged and discriminated against (Ernst 1999; Liebeskind 2002). For the first time in the medical history of Bengal, a tension was noticed among different medical practitioners based on their perceived hierarchy, superiority and scientific legacy (Gupta 1976: 370). Allopathic doctors, with their training in scientific biomedicine, placed themselves at the top of the hierarchy, whereas native medical systems were looked down upon and referred to as the "products of paganism and superstition" (Gupta 1976: 370).

Despite such institutionalization of Western biomedicine, indigenous medicine continued to be practiced at the private level "largely due to the continuation of the popular support it had received through the ages" (Bala 1991: 18). During the nineteenth century, a new sense of nationalistic politico-ideology emerged among the affluent and English-educated *voddorlok* in India, which motivated them to take part in the *swadeshi* movement.[2] The politico-historical significance of the *swadeshi* movement was far-reaching, which ultimately paved the way for India's political independence by compelling the British to quit the subcontinent in 1947. As far as medical history was concerned, the nationalistic *swadeshi* movement called for a revival of indigenous medicine. Ayurveda, Unani, Yoga and other forms of native healing systems became part of the broader nationalistic sentiment. The formation of the Committee on Indigenous Systems of Medicine in 1923 reflected the need to institutionalize alternative medicine, which further promoted teaching, research and training of *vaids* and *hakims* in Bengal (Bala 2007; Kumar 1998, 2002; Patterson 2001). Despite such initiatives for reviving alternative healing systems, biomedicine continued to dominate over other medical systems in the postcolonial context.

The decline of the British empire in 1947 realigned the Indian subcontinent into two different nation-states, India and Pakistan. Although part of Bengal for centuries, West Bengal, on the grounds of being numerically dominated by Hindus, belonged to India, whereas the then East Bengal, being dominated by the Muslims, constituted part of Pakistan (Chatterji 2007; Khan 2007; Pandey 2001; Tan and Kudaisya 2000). Except for religious similarity, there were virtually no geographical and sociocultural connections between East and West Pakistan. Such a disconnection resulted in a discriminatory attitude, political dominance and military invasion over East Pakistan by the West Pakistani rulers. Discontent ultimately broke out in 1971, when Sheikh Mujibur Rahman, the political leader of East Bengal, declared independence for Bangladesh. The nine-month-long liberation war ended up with the surrender of the West Pakistani Army on December 16, 1971, and Bangladesh emerged as a new nation-state on the world map.

Since independence, apart from consecutive military interferences and political antagonism, the achievements of the democratic government have been severely affected by poor governance, particularly widespread corruption and lack of accountability at all levels in the public sector (Ahmad 2002; Alamgir, Mahmud, and Iftekharuzzaman 2004; Sobhan 1993). For promoting good governance and effectiveness of the state apparatus, a number of initiatives had been taken, including divesting public enterprises, attracting local and foreign investments and promoting private entrepreneurs (Haque 2001: 1410). In order to accentuate these reform processes, a number of institutional changes were made, such as the establishment of the Privatization Board, Board of Investment, Deregulation Commission, Anti-corruption Commission and National Commission for Reforming Government (Haque 2001: 1412). The Bangladeshis have been waiting to see the general implication of such institutional reforms in terms of improvement in good governance, accountability of the state and restriction of widespread corruption.

Home to approximately 145 million people in an area of 147,570 square kilometers, Bangladesh is one of the most densely populated countries in the world. Agriculture is the main subsistence for the majority of the population, who live in villages. Their subsistence, however, is supplemented by other home-based small enterprises such as livestock and poultry farming, running small shops and simply supplying manual labour in others' agricultural lands. Nearly half of the Bangladeshi population lives below the poverty line. Although 85 percent of the total land area of Bangladesh is arable, it is not evenly distributed, since nearly 28 percent of the total rural population is landless (BBS 2001). The economic condition of the landless becomes miserable during the monsoon and off-seasons, when there is no agricultural work. One obvious consequence of having such a large population living below the poverty line is the widespread prevalence of malnourishment, particularly among the children and women (FAO 1999; Rahman et al. 2005; UNICEF 2006). An estimated 58 percent of children of pre-school age are malnourished and underweight, and 51 percent are stunted, whereas nearly 50 percent of women suffer from chronic energy deficiency (WHO 2000). The costs associated with such malnutrition are often very high in terms of both economic and human development, since the malnourished population is highly susceptible to different diseases due to their low body immunity.

The failure of the state to ameliorate pervasive poverty opened up a new space for NGOs to come up with different development projects, targeting directly the rural poor and vulnerable population. By the 1990s, the growth of NGOs was exponential, as the number increased from 494 in 1991 to 1,370 in 2000 (Devine 2003). NGOs are recognized as the "agents of development par excellence" (White 1999). The outcomes of NGO intervention in Bangladesh are remarkable, since thousands of NGOs reach millions of individuals and households in the rural areas with improvements in various developmental indicators. It is claimed that NGOs are the first to attack the root of poverty through microcredit programs. NGOs are considered the carrier of many observable changes in the areas of household income, asset accumulation, networking, awareness creation in contraceptive use, informal education and better toilet, sanitation and drinking water facilities (see, e.g., Chowdhury and Alam 1997; Hashemi and Morshed 1997; Hulme and Edwards 1997; Islam 2004, 2010; Khandker and Khalily 1996; Khandker 1993; Mayfield 1997; Yunus 1997, 1998, 1999).

The contribution of NGOs to promoting health is also impressive. Many NGOs prioritize promotion of contraception, water and sanitation as their central development agenda. Although the exact number is unavailable, an estimated 400 NGOs are actively involved in promoting preventive and curative health care services at the community level (Hashima-e-Nasreen et al. 2007: 15). Maternal, neonatal and child health care programs of the BRAC reach nearly 19 million people in rural Bangladesh. The BRAC trains thousands of health assistants (*Shasthya Sebika*) from its female savings group members, who are subsequently employed for promoting preventive, promotive and curative health care services at the community level. By visiting door-to-door, they disseminate health, nutrition and family planning messages, motivate people to use sanitary latrines and safe drinking water, promote safe motherhood, provide treatment for common illnesses and sell basic health commodities (Ahmed 2008; Hashima-e-Nasreen et al. 2007).

Following independence, the government had substantially invested in developing suitable health care systems in Bangladesh, which can broadly be organized into three sectors: the professional, the paraprofessional and the traditional.[3] Each of these sectors is described below.

The professional sector

The government adopted the PHC approach with a four-tier system: (1) community health workers at the village level, (2) satellite clinics/health posts, (3) the UHFWC at the Union level and (4) the UHC at the subdistrict level (Khan 2007; WHO 2000). Currently, through 3,178 UHFWCs, preventive health care and family planning services are provided at the village level (Bangladesh Health Watch 2007). These UHFWCs are usually run by HAs and FWAs, who generally make door-to-door visits for promoting awareness on public health and family planning issues. The UHC is the first referral health center in Bangladesh, which is usually a 50-bed hospital, and the doctors have at least an MBBS degree. Both ambulatory and twenty-four-hour emergency services are available. The services and medications, subject to availability, are free at the point of delivery. Currently, there are a total of 402 UHCs serving approximately 200,000–450,000 people each. Since many UHCs do not provide specialist health care services, patients who seek those services need to go to the district hospitals. The district hospitals are equipped with modern health care facilities, and the services are free at the point of delivery. Each district hospital has 50–100 beds for serving approximately 1–2 million people. Next to the district hospitals are the tertiary medical colleges and their adjunct hospitals located at the divisional headquarters. These medical college hospitals are the largest public hospitals, with 250–1,050 beds and provide tertiary health care services.

The government has substantially invested in developing medical infrastructure and a biomedical workforce. Currently, there are a total of thirteen government and thirty-two private medical colleges in Bangladesh, which have so far produced 38,000 MBBS doctors (Amin et al. 2008; WHO 2006a). Besides biomedicine, the government has also supported alternative healing systems. The establishments of the Government Homoeopathic Medical College and Hospital in 1984 and the Government Unani and Ayurvedic Degree College in 1987 are considered the greatest leaps towards institutionalizing homeopathy, Ayurvedic and Unani systems of medicine in Bangladesh.

Despite these various initiatives, problems are many in the public health sector (see, e.g., Aldana, Piechulek, and Al-Sabir 2001; Andaleeb 2000, 2001; Ashraf, Chowdhury, and Streefland 1982; Bhardwaj and Paul 1986; Feldman 1983; Islam and Bachman 1983; Kaosar 2004; Paul 1983, 1999; Stanton and Clemens 1989; Zaman 2004). Development and delivery of health care services remain severely limited by economic, logistic and human-resources constraints. In 2003, the annual budget allocation for health was only 5.8 percent of the total government expenditure (compared with 18.5 in the USA and 15.8 in the UK). The problem has been exacerbated by the lack of a qualified health care workforce, since the doctor–patient ratio is only 0.26/1000 (compared with 2.56 in the USA and 2.30 in the UK), and the nurse–population ratio is 0.14/1000 (compared with 9.37 in the USA and 12.12 in the UK), which is by any measure one of the lowest in the world (WHO 2006a). The consequences of such limitations and inadequacies are reflected in the poor outcome of the public health services in Bangladesh. One study reports that the "overall performance of the sector was unacceptably low by all conventional measures" (Andaleeb 2001: 1360).

Given such a poor public health system, prolific growth has been observed in the private health care sector, as the number of private hospitals increased from 288 in 1997 to 613 in 2000 (BBS 2001). The proliferation of expensive private health care services has further raised the question of equity and accessibility, since these private resorts are mostly based in the urban areas and provide high-tech medical facilities mostly to the upper-class and affluent section of the population. Poor people with low incomes mostly remain out of these services and have no access to them (Andaleeb 2000).

The paraprofessional sector

Influenced by the Chinese model of "barefoot doctors", the GoB, with the assistance of USAID, has launched an initiative to train rural traditional practitioners to create trained health practitioners called *palli-chikitshoks*. The one-year program was intended to provide basic understandings of anatomy, physiology, pharmacology, first aid, nutrition and family planning. Upon completion of training, an eligibility certificate was given so that PCs can practice medicine in rural areas. The underlying assumptions of the PC program were twofold: firstly, these trained health cadres were expected to replace the existing "traditional" and "quackery" services by providing skilled allopathic medicine to the rural populations, and secondly, this program would increase professional opportunities for educated individuals living in the rural areas who would be willing to serve the community by providing skilled allopathic treatment (Feldman 1983). Some researchers, however, argued that the introduction of PCs has further reinforced the existing polarization of health care utilization, since affluent families continue to seek health care services from professional biomedical doctors, and the less trained PCs remain as the last resort for the poorest people. As Feldman (1983: 1888) notes:

> [T]he PC program would reinforce an already class biased medical structure in which only minimal services, composed of the least trained, reach the poorest sectors of the society. The PC program, in effect, would institutionalize these differences since, given available resources, those who could afford trained practitioners would indeed be more likely to choose them.

The traditional sector

Traditional healing services are widespread in rural Bangladesh (see, e.g., Ahmed et al. 2000; Ashraf, Chowdhury, and Streefland 1982; Bhardwaj and Paul 1986; Feldman 1983). This sector comprises a wide array of practitioners, including but not limited to the untrained allopathic drug sellers, village *kobiraj*, magico-religious healers, herbalists, traditional birth attendants and untrained homeopaths. These traditional healers render a range of medical services, such as handling snakebites, removing supernatural or evil eyes and finding lost goods and properties. Many traditional healers practice privately at their homes, whereas others run herbal drug shops at the village market. One category of traditional healers extensively used by the rural villagers is the religious healers, popularly known as *hujur*[4] in many areas of Bangladesh, who provide various health care services such as blowing water (*pani-pora*),[5] providing amulets and *jhar-fuk*.[6] In most cases, their services are either free of charge or at a very nominal price, making them popular among the poor rural Bangladeshis.

Another common health service provider in rural Bangladesh is the untrained allopathic drug seller, known as the village doctor, who runs his own pharmacy cum chamber in the village marketplace for providing biomedical health care services. They sell allopathic medicine with or without prescriptions. What one needs to know is the name of a medicine, or even without this one can purchase medicine by just telling the symptoms of the illness. These village doctors often do not have any formal training in allopathic medicine; rather, they are apprenticed under a senior village doctor. Although the Drugs (Control) Ordinance of Bangladesh clearly mentions that "[n]o person, being a retailer, shall sell any drug without the personal supervision of a pharmacist registered in any Register of the Pharmacy Council of Bangladesh", these laws are rarely enforced (Drugs (Control) Ordinance 1982).

It has been quite evident in the foregoing discussion that Bangladesh has historically evolved into a land of diverse medical practices and the Bangladeshis have generous access to varieties of health care services. The health-seeking behaviour of the rural Bangladeshis is thus shaped by the presence of pluralistic medical systems. The emergence and sustenance of alternative healing services, which are quite pervasive, are guided by the popular support of the rural Bangladeshis. These burgeoning alternative healing services are not just popular resorts for many rural Bangladeshis, including arsenicosis patients, but are also considered as the only option against the downtrodden public health care services in Bangladesh.

Conclusion

It has been necessary to outline the history of medical systems in Bangladesh, the extent and causes of arsenic contamination and its resultant health impact to allow a transition to the following chapters. Arsenicosis is medically explained as a particular pathological condition which occurs due to drinking arsenic-contaminated groundwater. From a medical point of view, arsenicosis has been constructed through particular clinical and physiological manifestations such as melanosis, keratosis, hyperkeratosis, cancer and gangrene. The biological and anatomical explanations of arsenicosis emphasize the pathophysiological conditions which induce dysfunction in bodily systems. Thus, medical understandings of arsenicosis are grounded in scientific observation, diagnosis and management. Against this backdrop of medical and scientific explanations of arsenicosis, the next chapter will delineate how the actual arsenic-affected individuals and lay villagers understand, explain and experience this illness. An ethnographic analysis of arsenicosis will demonstrate how culture and ecology play a decisive role in creating a lay knowledge of public health in general and arsenicosis in particular.

Notes

1 Situated in the borderland between Bangladesh and India, the Farakka Barrage was constructed in 1975 to divert water from the Ganges to the Hooghly River in Kolkata. Such a construction creates huge controversy, as the barrage cuts off water flow from the River Padma in Bangladesh, resulting in huge environmental disasters such as drying out of the rivers, raised salinity level, ecological imbalance, hindered waterway navigation and the process of desertification, leading to huge public health crises in the northwestern region of Bangladesh.
2 The *swadeshi* movement was an anti-imperialist movement under the leadership of Mahatma Gandhi, who called for an end of British colonialism in India, largely because of its exploitative and discriminatory attitudes towards the Indian people. The major guiding strategies for the *swadeshi* movement were a call for boycotting Western products and the revival of indigenous culture and technology. The *swadeshi* movement later on paved the way for a broader anticolonial movement and the political independence of India.
3 I am fully aware of the limitations of such neat categorization of medical systems and the problems associated with the definition and "boundary" maintenance of different medical systems. They are often overlapping and syncretic in practice. However, these are just meant to facilitate easy reference and discussion of medical resorts in Bangladesh.
4 A *hujur* is usually the elder person of the village who is also the imam of the mosque to conduct prayers. Many people visit him for obtaining religious advice or curing diseases, which he does by using religious chants or by giving amulets.
5 This is a specific healing technique used by the traditional healers or *hujur*, who blow water while chanting from religious books. The patient is then advised either to drink the water or apply it externally.
6 *Jhar-fuk* is very common in rural Bangladesh, whereby the traditional healer or *hujur* chants from the holy book and blows on the body of the sick person.

4 *Ghaa*
The social construction of arsenicosis

Introduction

This chapter draws upon ethnographic data to demonstrate how arsenicosis is socially constructed within the broader framework of health and illness beliefs and practices in rural Bangladesh. By focusing on lay concepts, labels, categories, disease etiologies and practices, as explained and experienced by lay villagers, it is revealed how a biomedical category of arsenicosis has been vernacularized as *ghaa* in practice. An ethnographic analysis of arsenicosis will illustrate how this illness has been understood, explained and responded to by lay villagers who handle this illness in their everyday lives. At the end of this chapter, two issues would be understandable: firstly, how arsenicosis is explained using existing local terminologies and disease etiologies, and secondly, perhaps preeminently, how such social construction of *ghaa* departs from the biomedical and official explanations of arsenicosis. At this point it is necessary to describe how health and illness are generally understood and explained by rural Bangladeshis, which would allow a transition to the next discussion of how arsenicosis is vernacularized within such beliefs and practices.

Lay health and illness beliefs and practices in rural Bangladesh

Perceptions about health and illness in rural Bangladesh are socio-historically, ecologically and religiously prescribed, and are guided by at least two core ideas: (1) a coherent form of beliefs and practices about health and illness, and (2) these beliefs and practices being embedded in the experiences of the everyday lives of subjects, who live under particular socio-political and ecological constraints (Leslie and Young 1992). Although popular beliefs and practices about health and illness in rural Bangladesh have not been either systematically disciplined or institutionalized per se, they are patterned, flexible, pragmatic and based on everyday life and culture. Even though there is no written textbook or procedural protocols, these beliefs and practices are very much shaped by "some rule-of-thumb guidelines and some tried and tested remedies" (Craig 2002).

Research on health and illness in rural Bangladesh has focused mainly on the areas of government health care services and their utilizations (see, e.g., Andaleeb 2000; Feldman 1983; Islam and Bachman 1983; Paul 1983; Paul and Rumsey 2002; Stanton and Clemens 1989), pluralistic medical systems (Ashraf, Chowdhury, and Streefland 1982; Bhardwaj and Paul 1986), constraints in public health care services (Andaleeb 2001; Islam 2012; Paul 1999; Zaman 2004) and doctor–patient interactions in a clinical setting (Wilce 1995, 1997). There has been clearly a dearth of anthropological scholarship in the areas of lay health and illness beliefs and practices in rural Bangladesh and their implications in understanding, interpreting and managing a specific illness. The only exception is Rousham's (1994) study of mothers' knowledge and perception about children's intestinal worm infection and the respective use of health care services in rural Bangladesh. Current study on arsenic poisoning is unique in the sense that it aims to fill the gap in Bangladeshi medical anthropological literature with respect to everyday health and illness beliefs and practices and how these beliefs and practices shape understanding, meaning and management of a specific disease – arsenicosis in this context. The discussion that follows demonstrates the general health and illness beliefs and practices in rural Bangladesh and the ways in which arsenicosis has been understood and explained within such a framework.

Conceptualizing health (sustho) *and illness* (osustho)

One fundamental difficulty that I encountered during the very early days of conducting fieldwork in rural Bangladesh, a non-English-speaking community, was to examine whether Western labels, terminologies and categories, such as 'health' and 'disease', were applicable to a local context. To facilitate easy discussion with the local community, it was necessary to identify the local terms that villagers used to refer to health and illness. Such conceptual difficulty has already been documented and raised by others – for example, by Allen's study of illness behaviour among the Thulung people in Nepal (Allen 1976). In an effort to avoid such problematics associated with these terms, I did not predefine them. Instead, I engaged myself in an open-ended conversation with the informants so as to establish the local interpretations, labels, meanings and categorizations related to health and illness as perceived and used by the people. I learned from the local context that whenever one was asked about health (*sastho*), it generally referred to the physical and mental conditions of an individual. The local meanings of health are often associated with some other synonymous concepts, such as remaining healthy (*sustho*) or experiencing illness (*osustho*). Kleinman's (1980) explanatory model of illness, which basically asks such questions as "what do you call your illness? what do you think has caused your problem?", appears to be very directed, narrow and inapplicable in the context of rural Bangladesh. I agree with Pigg (1990) and Zvosec (1996) that such straightforward questions often lead to an answer like "how can I tell?" or simply, "I do not know". Instead, to understand disease etiologies and beliefs about health and illness, I had to follow the village norms and customs. During my initial fieldwork, whenever I met someone in the village, the first typical starting of a conversation was as follows:

Researcher: How are you? (*kemon asen*)
(This often led to either a positive or negative answer).
Respondent: (for positive answer): good (*valo asi*) or (for negative answer): just going on (*eito asi ar ki*), or, the body is not good (*shorir ta valo ney*)
(Excerpt from fieldwork diary)

Thus, following local norms, one is not expected to ask "how is your health?", but to begin with a general question like "how are you?" (*kemon asen*), which leads to other information about the physical and mental conditions of the individual. From the villagers' point of view, health and illness often come under the linguistic framework of being good or not (*valo thaka / na thaka*), which is frequently explained through multiple and subjective reasons. When asked about health, respondents mostly used a comparative perspective vis-à-vis healthy/sick others to denote one's own health condition. As one villager explained to me:

> I consider health and illness a matter of comparison (*tulonar bisoy*). You can never consider yourself healthy unless you compare your physical and mental condition with someone else who is sick. Look, right now I am fit both physically and mentally because at least I am not in a situation like Ali,[1] to whom being alive or dead is almost the same. Thanks to Allah that I am good and not in such a situation.

Health and illness are thus explained in comparison with someone else. When asked the question "how are you?" many respondents incorporated other issues unrelated to disease to narrate their personal concerns and troubles. These concerns came from diverse realities, such as finding a suitable bridegroom for a marriageable daughter, effects of drought on agriculture, price hikes for everyday commodities, frequent electricity failure or even the rise of miscreants who stole oxen, which tremendously influenced villagers' sense of being good or not. As Mr. Delwar, a 35-year-old man, expresses his concern about a stolen ox:

> How can I remain good? (*kivabe valo thakbo*). People will not allow me to stay good. Do you want to know why? My only pair of oxen was stolen last month, which were the only means of meeting many agricultural purposes. Now it is the time to plough lands and I am in trouble, and thinking most of the time how to manage money to tract land or to borrow others' ox. I am always worried in these days. If I miss this season, all my family members will have to starve.

Losing the only pair of oxen severely affects the life of this person, which made him anxious about continuing agriculture and maintaining the family. This may be unrelated to disease, but it upsets his mental condition and disrupts his everyday life, which subsequently affects the way of remaining good (*valo thaka*). In another interview, one mother of a female arsenicosis patient said:

> My daughter has reached her marriageable age (*biyer boyos hoyese*) but she is suffering from *ghaa*. I am really worried about her. How can I manage a groom for her? Who will marry my daughter who is suffering from *ghaa*? I am seriously worried about this matter.

Here, the mother is more worried about how to find a suitable bridegroom for her marriageable daughter than health consequences of arsenicosis. On many occasions villagers also informed me that they were anxious about the recent price hikes of everyday commodities, as it affected their ability to provide three meals a day for the family. Thus, the notion of health and illness has economic and class dimensions and is very much shaped by the experiences of everyday life of the villagers. Suffering illness and their expressions, however, differ across social classes in rural Bangladesh. For many poor villagers, who live from hand to mouth and by physical labour, less meticulous symptoms often remain unnoticed and are generally ignored. One day while I was travelling by a trishaw,[2] I informally spoke to the trishaw puller about his understanding of health and illness. He replied to me thus:

> Do not ask me about health. We have to think about what we will eat tomorrow; let alone thinking about health. Look, many times I have to work under sun and rain and often feel runny-nosed (*sordi*) and feverish (*jor jor vab*). But at the same time I have to think if I cannot pull my van today, my family would starve the next day. So I do not care about these small symptoms. For poor people like us, we are happy that we are still alive. We just have to work hard and live from hand to mouth. We have to work, eat whatever we get, and see what happens next.

Thus, in a poverty-ridden rural Bangladesh where most people have to work hard for merely managing three meals a day, minor issues of illnesses remain trivial to them. They often prioritize other issues, such as economic survival and earning cash for maintaining the family, ignoring minor health issues. Many villagers further perceive health as synonymous with the fitness of the body (*shorirer shokti*) and the ability to work. As one school teacher explained to me:

> Health is something that makes me fit for work (*kaaj korte pari*). If anything limits my ability to work (*kaaj korar shakti*), I would not be in good health. Right now I am fine and doing quite well in my work, both in the school and in agricultural land, and so I think I am healthy now.

Such a relationship between sickness and inability to work has already been documented by Parsons (1951), who argues that being sick means that one is in a mode of a "sick role", that he is exempted from normal social roles and responsibilities. Blaxter (1995) has also explained health as "physical fitness", meaning that good health is perceived as long as the body is found fit for work. Such understandings of health have been validated by a 65-year-old woman, who stated that old people are not healthy because they do not have enough bodily strength and, hence, are unable to work. She narrates:

> [I] do not find enough strength (*sorire bol pai na*), hands and legs shake, sometimes cannot stand up due to weakness. The eyes have become hazy. Doctors say I have high blood pressure. I am advised to take the red pill[3] every night. I am not healthy at all because I do not have any bodily strength.

In many cases, conceptualization of health or "remaining good" often comes in comparison with time, i.e., the past and the present. Many villagers frequently stated that the past days were good when they did not live in poverty and had lower population density and sufficient chemical-free[4] food, as opposed to the present day when utilization of chemical fertilizer (*sar*) and pesticides (*bish*) have become pervasive, which has severely degraded the quality of food, leading to the emergence of new diseases as a result of a weakened immune system. As one informant stated:

> Can you find any food in the market which has been produced without *sar* and *bish*? How can you expect good health having eaten such poisonous food? The water is poisoned, the air is polluted. What is left? Is it not enough that we are still alive? But in our times,[5] the condition was not like this. We had fresh water, big fish from the ponds, and fertilizer-free rice from the lands. We were happy that time.

From these statements, it is obvious that health is a subjective phenomenon. Health is considered positively when the school teacher considers physical fitness and ability to do work as good health, or when the trishaw puller ignores minor symptoms of illness so that he remains functional for an everyday livelihood. At the same time, health is also perceived negatively when the ill-fated farmer narrates his stolen pair of oxen, or an anxious mother is worried about finding a suitable bridegroom for her daughter. Clearly, health and illness are defined in subjective, multidimensional and holistic perspectives. The vocabulary used, the experiences encountered and the symptoms categorized are varied, complex and subtle. The social construction of health and illness is holistic and pragmatic and often narrates the ways individuals experience them in their everyday lives. As Dubos (1995: 9) rightly points out:

> Health and disease cannot be defined merely in terms of anatomical, physiological, or mental attributes. Their real measure is the ability of the individual to function in a manner acceptable to him and to the group of which he is part.

***Dietary rules and the concept of hot* (gorom) *and cold* (thanda)**

Mary Douglas in her book *Purity and Danger* argues that all societies have basic classificatory systems of binary divisions, which offer such classifications as 'clean' and 'unclean', 'pure' and 'impure', as she notes, "for us sacred things and places are to be protected from defilement. Holiness and impurity are at opposite poles. We would as soon confound hunger with fullness or sleeping with waking" (Douglas 1966: 7). In medical anthropology, binary classifications based on a humoral theory of disease, such as 'hot/cold' and 'yin/yang', have been well documented across cultures. Appreciating its sociological value, an entire issue of the *Journal of Social Science and Medicine* (1987, vol. 25[4]) was dedicated to understanding the cross-cultural dimensions of hot/cold phenomena. The elements of this humoral theory of disease have been found in the Greek, Ayurveda and Chinese medical philosophies, where it has been argued that excessive exposure to either hot or cold situations may trigger imbalances in the body's humoral condition, making one susceptible to illnesses. It requires a return to a balance by consuming foods with the opposite effects, a strategy that may also be used as a preventive measures (Laderman 1987; Manderson 1987; Messer 1987; Nichter 1987; Pool 1987).

In medical anthropology, food and foodways are of major interest given their significance in understanding and explaining health and illness. In many societies, food is considered both as a pathogen that induces disease and a remedy that leads to the recovery of strength, vitality and soul that are lost due to illness (Borré 1991; Cassel 1977; Lupton 1996; Mckay 1980). In the context of rural Bangladesh, dietary rules and their perceived hot/cold characteristics are culturally patterned and have provided a frame of reference for conceptualizing health and illness. The hot/cold classification, however, is not only applied in the case of dietary rules, it can also be applied in a variety of other contexts to illustrate weather, personal mood and bodily status. Thus, besides hot and cold food, there can also be hot and cold weather, a hot and cold person and a hot and cold body.

According to rural Bangladeshi health beliefs, one fundamental principle for avoiding many illnesses is to keep the body cool by reducing accumulated heat. There are different culturally constructed ways that rural people rely on to ensure this balance. Appropriate bathing has become one of the key ways of eliminating body heat and keeping it cool. In this connection, Nichter (1987) has mentioned two types of bathing in the Sinhalese context: a full bath (*nanawa*) "to cool the body and the mind" and a body wash (*anga sodanawa*) "to cleanse the body". Nichter's observation has some relevance to the context of rural Bangladesh, where an appropriate full bath (*gosol*) is perceived to be an important way of controlling body heat. Many villagers confirmed to me that at least one full bath is important for maintaining good health. The preference is for this to be performed at noon before lunch, since this time is considered to be the hottest period of the day and requires the body to be cooled down. Some villagers, who work as day labourers in the agricultural fields, perceived bathing as both a means of cleansing body parts and a source of regaining vitality by maintaining a balance between hot and cold.

Besides bathing, another practice to reduce body temperature in rural Bangladesh is the ingestion of liquids, which are perceived to contain cooling properties. According to Bangladeshi culture, whenever someone visits another's home, particularly during the summer months, a hand fan (*hatpakha*)[6] and a glass of cold water or *shorbot*[7] are offered. Offering these is an age-old practice among the rural Bangladeshis, particularly to those returning home from outside. These practices are common mostly during the summer, when the outside temperature is high and considered to be harmful. It is believed that exposure to such heat makes the body susceptible to runny nose (*sordi-gormi*), headache and blurred vision. A cooling agent, in this case the *shorbot*, or washing body parts with cold water is then required to counterbalance the heat and to prevent these illness symptoms. Moreover, sweating is regarded as the loss of body fluids – leading to the loss of energy and vitality of the body – which need to be replenished. Thus, in the guise of a customary prescription of offering *shorbot*, a culturally constructive framework of balancing body temperature and maintaining health is evident in rural Bangladesh.

Associated with this hot/cold framework is the classification of different foods as possessing hot and cold properties. It is believed that both hot and cold foods have promotive, preventive and causative capabilities, and are either prescriptive or proscriptive to certain groups of people. For example, the village *kobiraj* told me that pineapple is considered to be a very hot food and must be avoided by pregnant women, otherwise it may trigger fetal malformation or even miscarriage. Some foods are considered to be hot and must be avoided to get rid of certain illnesses. In this scheme, brinjal, Indian spinach (*puishak*), radish (*mula*) prawn, eggs and beef are considered to be hot foods, which may cause skin rashes, itching (*chulkani*) and allergies. In contrast, papaya, bitter gourd, bottle gourd (*lau*) and cucumber (*shosha*) are considered cold foods, and caution is advised for those who are prone to colds. The village *kobiraj* explained to me thus:

> If someone gets any skin problem (*chulkani-pachra*), he must avoid foods like brinjal, beef, and prawn, as these foods are hot and may exacerbate the condition. Some foods are favorable for digestion and the gastrointestinal tract. I will tell you to take some light cold foods like yogurt (*doi*), banana, plantain, wood apple and flatten rice (*chira*), as these foods are cold (*thanda*) and good for health.

I found that villagers have well-developed taxonomies to explain the ways in which the body can become hot. During field research, many informants told me that their "body has become hot" (*shorir gorom hoyese*), which was understood by such symptoms as yellow colour of urine, burning eyes, burning under the palm and feet and hot flashes. Such illnesses are believed to be caused by prolonged exposure of the body to excessive heat, which dries out the internal organs and leads to the noted symptoms. Many informants believed that besides external temperature, certain allopathic medicines can also induce heat within the body, as they are considered hot and can lead the body to be dry. The heating property of allopathic medicine is particularly experienced when someone recovers from illness but is still noticeably weak. As one village doctor explained to me: "Some high dose of antibiotic for a long time may cause the body to be weak, and it requires nutritious diet after the treatment to regain the general vitality and body strength."

The local terminology that villagers used to refer to dietary practice is *khao-dawa*, which basically has two different but interrelated meanings: *khao* (eating) and *dawa* (medicine), to reflect the saying that "good food is also a good remedy". In fact, considering food as medicine is not only evident in the Bangladeshi culture, Farquhar (1994) and Lu (1986) have already documented the role of food in the healing process in Chinese society. Nichter (1986) has also reported the classification of food and its health efficacy in the South Indian context. Mckay (1980) and Stone (1983) have demonstrated that there is a contingency between food and healing in Malaysian and Nepalese contexts. In rural Bangladesh, when someone recovers from illness, it is suggested that the person be put on a nutritious but easy to digest diet such as chicken soup, fresh fish and green vegetables, so that the recovery process can be hastened and the body regains its lost vitality. During their visit to doctors, many patients often ask, "What should be the diet?" (*khao-dawa ki korbo?*). Or, are there any dietary restrictions? One homeopathic practitioner in the village marketplace told me that foods which are considered hot, such as beef, prawn and brinjal, should be avoided during the course of treatment because it may interrupt the action of the medicine.

Thus far, I have demonstrated that the rural Bangladeshis have well-developed practice and logic about the hot-cold framework, in relation not just to illness but also to foods and their role in alleviating illness and maintaining good health. There also exists culturally patterned ways of maintaining balance between hot and cold through such practices as *gosol*, drinking *shorbot* or consuming the right food for maintaining good health and avoiding common illnesses.

Time, space and perceptions of health and illness

The idea of time and space and their contingency to disease causation has been well documented. In the Japanese context, Ohnuki-Tierney (1984) has described how the commonplace customs of maintaining daily hygiene are in fact part of a "complex series of activities" that the Japanese carry out throughout the day. Regular bathing and cleaning of body parts have been considered important to avoid people's dirt (*hitogomi*) or the bodily dirt of others, which is perceived to be a major mode of disease transmission. It is further argued that the daily practices are embedded in the broader Japanese symbolic structure, which defines the inside as pure and clean, whereas the outside is impure and dirty (Ohnuki-Tierney 1984: 31). In rural Bangladesh, understandings and explanations of health and illness have also been associated with the classification of time and space. These classifications are considered to be the guiding factors in shaping activities for maintaining health and hygiene in everyday life. According to rural Bangladeshi culture, certain periods of time are considered to be good, whereas others are bad.

Associated with these classifications are some culturally prescribed norms of what to do and what to avoid to remain healthy. Many informants told me that evening, particularly during the *magrib azan*,[8] is considered bad for infant and pregnant women. Expectant mothers and infants cannot stay outside the home at this particular time, as evil spirits (*shoitan*) may enter into their bodies to make them sick. One older woman explained this:

> The Evil (*shoitan*) cannot tolerate the sound of *magrib azan*. So, when the *magrib azan* is announced, the *shoitan* enters into the bodies of infant babies and pregnant women to hide himself. And if the *shoitan* enters anyone's body, he/she will become sick. So, pregnant women and infant babies must remain inside the home during that time to be safe from the *shoitan* and thereby avoid any kind of illnesses.

Some days in the week are also considered to be ominous (*oshuvo*), while other days are good (*shuvo*). Informants told me that Tuesdays and Saturdays are particularly *oshuvo* days of the week, thereby inauspicious and to be avoided for starting any business, travelling or doing any kind of work. One must refrain from taking any important initiative on these *oshuvo* days. Other days of the week, however, are considered *shuvo*, leading to successful outcomes. Many villagers strongly believed that if attempts are made on the *shuvo* days, they are likely to be successful, especially on Fridays, which is one of the consecrated days of the week. However, some educated and young informants described these beliefs as "old wives tales" and eccentric (*kusonskar*). They argued that there is no validity to such belief. Despite such refutation, many villagers informed me that they think twice before travelling or attempting anything on Saturdays and Tuesdays. Such a binary framework of *shuvo/oshuvo* has shaped the understanding of health and illness in rural Bangladesh. As the grandmother of one arsenicosis patient explained to me, the reason her grandson had gotten the disease is because he did not pay attention to her advice to avoid collecting grass for cows on Saturdays and Tuesdays. She suspected that he had come into contact with snake poison on these *oshuvo* days, which resulted in such a *ghaa* in his body.

There are some routine activities that are to be performed for maintaining good health and hygiene in everyday life. The local concepts of dirt (*moila*) and germs (*jibanu*) have been referred to as a mode of disease causation and transmission. According to rural Bangladeshi health beliefs, people come into contact with *moila* either through physical contact with other people or by consuming spoiled food or dirty water. Thus, to avoid disease is to avoid *moila/jibanu*. To achieve this level of hygiene, the first thing one must do is to clean the face and teeth (*mukh dhoa*) in the morning. *Mukh dhoa* bears a particular symbolic message because the mouth and nose are believed to be the specific routes for germs to enter the body. These entrance organs must be kept clean for the body to remain free from *moila/jibanu* and thereby ensure good health. In order to keep these passages clean, many people brush their teeth with fingers, and sometimes water alone is considered enough to clean the mouth.

Besides physical cleanliness, cooking utensils and homesteads must also be kept clean to be protected from *moila*. Many women are seen in the morning cleaning homestead areas and washing cooking utensils in the nearby ponds and wells. The process of cleaning everything in the morning bears the message that the starting of a day in a clean environment is conducive to good health and hygiene. The end of the day is also marked with specific activities. Cleaning body parts and homestead areas is an important task in the evening. Children are asked to clean their bodies before entering into the home, which not only implies physical purification but also symbolizes the transition between day and night, as well as the perception of the outside as dirty and germ infested, whereas the inside is clean and hygienic (Ohnuki-Tierney 1984: 31).

It is evident in the above discussion that the social construction of time and space has influenced the ways that villagers make sense of health and illness. The binary framework of *shuvo/oshuvo* has also shaped activities and practices for maintaining health and avoiding illness. Given the paucity of extensive ethnographic research on such concepts and categories of disease causations in rural Bangladesh, it is suggested that further research should be conducted on this interesting topic.

Fate (kopal/vagyo)

One of the classical documentations of disease causation was to contextualize it within religious domains (Evans-Pritchard 1937; Field 1937; Radin 1957; Rivers 1924; Turner 1968). Glick (1967: 32), for example, argues:

> It is common knowledge that, in many cultures, ideas and practices relating to illness are for the most part inseparable from the domain of religious beliefs and practices. Illnesses are said to be caused by gods, ghosts, angry ancestors, demons, spirits, and other so-called supernatural beings; or they may be attributed to human beings who are in some way able to mobilize unusual powers – witches, sorcerers, evil shamans.

Supplementing Glick's argument, Foster (1976) has proposed a model based on two basic etiological domains: personalistic and naturalistic disease etiologies. By personalistic disease etiology, Forster refers to any purposeful intervention of agents, whether human, non-human or supernatural, that is seen to induce illness in human beings. Naturalistic disease etiology, on the other hand, includes such natural forces or conditions as heat, cold, weather and winds, which stimulate illness due to the loss of equilibrium in the human body (Foster 1976: 775). One major drawback of such a neatly dichotomized model of disease etiology is that it fails to take into account the rich ethnographic narratives of personal illnesses, doctor–patient interactions in a clinical setting and wider politico-ecological factors that shape medical systems and health-seeking behaviour of lay individuals (Kleinman 1978). This has provoked Kleinman (1980) to propose an "explanatory model" of health and illness to incorporate different episodes of illness and treatment processes as experienced by actual patients. This model is, however, very much idiosyncratic, subject to change and influenced by personal and cultural factors (Good 1994; Young 1982).

Although Foster's theorization has been criticized as limited and narrow, it nonetheless offers a powerful explanation of disease etiologies across societies. Fate, bad luck and misfortune, as forms of personalistic disease etiology, have been systematically conceptualized as underlying causal factors of illness in many societies. Stone (1976), for example, has found that in Nepal one's fate is determined by the alignment of the planets. If a planet is inauspiciously misaligned (*graha bigrayo*), one is susceptible to misfortune, illness or even death. Zvosec (1996) has also documented that the fate of a person is set by the astrological positioning of the planet during one's birth, which plays a significant role in determining bad luck, misfortune or illness for the rest of one's life. Similarly, in Thailand, Naemiratch and Manderson (2007) observed that the cause of type 2 diabetes is *kam*, or the fate of a person, which has been set due to one's negative effects of past behaviour. Fabrega and Nutini (1993) also found that the Tlaxcalans in Mexico explain disease, illness and death as the will of the Christian God, fate or destiny.

Within the rural Bangladeshi context, one's fate (*kopal* or *vagyo*) is central to the popular perceptions of illness. Although many respondents synonymously used both *kopal* and *vagyo* to refer to the inevitable ascription of a person, there are terminological differences between them. *Kopal*, or the forehead, is the place where respondents believe that the *vagyo* is written. Thus, the conceptualization of *kopal* or *vagyo* has its link to the religious doctrine that one's fate-write-up (*vagyo lekha*) has been written on one's forehead (*kopal*), which is determined by Allah prior to one's birth. According to rural Bangladeshi belief, *kopal* or *vagyo* can be both auspicious and inauspicious. It can be auspicious when attributed to birth, prosperity, marriage, a good job or any kind of achievements, whereas illnesses, misfortune, death, mishaps, loss of property or any kind of sufferings are attributed to the inauspicious properties of *kopal*/*vagyo*. Thus, the ways in which the rural Bangladeshis make sense of illness are invariably shaped by the framework of *kopal* or *vagyo* that has been predetermined and deemed to be obvious for a person. As one respondent explained to me about the link between disease and *vagyo*:

> Disease (*oshukh*) is written here (showing his forehead). This is a matter of *vagyo*. Allah has written it there before we are born. The written of the *kopal* can never be avoided.

Villagers have a well-developed logic to justify disease, illness, misfortune and sufferings within the framework of fate, or *kopal*, which is guided by the Islamic religious belief about the afterlife. Illness is considered to be a mode of abolishment of past bad deeds (*pap mochon*). Villagers explained to me that through the sufferings of illness, one would get rid of the past sins, as the sufferings of illness relieve one from the burden of sin. The *hujur* of the village mosque clarified:

> Illness (*oshukh*) is an examination from Allah. Allah wants to examine our level of patience by giving us many sufferings. Those who successfully pass

the examination, they are the true followers of Allah. Sometimes Allah forgives ones' past sin by giving disease. So, (one) should not worry when disease comes; rather, consider that there must be something good in it. It may be a means (*osila*) of purification (*pap mochon*).

Thus, the sufferings of illness are justified in two ways: Firstly, through a framework of *pap mochon*, whereby illness is perceived as an examination from the God. The individual is hence gratified with the loss or sufferings of disease and misfortune. Secondly, illness is perceived as a means of purification, whereby the sufferings of illness make someone clean by washing out past bad deeds or sin. Conceptualizing illness as an examination from God and a means of purification is not unique in the context of Bangladeshi culture. Adib (2004) has already documented such an example in the Middle Eastern context, where illness is considered to be a test from God, the successful passing of which results in a reward in the afterlife. Adib notes, "They are being tested and purified from sins and, if they accept the will of Allah and bear their ordeal patiently, they shall be rewarded" (Adib 2004: 700).

Is *kopal/vagyo* alterable? Some respondents believe that *vagyo* or *kopal* can be changed through observing specific rituals, following strict Islamic regulations, praying to Allah and doing good deeds. This argument is particularly important when someone survives a serious illness, injury or fatal accident, which is explained as a result of past good deeds that has altered the inevitable destiny of death. Thus, any patient who goes to see a *hujur* for religious healing is first advised to get pardoned by Allah for his past bad deeds that might have triggered illness or misfortune to him. Others hold firm views about the non-changeable characteristics of fate. As one 52-year-old villager explained:

> Fate cannot be changed at all. Since we cannot see what has been written in the *vagyo*, how do we know what has been changed? When time comes, everyone has to face death. When time comes, everyone has to face illness.

The conceptualization of bad deeds (*pap kaj*) in the Bangladeshi context differs slightly from what Zvosec (1996) has illustrated as *karma* in the Nepalese context. *Pap kaj* refers to only past bad deeds, not the good deeds, whereas *karma* can be either good or bad. It is bad *karma* that accounts for illness in both contexts. Rural Bangladeshi villagers have a further well-developed categorization of *pap kaj* to classify the severity of illnesses. The more severe and prolonged the disease and sufferings, the worse the past bad deeds were. The *hujur* of the village mosque explained to me why one has prolonged or chronic illness, whereas others have relatively shorter durations of illness:

> If someone has done a grave bad deed (*boro pap kaj*) like infidelity, Allah may not forgive him or if (Allah) forgives, the means (*osila*) would be very bad. If the *osila* is a disease, it will be a serious disease (*boro oshukh*) . . . [the person] will take a long time to recover. You will be punished slowly . . . and one day

Allah will forgive you. If someone does a minor bad deed (*soto pap kaj*) . . . (Allah) still records it, but a minor disease will occur to him from which he will recover in a few days, and then Allah will forgive you.

Many villagers thus believe that bad deeds can be either grave or minor with corresponding consequences. Grave bad deeds refer to the violation of strict prohibitions of Islam such as adultery, killing a human being and faithlessness to God, resulting in chronic diseases, whereas small bad deeds refer to the violation of minor religious regulations of various types, resulting in minor illnesses. Villagers also have a neat categorization of different diseases. On many occasions, villagers explained to me that chronic diseases are those which are severely painful, take a long time to cure, have no remedy or require very expensive treatment and can even lead to death. Examples of such diseases are heart disease, bronchitis, chronic blister (*jotil ghaa*) and rheumatism (*baat*), whereas minor illnesses refer to those conditions which disappear quickly and are less painful, require little or no remedy and usually do not appear as life threatening. Examples of such illnesses are headaches, gastrointestinal problems, minor fever, runny nose and cough (*sordi-kashi*).

Clearly, the idea of fate has profoundly shaped the understanding of illness in rural Bangladesh. It is believed that illness is predetermined and is written in *kopal*, which is inevitable. Illness is justified as an examination from God and a means of purification from past bad deeds. Later on in this chapter I will describe how such an understanding of *kopal* shapes who will suffer from arsenicosis illness.

Bad weather (kharap abhawa)

Cross-culturally, people routinely explain illness as a result of abrupt changes in weather conditions. The basic etiological explanation comes from the notion of loss of equilibrium in bodily humoral factors due to changes in weather. If the body fails to adjust with the changes, one is susceptible to being ill. Yan (2000) has found a strong correlation between changes in weather and a rise in mortality in Hong Kong. He demonstrated that changes in climate collapse the human physical defense mechanism, leading to respiratory and cardiovascular diseases (Yan 2000: 420). Donohoe (2003) has argued that the adverse impact of environmental degradation on human health stems from overpopulation, air and water pollution and global warming. Laderman (1981) further shows that the Malays believe in seasonal variations over the year (*musim banjir*, *musim sejuk* and *musim kemarau*), which govern one's humoral circumstances, and any changes in the condition may result in imbalances, leading to increased susceptibility to illness.

Particular seasons of the year are believed to be the causal factors in hastening particular illnesses. Reeve (2000) notes that the Caboclo people of the Lower Amazon attribute specific illnesses to particular seasons – for example, flu in the summer and diarrhoea in the winter. Shawyer et al. (1996) also demonstrated that in the Thai folk taxonomy, *tong tai* or diarrhoeal illness, is perceived to be the result of exposure to sunshine or an abrupt change in the weather. In India, Chatterjee (1991) notes that women are susceptible to various illnesses in winter because of their inadequate clothing while fetching water in the early morning or gathering fuel for household cooking. Additionally, Indian women's long stay in smoky kitchens often culminates in different illnesses, including respiratory disorders such as bronchitis, pneumonia, tuberculosis and asthma. Such findings are further corroborated by Koblinsky, Campbell and Harlow (1993) and Kettel (1996) that women's occupation as close to nature further increases their susceptibility to climatic illnesses.

In the context of rural Bangladesh, villagers often refer to climatic changes that cause different illnesses. Perceptions of climatic changes often come from a comparative perspective: the past versus the present day. It is believed that climatic conditions in the past were conducive to good health, as opposed to the present climatic conditions, which have become unfavorable to good health. Many older people in rural Bangladesh often say, "The weather has gone bad in these days", as one senior villager explained to me:

> We never experienced such bad weather in the past. You see what a heat has fallen in the summer and what a cold in the winter. How can we survive in such extreme conditions? (We) cannot go outside; the skin seems on fire. In our times rain used to come rightly during monsoon, hot in the summer, and cold in the winter. But nowadays, there is no schedule. . . . (Climate) does not follow calendar. You see it is monsoon now . . . but no rain . . . so heat as if summer has set in.

Many villagers referred to such changes in the weather as being responsible for spreading many illnesses. The body is perceived to be vulnerable during the transition period between two seasons, since it has to adjust to these altered conditions. It is believed that young children, pregnant women and the elderly, who are not physically strong enough to adjust to such changes, are particularly at risk. The village *kobiraj* said:

> When weather changes from summer to winter or to the rainy season, the temperature also changes. The body will have to adjust to such changing temperature. If the body cannot adjust to the outside temperature, people become sick. Do you see many people suffer from cough, fever, runny nose and sore throat during seasonal change? It is because their body fails to adjust to the changing temperature.

Thus, adjustment to the temperature because of transition from one to the other season has been perceived as an important etiological factor for many illnesses. Many villagers mentioned that sudden fluctuations of temperature can induce illnesses such as fever and cough. Family members, particularly young children, are advised by the elders to be careful and maintain good health by balancing between hot and cold elements so that they do not get sick. Villagers often mentioned that the temperature nowadays veers towards extremely hot or cold during the summer and winter. Sometimes the temperature exceeds 40° Celsius in summer or may fall as low as 5° Celsius in winter. Both of these extreme conditions are considered bad weather (*kharap abhawa*), which can inflict illness upon exposure.

It is believed that exposure to such hot weather may cause diarrhoea, headache, swelling or inflammation. Exposure to cold weather, however, can cause headache, runny nose or asthma (*sash kosto*). Appropriate dietary rules and suitable clothing for maintaining bodily humoral equilibrium have been suggested to adjust to such changes and avoid illnesses. People who are already sick are advised to be careful about such changes in weather. One asthma patient informed me that he was worried about the coming winter's temperature falling, which increases his asthma symptoms. Another arsenicosis patient told me that his condition was aggravated during the winter months, causing him some concerns.

The above discussions thus far have demonstrated the general health and illness beliefs and practices in rural Bangladesh. It is quite evident that disease etiologies in rural Bangladesh are shaped by many sociocultural, humoral, religious and environmental factors. The terminologies used, the experiences encountered and the symptoms classified to refer to health and illness are far from clinically defined and scientific biomedical categories. A number of sociocultural factors, such as the hot/cold framework, perception of time and space and religious factors, such as fate, appear crucial in shaping lay understandings of health and illness. Disease etiologies in rural Bangladesh are also ecologically prescribed, as *kharap abhawa* is believed to influence the body's humoral balance, leading to various illnesses. Thus, personalistic, naturalistic and ecological factors are important in shaping the ways that Bangladeshi villagers make sense of health and illness. Having outlined the general health and illness beliefs and practices, the following section demonstrates how arsenicosis is perceived and explained within such a cultural framework.

Ghaa: the social construction of arsenicosis

This section describes how arsenicosis has been culturally understood, explained and categorized by patients, other members of the family and the community. Drawing upon local terminologies, folk taxonomies, personal experiences and lay disease etiologies, an ethnographic analysis of arsenicosis has been activated to illustrate how this biomedical category, which is officially labeled as arsenicosis, has been vernacularized as *ghaa* in everyday life.

Arsenicosis as **ghaa**

Initially when I was thinking about the suitability of conducting anthropological research on arsenicosis in rural Bangladesh, I asked myself if I knew the local term that villagers use to refer to this illness. I did not find the answer, as I did not know the exact local terminology that people used to describe this illness. Later on, while conducting the actual fieldwork, I realized how decisive this question was. On the very first day of my fieldwork, a strange thing happened when I was trying to find arsenicosis patients in the village. I asked people gathered at the tea stall if they knew any arsenicosis patients living in the village. Not surprisingly, none of the villagers I encountered in the local tea stall knew of any such patients, although I knew from the BAMWSP website that there were at least seventeen such patients in the village. I was bewildered and wondered how to proceed. I then went to the local DPHE office to seek their help. They provided me with a list of patients and their names that they found while surveying the village.

Having acquired that list, I returned to the village the next day and asked the owner of the tea stall if he knew the name of a person from that list. The person promptly replied, "Oh, are you talking about [the man] who is suffering from *ghaa*? His condition is very bad. You cannot believe [it] unless you see [him] with your own eyes." Only then did I first realize that the villagers used the word *ghaa* to refer to arsenicosis. I understood that arsenicosis was an alien term and a biomedical description, which was mostly unrecognized by the local villagers. This exemplifies the problematics associated with naming and labeling diseases in the biomedical context, and how this does not match the reality of ethnographic research.

Most health education messages, bulletins, leaflets and billboards portray such *ghaa* as arsenicosis, which has appeared as an official or biomedical term preferred by the public health officials, medical practitioners and educated individuals. But most arsenicosis patients I interviewed and other people in the village I spoke to used the term *ghaa* to refer to the illness symptoms associated with arsenicosis. In rural Bangladesh, *ghaa* is literally a general category of skin disease. Varieties of skin diseases such as blisters, warts, scabies and eczema are locally called *ghaa* and are very common in rural Bangladesh. Given the symptomatic similarity with other skin diseases, villagers labeled arsenicosis as *ghaa*. Thus, while looking for arsenicosis, I found *ghaa* in rural Bangladesh.

The use of the term *ghaa*, however, has become problematic because of its wider meaning, classifications and applicability in the local context. The village *kobiraj* informed me that some forms of *ghaa* are soft with pus inside, whereas other forms are relatively dry. Some of them can be very itchy, while others are relatively non-itchy. Some forms of *ghaa* are transmittable, while others are not. Many villagers informed me that *ghaa* has different names according to its characteristics, such as dry *ghaa* (*sukna ghaa*), *ghaa* with pus (*rosh ghaa*), itchy *ghaa* (*chulkani-pachra*) and ringworm (*daad*). Given such varieties of meanings and classifications, it is interesting to explore how villagers differentiate arsenicosis *ghaa* from other types of skin diseases. The following table illustrates the local terms that villagers use to explain symptoms of arsenicosis:

Table 4.1 Local terms used to explain *ghaa*

Symptoms in Local Terms	Translated into English
Chulkai	Itchy
Jala pora kore	Burning sensation
Rosh-koshani ber hoy	Pus and watering discharge
Haat paa fule jai	Hand and legs become thickened
Chamrai kalo daag	Black spots on the skin
Shorir durbol hoy	The body becomes weak
Haat paye gota hoy	Hard eruptions on hand and leg

58 *Ghaa: the social construction of arsenicosis*

Following this ethnotaxonomy, the local term *ghaa* is used throughout the rest of this analysis to refer to a particular skin disease which is medically labeled as arsenicosis. Obviously, *ghaa* has been constructed by the lay individuals as they experience it while managing this illness in their day-to-day lives. To differentiate *ghaa* from other skin ailments, villagers use a binary perspective. The discussion that follows describes these binary classifications that villagers use to explain *ghaa* and its symptoms and etiological processes.

Ghaa from snakebites: strong poison vs. mild poison

When I asked the local people if they had heard of the word "arsenic", most of them replied that arsenic is a kind of poison (*bish*) without any further detailed knowledge about it. In one study, Ashraf, Chowdhury and Streefland (1982: 2043) demonstrated that it is a predominant belief among the rural Bangladeshis that skin diseases occur as a result of blood poisoning. Thus, the concept of poison and its classifications are important for understanding how villagers perceive arsenicosis and its etiologies. My ethnographic evidence reveals that rural Bangladeshi villagers have well-developed nomenclatures for *bish* – particularly its varieties are organized according to severity and potency. Some poisons are perceived to be very strong (*kothin bish*) and life threatening, whereas others are relatively mild (*norom bish*) and considered to be not so dangerous. Villagers informed me that there can be two sources of *bish*: one is the pesticides used for pest control in the local agriculture, and the other is from snakebites. Such conceptualization and categorization of snake poisoning came from the villagers' living experience under a particular ecological condition where snakebites were a frequent occurrence. Many villagers informed me that *ghaa* could be the result of poisoning because of snakebites. One 45-year-old patient, whose leg up to the knee had been amputated because of *ghaa*, explained to me how he got this disease:

> On that night I had been returning from the bazaar. It was late at night, nearly 11 pm. I did not have any bicycle with me and was walking alone to my home. That night had a full moon, and everything was clearly visible. I had been walking fast, since it was already late at night. When I reached near to the school, I saw something like a rope laid down on the street. While I crossed the rope, I felt something bite me near my ankle. It started burning and I thought something went wrong. I thought it might be a snake. With that condition, I ran straight to the *kobiraj* and showed him the condition. He put some herbal medicine on my tongue and opened up the wound to suck the blood. I felt less burning after that and came back home. I still felt burning next morning. I had some prior experiences of snake bite, which was recovered through *jhar-fuk*.[9] But that time the burning continued and I spoke to my father, who suggested that I go to the *hujur*. I went to him and he gave me *pani-pora* to drink. After two days, I again felt burning and went back to *hujur*, who suggested that I have a bath using the *pani-pora*. I did that and felt well. After

some months, I found that this *ghaa* appeared on my hands and feet. I think this is a different kind of poison . . . very hard poison. . . . The whole body seemed to have become poisoned.

Clearly, the patient believed that *ghaa* was a result of snakebite. He realized that such poison could only be removed by herbal medicine (*gasra oshud*) and chanting (*jhar-fuk*), which prompted him to visit the village *kobiraj* and religious *hujur*. However, since these healing options could not cure his illness, he further categorized such poison as very strong (*kothin bish*), which seemed to have poisoned his whole body. Thus, the conceptualization of *ghaa* and its etiology are very much shaped by the everyday life experiences and constraints of living in unfavorable conditions where snakebite is a frequent occurrence. The appearance of *ghaa* because of snakebites is confirmed by another 50-year-old patient who had long been suffering from this illness. He explained to me how such *ghaa* developed in his body:

> One day I went to the field to collect grass for the unfed cows. While I was cutting grass, my hands came into contact with *era-bish*. Do you know what *era bish* is? [Since I replied no, he explained] The *bish* which you can find in the field as a bubble form left by the snakes is called *era-bish*, which came in touch with my hands. After some days, I found such *ghaa* [showing the *ghaa* on his hand], which extended in both my hands and legs. I think this *ghaa* is because of such *era-bish*, which is not healing at all. It seems this *era-bish* is very strong and that's why the *ghaa* is not healing.

It is quite evident in this narrative that the patient understands *ghaa* as a result of *era-bish*, which he came into contact with while collecting grass for cows. He believes that this poison is very strong, since the *ghaa* cannot be cured. In another interview, a *ghaa* patient told me that if poison cannot be fully expelled from the body, the remnants of it can cause *ghaa* later on. He recalled, "After I was bitten by a snake, I went straight to the *kobiraj*, but he could not fully expel the *bish* from my body. I still had burning on my skin and the *ghaa* appeared. This *ghaa* is because of that *bish*, which was very strong." Some other patients also confirmed that they got such *ghaa* because of snakebites, as another 45-year-old patient explained:

> It was in a night previous to the last monsoon when I was sleeping on my verandah. My leg came in touch with something and I kicked it away. Suddenly I felt something had bitten my right leg and it started to burn. I shouted and my parents came out and found a snake escaping the scene. They killed the snake and brought me to the *kobiraj*, who told me that it was a poisonous snake. He tried to expel the poison using herbal medicine. But I think it was that poison which resulted in this *ghaa*. Otherwise how could it happen?

60 *Ghaa: the social construction of arsenicosis*

From these lay narratives, a clear link is found between snakebites and the appearance of *ghaa*. Other patients believed that not all poisons can cause *ghaa*. The poisons that cause *ghaa* are of higher severity and potency, which cannot be completely removed from the body. Thus, a binary perspective of strong *bish*/mild *bish* is used to categorize poisons based on their degree of severity. Some poisons are believed to be stronger and life threatening, whereas others are relatively milder and less harmful to health. As one patient said, "I had snakebites before, but I did not see such *ghaa*. The last snakebite was very poisonous, which resulted in this *ghaa*. This poison must be stronger than other poisons."

Villagers also used a binary classification to explain the differences between arsenicosis *ghaa* and other skin diseases. When asked how *ghaa* was different from other skin ailments, one patient explained to me:

> I have seen many villagers suffering from other *ghaa* such as blister, eczema, ringworms and so on. But when medicine is taken, these *ghaa* disappear. But in my case, even after trying whatever available treatments there are, the *ghaa* is not healing. It is returning. Don't you think this *ghaa* is different? It must be due to very strong poison.

Thus, many villagers believe that chronic and recurrent characteristics of arsenicosis *ghaa* make it different from other skin diseases. In another interview, one villager told me that *ghaa* is different from other skin diseases because of its incurability. He said that *ghaa* comes back, even though medications are taken. It is believed that the poison that causes *ghaa* is stronger than those causing other skin diseases. Thus, the severity of poison and the failure of medications to cure *ghaa* are perceived to be important markers that distinguish arsenicosis *ghaa* from other skin diseases. Many patients also explained to me that arsenicosis *ghaa* is resilient, recurrent and drug-resistant, unlike other types of skin ailments.

Inside, outside and the poisoned body

My ethnographic evidence further suggests that cultural understandings of *ghaa* are shaped by the ways in which villagers perceive the human body (*shorir*). Although physiological implications of arsenicosis have been well documented in biomedical research, it is interesting to explore how such physiological processes are culturally understood and explained. Rural Bangladeshi villagers perceive the human body as having two components: (1) inside (*vitor*), meaning the internal organs, which cannot be seen and remain inside the body, such as blood, intestines, arteries and heart, and (2) outside (*bahir*), referring to the external organs, which can be seen, such as the skin, hair and nails. Pigg (1995) has already documented such a classification of the human body in the context of the Nepalese, who believe that some illnesses occur "inside" the body (*bhitrako betha*), whereas others are perceived as external disturbances. In the context of my research, there is a predominant belief that *ghaa* is a disease from inside the body. The rural Bangladeshi believe that although *ghaa* surfaces on the skin, it has in fact originated from inside the body. One arsenicosis patient thus explained to me:

> (Showing the palm of the hand) The *ghaa* as you are looking here, it comes from inside the body. I think the poison has entered deep into the body and from there the *ghaa* comes out. (If it does not come from inside,) why after even using *shuku molom*[10] is the *ghaa* still not healing?

Another arsenicosis patient explained to me that *ghaa* first attacks the internal organs of the body and then appears on the skin. This confirms the widespread belief that *ghaa* is not merely an external phenomenon, but an illness from inside the body (*vitorer ghaa*). Recently, biomedical research has also established the fact that arsenic poisoning affects many internal organs of the body, such as the liver, kidney and heart (Mazumder 2005). In this sense, the social construction of the human body, as reflected in the villagers' understanding of arsenicosis disease etiology, corroborates the biomedical explanations of human physiology.

Closely linked to the above perception of the human body is the social construction of blood, which shapes the understanding of *ghaa*. According to my informants, blood (*rokto*) is the main substance of the human body. If the blood is found to be good, the body will remain well. Villagers believed that pure blood (*valo rokto*) would help create bodily resistance against many diseases, and if blood becomes impure (*kharap rokto*), many diseases would attack the weakened body. Thus, the lay notion of blood as pure or impure provides a powerful cultural framework to explain *ghaa* etiology in rural Bangladesh. Many patients believed that *ghaa* appears because of poisoned blood (*bisakto rokto*). Some others perceived that their blood had become poisoned because of snakebites, which resulted in such a *ghaa* on their bodies. As one patient explained to me:

> I think my blood has become poisoned. If blood were pure, it [the *ghaa*] would not happen. Why would it happen to me, if the blood is pure? You see the pus and discharge, these are the poisons that entered into the blood and are now coming out. Since the poison entered into the blood, the blood has become poisoned and comes out as *ghaa* on the skin. The doctor has given me medicine to purify the blood. If the blood becomes clean, the *ghaa* will disappear.

Thus, villagers understand that *ghaa* is due to poisoned blood, and discharges of *ghaa* are believed to be the sign of such impure blood. They also believe that blood can be poisoned, if something poisonous enters into the body either through consumption or by inhalation. In rural Bangladesh, snakebites and consumption of poisoned food are the two most cited reasons for blood poisoning. Some villagers mentioned that the consumption of food, which is produced using chemical fertilizers and pesticides, might intoxicate the blood of the human body. Thus, for most villagers, perception of the impurity of blood is central to arsenicosis disease etiology, which in turn shapes the choice of treatment options – for example, seeking medications that purify the blood.

In sum, the social construction of the human body, as constituted by internal and external organs, is important in conceptualizing *ghaa* etiology in rural Bangladesh. Although *ghaa* appears externally on the skin, it is believed to have originated internally. Additionally, the perception of blood as a vital fluid inside the body has significantly contributed to explaining arsenicosis disease etiology. It was a prevailing belief amongst the informants that arsenicosis *ghaa* is a result of blood poisoning due to snakebites.

Increase, decrease and recurrence

Another frequently cited *ghaa* etiology in rural Bangladesh is its perceived symptomatic characteristics experienced by the patients. My ethnographic evidence confirms a well-developed ethnotaxonomy that patients use to illustrate this illness. Such ethnotaxonomy is explained under the framework of increase (*bare*), decrease (*kome*) and recurrence (*fire ase*). I came to notice such characteristics of *ghaa* during the initial period of my fieldwork when my key informant told me that if I was interested, he could introduce me to a 50-year-old man who was known to be a chronic *ghaa* patient. I instantly agreed. One afternoon, we went to his home but his wife informed us that he was not there. She suggested that we come back early the next morning. My key informant had earlier told me that the person had been suffering from serious *ghaa*, which he emphasized that "you would not believe, if you do not see his condition with your own eyes". When we met the person the next morning, we found no *ghaa* in his body except some black spots on the skin. My key informant was surprised and asked, "What happened to your *ghaa*, have you recovered? I heard you had to remain in bed as you could not stand up because of your *ghaa*. Are they gone?" The person replied:

> Yes, you are right that I had a very serious condition during last summer. It seemed to me that the skin became rotten . . . the skin was falling to pieces from my hand and feet. People used to cover their noses when they came to visit me. I thought I would rather die than live in such a condition. By the grace of Allah, the condition is better now. In fact, the *ghaa* increases in the months of *Falgun* and *Chaitra* and in *Poush* and *Maagh*.[11] The condition remains dormant during the monsoon. But it never recovers. . . . (I)t comes back (*fire ase*). I do not know when Allah will relieve me from such *ghaa*.

Clearly, the above narrative demonstrates that the symptoms of *ghaa* fluctuate over the seasons. The symptoms increase at times, while remain dormant at other times. In the case of this person, the condition of *ghaa* worsened during the months of summer and winter and improved during the monsoon. Thus, one most remarkable characteristic of arsenicosis *ghaa* is that it is never cured, but it comes back (*fire ase*). Although the condition of this person was very bad during last summer, the situation improved when I saw him during the fieldwork.

In another case, when I went to see a 16-year-old boy who was suffering from *ghaa*, his mother told me that he was not at home and had been working in a shop as a sales assistant. His mother explained to me that when her son is in a good condition, the shop owner allows him to work, but when *ghaa* reappears, he is forced to take leave. Since his condition was good then, he had been continuing his job. A 55-year-old patient who worked as an assistant in the village mosque also explained to me that he could only work on the days he did not have *ghaa*. Since his condition had worsened since last year, with a terrible discharge from *ghaa*, people abhorred him and did not want him to continue the job. He had to give up the work early, since people disliked to be served by a person with dreadful *ghaa* on his hands and legs. In another case, the education of a 13-year-old girl patient was affected by *ghaa*, since she had to refrain from attending school when the *ghaa* appeared and could only go to school when the condition improved.

Thus, the persistent characteristics of *ghaa* appear to be a powerful cultural framework to explain arsenicosis. Villagers believe that other skin diseases can be cured with medications but *ghaa* persists, even though medications are applied. Such chronic characteristics of *ghaa* are believed to be different from those of other common skin diseases. Many patients informed me that the symptoms of *ghaa* appear sometimes in a violent form, become dormant for some time, and then reappear, unlike other skin diseases. They also admitted that when *ghaa* appears, it sometimes takes on a serious form, while at other times, it is hardly noticeable that the patient has suffered from such a terrible *ghaa*. Most patients I interviewed informed me that *ghaa* increases in the months of summer and winter, while becoming dormant during the monsoon. It comes back routinely, as it is never permanently cured. Therefore, a socially constructed framework of increase/decrease and recurrence proves to be a powerful analytical tool to explain arsenicosis *ghaa* in rural Bangladesh.

Fate and the curse of Allah

While explaining arsenicosis disease etiology, a common factor that was cited most frequently was fate (*kopal*). Almost all patients I interviewed invariably referred to *kopal* as the most decisive factor in arsenicosis disease causation. The reference to *kopal* was particularly evident while illustrating the question "Why is *ghaa* happening to me?" Villagers realized that all family members were drinking water from the same tubewell, but not all of them were affected by *ghaa*, which pushed them to believe that *ghaa* is inevitably written in their *kopal* and it is fated. One informant explained to me that he got his *ghaa* because it was written in his fate. He explained to me thus:

Researcher: Do you think arsenic comes from water?
Informant: (thinking a while) . . . Yes . . . people said that.
R: Do you not believe that?
I: Yes. But I do not know much about it.
R: Why? What do you think?
I: People say that my tubewell has arsenic, but all my family members are drinking water from it for a long time. Some neighbors also

64 *Ghaa: the social construction of arsenicosis*

               come to collect water from it. They do not have *ghaa*, but I have. Why?
R: Why? What do you think?
I: I think it is in my *kopal*. If it (*ghaa*) is written in my *kopal*, no way that it can be avoided. The *ghaa* will occur even though I drink bottled water.[12] Otherwise, tell me why they do not have *ghaa* but I have? It is because of *kopal*, nothing else.

As this discussion suggests, *ghaa* has been perceived as preordained and beyond human control. It is believed that *ghaa* can occur to anyone, if it is written in one's *kopal*. Fate is thus rationalized through the belief that many others have been drinking water from the same arsenic-contaminated tubewells, but only a few of them are affected by *ghaa*. One patient thus explained to me that such *ghaa* is predetermined and written in his *kopal*, and it will happen to him no matter what kind of water he has been drinking. Being guided by such understandings, many villagers continue to consume arsenic-contaminated water from the tubewells marked as red,[13] a sign of danger, despite prohibition notices by NGOs and government agencies. When asked why he did not collect arsenic-free water from the water treatment plant, one villager explained to me:

    Water from the plant and red tubewells do not make any difference to me. If *ghaa* is written in *kopal*, water from the plant cannot protect me. I have been drinking water from the tubewell for a long time, but I do not have any *ghaa*. My fathers and forefather did not have this *ghaa* and thus this would also not happen to us.

Therefore, the social construction of fate appears crucial not only in explaining arsenicosis, but also in making development projects successful. Most villagers, who did not subscribe to arsenic-safe water, told me that the treated water cannot protect them from this *ghaa*, since it is predetermined by *kopal*. The village headmaster, who was the head of the management committee of the village water treatment plant, also confirmed to me that many villagers could not be motivated to subscribe to an arsenic-safe water supply because of their strong belief in fate.

Besides fate, there are other religious understandings of arsenicosis. Many villagers considered *ghaa* as a "curse from Allah" (*allar gojob*) and explained it as a consequence of past bad deeds (*paap kaj*), as one respondent explained to me thus:

    I think this (*ghaa*) is a curse (*gojob*) from Allah. We surely have done some sin (*paap kaj*). This (*ghaa*) must be a punishment because of our sin. Allah has indeed thrown such *gojob* upon us in order to abolish our past sins. We are not likely to get rid of this curse, unless we appeal to Allah with real admission of guilt.

Clearly, *ghaa* is understood and explained as a curse from Allah, which is inscribed in one's *kopal*, because of past transgressions. In order to get rid of such *gojob*, it is believed that these bad deeds must be abolished, either through good deeds or by solemn prayer to Allah. The village religious *hujur* also confirmed to me that the pervasive outbreak of *ghaa* is because of villagers' disobedience to Allah. He mentioned to me that:

> Do you not see that many people have become disobedient in these days? Villagers are involved in many misconducts which Allah never permits. They have totally forgotten Allah's rule. This *ghaa* is nothing but a curse from Allah, only Allah can protect us from this disaster. We need to be apologetic to Allah, we need to pray so that Allah forgives us.

Thus, in a predominantly Islamic society in rural Bangladesh, religion appears to be crucial in explaining arsenicosis. *Ghaa* is believed to be a punishment from Allah. Such religious understanding deeply influences the subsequent health-seeking behaviour of patients, as they prefer seeking religious healing to biomedicine. To many villagers, solemn prayer and apology for previous transgressions are considered to be more rational and effective than drinking arsenic-safe water. Thus, a framework of transgression and its abolition through punishment by diseases strongly influence the lay understandings of *ghaa* in rural Bangladesh.

Conclusion

Drawing upon these ethnographic findings, it is argued that a biomedical category of arsenicosis has been socially constructed as *ghaa* in practice. Rural Bangladeshi villagers explain *ghaa* as they experience it in their everyday lives, which is predominantly shaped by specific sociocultural, religious and ecological constraints in southwestern Bangladesh. A clear mismatch between biomedical and lay constructions of arsenicosis is evident here. From a biomedical perspective, arsenicosis is believed to occur because of drinking arsenic-contaminated water, whereas lay villagers consider arsenicosis as a kind of *ghaa* which is a result of blood poisoning due to snakebites, ill fate and past transgressions. Such a mismatch in understanding arsenicosis demands another important question to answer: What are the implications of such lay understandings of arsenicosis in terms of health-seeking behaviour and response to mitigation strategies? The next chapter will delineate this issue to demonstrate how the social construction of *ghaa* shapes the health-seeking behaviour of patients in medically plural rural Bangladesh.

Notes

1 Ali is a 45-year-old man who has been suffering from arsenicosis, and his one foot has been amputated due to gangrene – the last stage of arsenic poisoning. Now he uses an elbow crutch for walking. Everyone in the village knows him as an unfortunate victim of *ghaa*.
2 In rural Bangladesh, the tricycle, a local vehicle called a van, which can carry as many as five to seven people, is a very common form of transportation of both goods and passengers. To move from one place to another, a van is one of the major modes of transportation used by the villagers in my study area.

3 Many patients in the village neither memorized nor understood the brand or name of the medicine, which is written in English. However, they usually referred to the colour of the medicine, memorized the specific disease for which the medicine was prescribed or stored the empty strips of the medicine to show the medicine sellers for their next purchase from the village pharmacy. When I asked to see the pill, a woman villager brought a box full of many empty strips and homeopathic medicine bottles. She showed me the red pill, which I read as Camlodin (amlodipine besilate) 5 mg, for lowering blood pressure.
4 While talking about contemporary food quality and food intake behaviour, many villagers expressed their concern over utilization of chemicals and pesticides in agriculture and aquaculture. Consumption of these foods, as the villagers were convinced, is one of the main causes of deteriorated health conditions in recent times.
5 "In our times" (*amader somoy*) is often used symbolically by the older people to refer to their past times, which are often portrayed as "good" and seldom polluted.
6 *Hatpakha* is a very common household stuff in rural Bangladesh, which is usually made from the leaf of a palm tree and used by hand for producing air to make the body cool.
7 *Shorbot*, a kind of drink, refers to a mixture of water, sugar and lemon juice, which is locally considered as containing cooling properties. However, the preparation of *shorbot* differs widely depending on the availability of the ingredients and one's capability of buying them.
8 *Azan* is a local term to refer to a call to prayer for Muslims. *Magrib azan* refers to a call to prayer in the evening.
9 *Jhar-fuk* is a Bengali word used widely in the rural areas to refer to the use of a mantra by the village *kobiraj* or the religious *hujur* to cure different illnesses.
10 *Shuku molom* is a kind ointment that has been sold by the hawkers in the open streets. Although there are different names and varieties of *shuku molom* in the market, almost every household keeps this in their home for immediate cure of eczema, blisters, ringworm and other skin diseases.
11 *Falgun* and *Chaitra* are two Bengali lunar months, which roughly fall in summer when the temperature rises as high as 41° Celsius. Whereas, *Poush* and *Maagh* constitute winter when the temperature falls as low as 5° Celsius. The villagers informed me that skin diseases are particularly aggravated during these two seasons.
12 Bottled water has been processed and bottled to be sold in the market, which is claimed to be clean and free from arsenic.
13 Under the BAMWSP project, water quality of the tubewells was carried out nationwide. The main objective was to map out the pervasiveness of arsenic-contaminated tubewells. The tubewells which are found with arsenic concentrations higher than the permissible level are coloured red so that people become aware not to drink water from those tubewells. The others, with arsenic concentrations within the permissible range, are coloured green and people are allowed to drink water from those tubewells.

5 Arsenicosis as *ghaa* and health-seeking behaviour

Introduction

This chapter examines how the social construction of arsenicosis as *ghaa*, as discussed in the previous chapter, shapes health-seeking behaviour of subjects in a medically plural context of rural southwestern Bangladesh. Drawing upon lay diagnosis, management and therapeutic options that are used by the persons affected by arsenic poisoning, it is argued that the health-seeking behaviour of patients is predominantly shaped by the ways illness is understood and acted upon. Ethnographic evidence presented in this chapter clearly shows that the predominant use of alternative healing by arsenicosis patients is not a surprise, but rather a reflection of their understandings that *ghaa* is better managed by traditional healers. This chapter begins with a description of everyday home-based management of *ghaa* using rudimentary healing techniques, followed by a discussion of different types of healing services that are available to and used by the patients. The ways in which local villagers make sense of these various health care options and the factors that shape their decision-making process in utilizing these services are explored. While examining these issues, the focus has always been on the perspectives of the patients, their family members and different health service providers in order to have a comprehensive ethnographic understanding of the diagnosis, treatment and management of *ghaa* in rural Bangladesh.

Ghaa and health-seeking behaviour in rural Bangladesh

As has been described already in the earlier chapter, one of the remarkable features of rural Bangladeshi health care organizations is the juxtaposition of Western biomedicine and a wide array of traditional healing options, which perfectly exemplifies the model of a medical supermarket, as described by Churchill (1989). According to this model, healing options that are chosen by the patients are a reflection of the freedom and choice enjoyed being in an environment with multiple healing services. Patients are in a context that is just like a marketplace, where a range of health care services are available to be bought and sold. Patients, who are the subjects of medical consumerism, shop around, being guided by pragmatic decisions on which health care services are believed to be helpful. As Churchill (1989: 179) rightly points out:

> Under this model, doctors, nurses, and other health "professionals" become "providers," while "patients" become "consumers." Consumers are then expected to choose from the vast medical supermarket which items or procedures for life maintenance they "want." (Note here how "need" is usurped by consumer preference.) The possibilities seem endless – antibiotics, respirators, chemotherapies, resuscitation (at a variety of levels), defibrillators, naso-gastric tubes, and on and on.

In the context of rural Bangladesh, arsenicosis patients are precisely in the situation described above. One major objective of this book is to explore the existing healing options that are available to arsenicosis patients. In so doing, I focus on the healing options that are actually used by the patients, rather than just surveying or enumerating the existing health care services in rural Bangladesh. The principle guiding question is: What do patients do to alleviate the sufferings of *ghaa*? The pursuit of this question reveals a broad range of perceptions, practices and assessments in relation to the therapeutic management of *ghaa*. I found that arsenicosis patients used at least three different healing resorts: self-treatment by using home-based remedies, traditional healing services at the village and professional biomedical treatment. Each of these healing strategies is described below with ethnographic narratives to illustrate how arsenicosis *ghaa* is managed in rural Bangladesh.

Barir chikitsa: the home-based remedy of *ghaa*

The initial treatment of *ghaa* usually starts at home with self-treatment using either home remedies or herbal medicines that are known to be effective in treating specific diseases based on indigenous pharmacology. The concepts of self-treatment or home-based treatment, however, appeared problematic to me, since I did not find exact terminology in the local language that denoted these terms. Jackson and Jackson-Carroll (1994) encountered the same situation when exploring routine health behaviour among the Tamang people of Nepal, who do not consider home treatment to be a significant healing option. Jackson and Jackson-Carroll (1994: 1008) note:

> If asked, "What do you do at home if your son or daughter has cherba?" People uniformly responded, "We don't do anything, we don't know what to do, only the bombo knows what to do, we go to the bombo."

I faced similar difficulty when exploring the routine management of *ghaa* at home. A question like "what do you do when *ghaa* appears?" simply yielded answers like "we do not do anything . . . we go to the doctor" or resulted in a description of treatment processes received outside the home. The standard local word that is commonly used to refer to treatment is *chikitsa*, which literally means treatment received outside the home or provided by healers or doctors. Although my interest was to explore the rudimentary home-based treatment of *ghaa*, villagers frequently referred to *chikitsa* or the treatment processes that are received outside the home. Later I came across the term *barir chikitsa*, which literally means home treatment that local villagers use to refer to the practices and activities associated with the treatment at the household level.

As has been demonstrated previously, *ghaa*, a general skin disease, is very common in rural Bangladesh. Often patients do not recognize the onset of such *ghaa* unless it takes a severe form and limits their ability to engage in physical activities. Most patients informed me that they did not do anything when they first noticed small blisters or *ghaa* on their body. It only becomes a matter of concern for them when they first notice a discharge from the *ghaa*. *Barir chikitsa* generally starts with an adjustment in dietary intake and the use of common remedies that are available at home. Since recurrence is one common feature of *ghaa*, many patients informed me that they do not take any extra care when *ghaa* remains in a dormant stage. However, there are particular seasons when *ghaa* reappears and sometimes takes a severe form. Cleaning discharge from *ghaa* would then become a routine activity for patients and their family members. It was usually the mother or other female members of the family who help in cleaning the *ghaa*. Small pieces of cloth were used to clean the affected areas. Some patients used liquid dettol as an antiseptic for cleaning purposes, while many others, who could not afford dettol or were unaware of the use of antiseptics, used only boiled water. Many patients also used boiled water with the leaf of the Margosa tree (*neem pata*) to clean the *ghaa*, as they believe it has particular healing properties.

While interviewing *ghaa* patients, I came to know about the uses of different plants, herbs and chemicals that were integral parts of *barir chikitsa*. Some plants are grown nearby the homestead, while others are collected from areas where they are known to be found. Two herbs that are commonly used for healing *ghaa* are turmeric (*halud*) and the *neem pata*. Sometimes these ingredients are mixed together and applied directly onto the *ghaa*, while at other times they are used separately. Many respondents informed me that *halud* and *neem pata* have particular healing efficacies, especially in preventing pus (*rosh-koshani*) and reducing itchiness (*chulkani*). One mother of a 14-year-old patient explained to me:

> When the *ghaa* comes back and discharge starts, *holud* and *neem pata* work very well. When *halud* is used, the pus stops. They can be used separately, or if used together, the combination works fast. Sometimes *neem pata* is boiled with water and used to clean *ghaa*. It works very well to stop discharge and itching.

Herbal medications, which are popularly known as *gasra oshud*,[1] are widely used in rural Bangladesh for treating various disease conditions. *Gasra oshud* can either be consumed by making a juice out of them or by directly applying them as a paste on the affected area. *Neem pata* is believed to be particularly effective in treating numerous skin diseases. Many *ghaa* patients in the village believe that a patch of *neem* and *halud* effectively stops the discharge from *ghaa*. One patient stated, "*Holud* and *neem pata* should be mixed together to make a paste and apply on the *ghaa*. It works very well to stop pus discharge. It also stops itching." Other patients informed me that they would take a bath with mildly hot water that had been boiled with *neem pata*, which is believed to be effective in purifying body odors that occur as a result of pus accumulated from the *ghaa*.

Ingesting small quantities of the juice of the *neem* leaf is believed to be effective in healing *ghaa*. As mentioned earlier, since *ghaa* is perceived to have originated from inside the body because of blood poisoning, a treatment method is preferred that would cure *ghaa* from within the body. Thus, besides the external application of *neem* and *halud* paste, juice made from *neem pata* is consumed, which is believed to have blood purifying efficacy. The village *kobiraj* explained to me that:

> The juice of the *neem* leaf is very good for health, although the taste is very bitter and not everyone can drink it – but if you can, it is very good for your body. It cools down the body. It is also good for the digestive system and it helps to remove dirt from inside the body. It purifies the blood and heals *ghaa*, eczema and many other skin diseases.

While conducting fieldwork I found many villagers with pink plasters on their *ghaa*. When I enquired about this, they informed me that it was a plaster of potash,[2] a diluted solution of potassium permanganate ($KMnO_4$), which is believed to be very effective at reducing swelling of *ghaa* if directly applied on it. Many patients informed me that they had been using potash since the *ghaa* first appeared on their skin. They believe that potash is generally effective against many skin diseases and fungal infections, which has led the villagers to believe that it should also work for *ghaa*. As one older patient explained to me:

> Why should it not work for this *ghaa* when it works for other *ghaa*? We have been using potash for many years. For itching and eczema, it works very well. I think it can also work for this *ghaa*.

Thus, potash has been used on a test and trial basis, as villagers believe that it works for other skin diseases. Younger *ghaa* patients, however, know very little about the use of potash and its effectiveness. For them, the decision to use potash comes from older members of the family. One 14-year-old girl told me, "I don't know much about it . . . but I know this is called potash. My mother brought it for me and she showed me how to use it. And I use this accordingly." Potassium permanganate is available in the village pharmacy at the price of 10–12 taka[3] per bottle. The village pharmacy has a regular stock of potash, but sometimes it runs out of supply and the villagers have to go to the Kalaroa bazaar to buy it.

At this point, at least two aspects of *barir chikitsa* have become evident from this study. Firstly, the practices undertaken and the substances used at home to cope with *ghaa* are quite rudimentary. Many villagers often overlook and ignore these practices as treatment, unless they are asked to tell about them. Since *ghaa* is a common skin disease in rural Bangladesh and many people experience this illness to varying degrees, they do everything that is perceived to be effective to manage the condition. This may range from letting out the pus using needles, cleaning the *ghaa*, to applying various herbs and substances on it. Because of its rudimentary nature, many respondents do not even consider *barir chikitisa* as a healing option. They typically consider treatment to refer to health care services that are sought from outside the home. Thus, villagers become quite reluctant or bewildered when asked to illustrate what they do at home to treat *ghaa*.

The second notable aspect of *barir chikitsa* is the use of herbs and plants, locally known as *gasra oshud*, to treat *ghaa*. It is believed that such knowledge has been decreasing, as many people are now going to the village *kobiraj* and allopathic doctors for treatment. When asked to name some common herbal remedies and their respective healing efficacies, many respondents could name only one or two, and often replied: "I do not know much about this, but I ask the older people which herb is to be used for which diseases." It is mostly the older people who could name some herbal remedies and their pharmacological efficacies. The knowledge of herbal medicine is particularly very low among the younger generations, who show less interest in *gasra oshud*. Many respondents also do not know how the herbs work, but they believe that they do work in some way. When asked why and how *neem pata* and *halud* work to heal *ghaa*, most patients replied, "We don't know how, but it works. We came to know about it from our elders and it has been effective since the olden times." Thus, the question of how these herbs work is irrelevant for them; rather, the practical result in the form of healing efficacy appears to be much more important to them.

Hujur: the religious healer

Seeking religious healing services from the *hujur* is a very common feature in rural Bangladesh. During fieldwork, when I spoke to many villagers, they frequently talked about the *hujur* and his religious healings. The *hujur* is a respectable figure in rural Bangladesh (Karim 1988: 280). The label *hujur* has several different meanings that are used to refer to different occupational groups. The teachers from the local madrasah,[4] the imam and his assistant of the village mosque are also referred to as *hujur*. The *hujur* in the village was a dual occupation holder. Besides his primary occupation as an agricultural worker, he also conducted prayers in the village mosque on a voluntary basis. He provided healing services only occasionally and on a non-professional basis. Although services from the *hujur* are free of charge, many villagers offered him a gift in monetary form or goods, if they were pleased with the services received. There was no fixed consultation fee for his services, as one *hujur* said, "We do not want to sell the Qur'an and hadith for taka. We do it for the benevolence of the people. We will be happy if people are happy. My purpose is to make Allah happy." Thus, the healing services provided by the *hujur* are considered voluntary and for the benevolence of the community, in contrast to the professional practitioners, who serve on a fee-for-service basis.

At least three types of techniques are used by the *hujur* to cure illnesses: blowing water (*pani-pora*), removing spiritual possession (*jhar-fuk*) and providing amulets (*tabiz*). For *pani-pora*, the *hujur* generally chants from the holy Qur'an and blows into the water, which he then advises the patient to drink. He can also blow on oil, which is then applied externally on the affected areas. The *hujur* provides services for a wide range of issues. Besides health and illness, villagers bring to the *hujur* many other problems that they are worried and concerned about. One example I found had to do with protecting cows from being stolen. I came to know about this issue one afternoon while I was talking to a group of people who were relaxing and watching young boys playing football. During the course of a casual discussion, one man suddenly said that he was worried about how to protect his cows from being stolen. I enquired, "What did you do then (to protect your cows)?" He smiled a little and explained:

> I went to the *hujur* and discussed the matter with him. He asked me to see him after the *magrib* prayer. I went to him accordingly and he gave me four small pieces of paper with something Arabic written on it in red. He asked me to put these papers into a pot made of clay and place them in four corners of the cowshed. He said that he has arranged to close the cowshed so that thieves cannot take away the cows.

Such services, although apparently unrelated to health and illness, exemplify the comprehensive services provided by the religious healers, which hold a high practical value in the context of rural Bangladesh. They provide people with peace of mind and alleviate their anxieties, something that biomedicine cannot provide. The *hujur* also provides healing services for many *ghaa* patients. In fact, all of the *ghaa* patients I interviewed had consulted the *hujur* at some point of their treatment-seeking process. As discussed earlier, many patients perceive *ghaa* as being a result of snakebites and blood poisoning. Such perceptions lead them to seek health care services either from the *hujur*, who helps to remove poison from the body by chanting and blowing water, or from the village *kobiraj*, who uses *gasra oshud* to remove poison. One *ghaa* patient explained: "Where can I go except the *hujur*? Only the *hujur* can give *pani-pora* to remove *bish* (*bish namano*). So, I went to him to get the *pani-pora*."

During my fieldwork, I frequently visited the home of Rahima, a 13-year-old girl who had been suffering from *ghaa* for two years. I engaged this family in conversation whenever they were free to speak with me. One afternoon, while I was sitting on their verandah, Rahima and her mother shared with me how Rahima's *ghaa* had been treated so far:

Me: When did you first notice this *ghaa*?
Rahima: I don't know when, but one morning I found a *ghaa* full of water on top of my feet.
Me: What did you do then?
Rahima: Using a needle, I let out the water.

Me:	What happened then?
Rahima:	I did not see (the *ghaa*) for some days but the condition became very bad and it was very painful. I told my mother.
Mother:	Yes, she told me she had a blister on her right foot. I did not care that much.
Me:	What did you do then?
Mother:	I thought it was a common *ghaa* and I told her to put some turmeric powder on it.
Me:	Did it work?
Rahima:	(hesitantly) a little bit.
Me:	What did you do then?
Mother:	I told her to see if the *hujur* could do something. Because last time when she had fever, *pani-pora* worked very well. The *hujur* gave her tabiz to protect her from awful nightmares.
Me:	Did you go to see the *hujur*? What did he do?
Rahima:	He gave me *pani-pora* to drink.
Me:	Did it work?
Rahima:	(hesitantly) . . . It remained dormant (*thom thoma*) for some days. The itching was reduced, but it was not permanent, seems nothing beneficial happened.
Me:	Did you seek any other treatment?
Mother:	Many things . . . many things . . . nothing left. Nothing worked. It (*ghaa*) came back. I am worried about how I can get my daughter married. It is in her fate. Nothing to do. I think Allah will cure it through some means (*osila*).

Rahima's case is not an isolated one. My interviews with other villagers revealed that many patients routinely visit the *hujur*. Blown water and blown oil are generally used in sequence, rather than simultaneously. First, the *hujur* provides blown water to drink and advises the patient to wash the *ghaa* using this water. If blown water fails to achieve the desired result, blown oil is then provided to be massaged onto the *ghaa*. Many patients informed me that blown oil is very effective in reducing the itching. Ali explained this to me as follows:

> Blown water has to be drunk and works from within the body, whereas blown oil is only for external application. For *ghaa*, blown oil works better because you can apply it externally, but the result is not permanent. It (*ghaa*) comes back.

Some of the patients I spoke with believed that allopathic and herbal medicine became effective for them because the poison of the *ghaa* was reduced earlier by using *pani-pora*, *tel-pora* and *tula rashi*[5] (the Libra astrological sign, which will be illustrated below). One patient explained to me:

> When I first went to see the *hujur*, he gave me *pani-pora* and *tel-pora*, which worked a little bit, but the *ghaa* did not completely heal. Then, I went to

see the village doctor to get allopathic medicine. That medicine worked well because the poison had already been reduced by *pani-pora* and *tel-pora*.

Thus, it is believed that biomedicine becomes effective when used along with *pani-pora* and *tel-pora*. Biomedicine can only be effective when high toxicity is initially reduced with the use of alternative methods. In this sense, alternative healings and biomedicine are perceived to be complementary and not contradictory.

On many occasions I met the village *hujur*, a white-bearded gentleman in his mid-60s, whom I found to be very polite and friendly. He had been attached to the mosque for the last twenty years. Besides his voluntary profession of conducting prayers in the mosque, he also had small plots of land that he cultivated for his own household consumption. In addition, he earned a small amount of money teaching Arabic to young children on the premises of the mosque. While we met many times at the mosque, the tea stalls and the market, I had the opportunity to talk to him about many issues, including but not limited to politics, economics, NGO interventions and health and well-being. He explained my questions using reference from the holy Qur'an and hadith. He was fully aware of the recent surge of *ghaa* in the village and considered it to be a "*paper-fol* of the people"[6] and "a curse from Allah". He believed that only the solemn observance of Allah's ordinances could save human beings from such deadly diseases. He explained *ghaa* etiology as such:

> Don't you think this *ghaa* is because of *paper-fol*? This is a curse from Allah. Human beings have plunged themselves into many sins. The sufferings and diseases are consequences of human beings' bad deeds. However, there are medicines in the Qur'an and hadith. What you need to do is to believe in it. We do not know many things that are written in the Qur'an and hadith. (If we knew) we could find many solutions. The *ghaa* must be healed through some *osila*. We can only give it a try. It is ultimately Allah who decides the healing.

This statement clearly demonstrates that *ghaa* is perceived to be a *paper-fol* and therefore a curse from Allah. Such a religious explanation of *ghaa* is shaped by the Islamic religious belief that any suffering or misfortune is a consequence of past bad deeds or disobedience to Allah. *Ghaa* is thus predominantly believed to be a consequence of transgression. Many patients I interviewed believed that only a *hujur* could suggest what is to be done to get rid of the *ghaa*. As one patient explained to me:

> This *ghaa* is a punishment from Allah because of our disobedience. What else, if it is not because of our sins? We should go to the *hujur* and talk to him about how we can get rid of it. We must be repentant to get rid of this *ghaa*. Only Allah can save us from this disaster (*gojob*).

Thus, many patients consulted the *hujur* to obtain an appropriate remedy for *ghaa*. Easy accessibility to the *hujur* was also considered to be one of the reasons for the widespread use of his services. The *hujur* is a member of the community and has a fictive familial relationship with most of the villagers. Everyone calls him uncle (*chacha*), which illustrates his warm relationship with them. People can visit and consult him at any time and, most importantly, without any charges. These characteristics of the village *hujur* are in direct contrast to the biomedical professionals, to whom villagers would have to travel nearly 5 kilometers and wait a long time before they could consult a doctor. Economic factors are also crucial in shaping people's decision to seek religious healing, since many villagers cannot afford the high consultation fees of private allopathic doctors as well as the cost of the medicines that are prescribed.

Another factor crucial in influencing the treatment-seeking process of *ghaa* is an individual's understanding of the disease causation, particularly the lay categorization of illnesses that shapes the understanding of which diseases are best treated by which health service providers. As has been mentioned earlier, many villagers perceive *ghaa* to be a result of poisoning from snakebites. This leads them to believe that the *hujur* is the right person to remove poison from the body using *pani-pora* and *jhar-fuk*. Thus, many *ghaa* patients first go to see the *hujur* with a hope that he can remove poison from the body. Other villagers, however, consider his services as simply a test and trial to see if it works before seeking other types of medical services. If alternative healings can cure *ghaa*, there is no need for them to seek other treatment methods that require money and time. One 45-year-old patient told me:

> Before I go to seek allopathic medicine, I first go to the *hujur* to see if he can cure the disease. If he can, it is fine. Why should I spend more money on allopathic medicine? If the *hujur* cannot cure the disease, I then go to other doctors.

Another patient explained to me that he rarely visited biomedical doctors, as they always give painful injections and administer tests that require collection of blood using needles. Yet, others expressed their dissatisfaction with the behaviour of the biomedical doctors. One patient stated: "They (biomedical doctors) never treat us like human beings. We go there to consult him but he treats us impolitely. He never listens to us properly."

In sum, it is evident from the discussions above that the decision making for seeking religious healing from the *hujur* is much more pragmatic, complex and dynamic and is not based on just one single factor. Despite such a high prevalence of religious healing in rural Bangladesh, there has been hardly any ethnographic research conducted on this issue. Additional anthropological research is required to determine the extent and nature of these skills, knowledge and practices.

The village *kobiraj*: belief as medicine

Before conducting my fieldwork, I learned from Feldman (1983: 1889) that a "*kobiraj* refers to a practitioner who prescribes herbal medicines usually prepared by the practitioner himself from locally grown herbs". During my fieldwork, however, I found that such an understanding of the *kobiraj* is too simplistic and generalized to apply in the context of my studied village. In southwestern Bangladesh, I came to know that *kobiraji* treatment is much more complex and syncretic in terms of techniques used and methods applied to heal illnesses. I found one *kobiraj* who relied only on herbal medicines, while two others combined a range of other techniques such as herbal medicine, allopathic medicine, chanting, the use of the Libra astrological sign (*tula rashi*) and sorcery or magico-religious techniques to find out lost properties. Thus, the range of services a *kobiraj* provides is much more diversified and syncretic than outlined by Feldman.

There are at least three *kobiraj* in the village who had been actively rendering healing services to *ghaa* patients. One was a full-time professional, whereas the other was a trishaw puller by profession and occasionally administered *kobiraji* treatment. The third *kobiraj* runs a small chamber at Kalaroa bazaar. None of these *kobiraj* had any formal training; rather, they had learned medicine through apprenticeships under an elder *kobiraj*. In order to exhibit their healing competencies, many pictures of successfully healed patients were hung in the chambers of the *kobiraj*. When asked if he had any certificate of apprenticeship, one *kobiraj* replied, "The patients (*rogi*) are my certificate; you go and ask them how successfully they were healed." He instantly uttered names of many successfully healed patients and asked me to check with them if I wanted to be sure of his competencies. Thus, successfully healed patients act as the competency certificate for the *kobiraj*.

The perceptions of *ghaa* and its etiology differ between the *kobiraj* in the village. When asked about *ghaa*, one *kobiraj* explained to me:

> Ringworm and eczema are not arsenic *ghaa* which occur in between the fingers, hands and feet. Arsenic *ghaa* is itchy and the skin is dismantled. Arsenic *ghaa* looks like a burn. Eczema, blisters and other *ghaa* have pus inside and are painful, whereas arsenic *ghaa* is less painful. Ringworm and eczema are communicable but arsenic *ghaa* is not. Arsenic *ghaa* comes from blood poisoning and it is not communicable. They are different.

Thus, it is stated that arsenicosis *ghaa* is different from other skin diseases. Although he considers that *ghaa* is a result of drinking contaminated water, he further believes that such *ghaa* is a result of poisoned blood (*dushito rokto*), which first affects the body's internal organs. The external appearances of *ghaa* are merely a symptom from within the body. He categorizes the human body as being either hot or cold and believes that individuals with a cold body type are more susceptible to *ghaa*.

On the other hand, Nimai *kobiraj* holds a different view about the causation of *ghaa*. According to him, *ghaa* is a result of poisoning from snakebites. He believes that the poison had not been fully removed earlier from his body, and that it was the remnant of poisons that causes *ghaa* in the body. Thus, it is clear that these two *kobiraj* hold rather different notions of the *ghaa* etiology. However, corroborating the lay understandings of *ghaa* held by the villagers, both of these *kobiraj* share the similar knowledge that *ghaa* might have occurred because of people's transgression or disobedience to Allah. Such similarities in understanding *ghaa* etiology between the villagers and the healers are believed to be a major motivating factor for seeking alternative healing services in rural Bangladesh. Bangladesh is not unique in this regard, as other studies, in Africa (Beckerleg 1994; MaClean 1969; Wooding 1979) and in Russia (Lindquist 2002), have confirmed that patients and health service providers feel comfortable when they have a shared understanding of disease etiology.

In terms of healing techniques, different methods are employed by different *kobiraj*. Nimai *kobiraj*, for example, prescribes both herbal medicine and biomedical ointment for external application. He purchases the ointment from pharmacies at the Kalaroa bazaar and resells it to patients who want quick results. As he explained:

> Some patients want quick relief from itching and pain which herbal medicine cannot provide. It takes a longer time to heal. Patients do not want to wait until that time. To keep the name as a good *kobiraj*, sometimes we have to give allopathic ointment which shows quick results and patients also become happy. They come back to see me again.

Thus, the incorporation of both biomedicine and herbal medicine in his treatment procedure is perceived to be a mechanism for spreading his reputation and making patients satisfied so that they continue visiting him. Besides herbal and allopathic medicine, he also uses shamanistic healing by means of the Libra astrological sign (*tula rashi*) to remove poison from the body. One *ghaa* patient explained to me that biomedicine worked well for him because the toxicity of poison was previously reduced by using *tula rashi*. Another patient, who did not go to a *kobiraj*, voiced his grief by saying: "I made a mistake. If I would go to see the *kobiraj* immediately after I got this *ghaa*, he might have given me *jhar-fuk* to reduce the poison. I think allopathic medicine works well after *jhar-fuk*." Thus, in the context of rural Bangladesh, traditional healing and biomedicine are not contradictory but are believed to complement each other.

Another very crucial aspect of *kobiraji* treatment is that patients must keep faith in medicine. Nimai *kobiraj* in the village explained to me that if patients do not have trust in what the *kobiraj* prescribes, the medicine might not work well for them. Patients must not hold any doubts about the medical authority and skill of the *kobiraj*. Thus, it is predominantly believed that maintaining trust and faith in the *kobiraj* and his medicine are crucial in the treatment process to achieve effective healing. Raju *kobiraj* explained it in this way:

> This is up to your belief. If you take medicine with the belief that it would cure your illness, whatever may be the disease, be it *ghaa*, cancer, or whatever, it would be healed effectively. You have to keep trust in what you are taking. Everything depends on your belief. If you believe in medicine you will be cured. If you do not have faith, then whatever medicine you take will not work for you. Everything depends on belief.

Thus, belief in medicine is considered to be more effective than the substance of the medicine itself. The material aspects of the medicine can only be effective if they are substantiated by a strong belief in their curative properties. Many patients who visited the *kobiraj* also told me that easy accessibility to a *kobiraj* is another crucial factor for them to seek healing services. The *kobiraj* is a member of the village and is accessible most of the time, unlike the allopathic doctors who stay at the Kalaroa Upazilla headquarters. A 58-year-old patient explained to me:

> In order to go to the hospital, we have to go to Kalaroa. This is far away from us and we are not sure if we will get to see the doctor. The *kobiraj* lives in the village and we can see him anytime we want to. If he can cure the disease, it is okay. But if he cannot, we go to the hospital.

Another patient told me: "Since this *ghaa* is not curing permanently and coming back again and again, we have to seek treatment regularly. Who has time to see the doctor in the hospital regularly? The *kobiraj* is in our village and we can see him anytime." Many other patients shared the same view that accessibility matters a lot to them. One worried mother of a *ghaa* patient said, "My daughter has been suffering from *ghaa* for a long time. She cannot go to the hospital alone. Either her father or I have to take her to the hospital. Who has time to go there regularly? That's why we go to the *kobiraj*. He is very close to our home." Thus, in rural Bangladesh, easy accessibility to the *kobiraj* is one of the important factors for many *ghaa* patients to seek their healing services. Affordability of herbal medicine is another factor that has attracted villagers to seek their services. The village *kobiraj* does not charge a fixed consultation fee and treatment is often offered in a package that includes both a consultation fee and the cost of medicine. When asked about the expenses of herbal treatment, one *ghaa* patient explained:

> For herbal medicine, the *kobiraj* does not charge you a lot. If you go to consult a doctor, he will charge you as high as 200 taka. But we give only 10–20 taka for herbal medicine. He never presses us to pay much. This is very convenient for us.

Another patient said: "Allopathic medicine will cost 200–300 taka. We are poor people. How can we afford such expensive medicine?" Yet other patients informed me that the *kobiraj* did not charge them in cases of minor illnesses such as a runny nose, cough or fever. The most convenient aspect of *kobiraji* treatment, however, is that it can be sought through credit. In rural Bangladesh, many villagers do not have enough ready cash to seek health care services. Thus, the *kobiraj* offers treatment on credit, as has been explained by one patient:

> If someone is sick and needs to see the *kobiraj* but does not have enough money to pay him, there is nothing to worry about. We can pay him later when we have enough savings. He is very kind. He does not mind giving us medicine on credit (*baki*); we can pay him later.

Thus, many patients seek *kobiraji* treatment on credit which they pay later on, particularly during the harvesting period when villagers have enough cash in their hands. Such flexibility in payment and the economic affordability of herbal medicine motivate people to seek health care services from the village *kobiraj*. Most of the patients I spoke to had begun their treatment with *kobiraji* medicine, but later on they went to seek allopathic medicine. However, their dissatisfaction with biomedicine caused them to come back to *kobiraji* treatment again. One such patient explained to me that:

> I first went to see the *kobiraj* to seek herbal medicine. Although the *ghaa* improved a bit, it came back again. My friend suggested that I seek allopathic medicine from the Kalaroa hospital. I thought allopathic medicine might heal this *ghaa*, but it did not. The *ghaa* came back again and again, and I went to the *kobiraj*, who said that it would take some time to remove the poison from my body to heal the *ghaa*.

Another patient, who spent a good amount of money for allopathic medicine but did not see any improvement, informed me with much discontent: "All my money I spent for allopathic medicine has gone to the water. I do not see any improvement of my *ghaa*. What kind of *ghaa* is this that the doctor cannot cure it? What can I do now? I go to the *kobiraj* if he can heal this *ghaa*." Clearly, patients were often disappointed with the failure of biomedicine to cure *ghaa*, which led them to seek alternative healing services.

It is now quite evident that *kobiraji* treatment is much more popular than many other healing options in rural Bangladesh. In order to meet the demands of patients and make them satisfied, the village *kobiraj* often crosses the therapeutic boundary to incorporate biomedical and spiritual healing techniques, including *tula rashi*. The decisions that individuals make to seek *kobiraji* treatment are pragmatic, socioculturally prescribed and guided by particular disease etiology held by the patients. One important reason why local villagers prefer *kobiraji* treatment for curing *ghaa* is that they believe such *ghaa* to be a result of snakebites, which only a *kobiraj* can cure using his herbal medicine and spiritual healing techniques.

Doctor without degrees: the village doctor and his pharmacy

Despite burgeoning village pharmacies, locally known as *oshuder dokan*, and the essential role of the village pharmacists and sales assistants in rendering health care services to the bulk of the rural Bangladeshis, hardly any ethnographic study has so far been conducted on this issue. In Bangladesh, both in urban and rural areas, drugs are available and within the reach of everyone through these pharmacies. All sorts of drugs, including antibiotics, analgesics and multivitamins, are available without any prescription. Biomedical drugs in Bangladesh have become an everyday commodity, like anything else that is bought and sold at the neighboring shops. During my fieldwork, the local village pharmacy situated at the village bazaar became one of the crucial entry points into the study of *ghaa* patients.

On many occasions, I used to sit in the pharmacy cum village doctor's chamber, not just to chat but to engage in careful observation of the interactions that took place between the village doctor and patient. On one occasion, a woman in her mid-30s presented with complaints of itching and discharge from *ghaa*. The interaction that took place was as follows:

Patient: (throwing the prescription on the table) Why does none of your medicine work? The *ghaa* is very itchy and painful, and pus is also coming out.
Doctor: Sit here. Did you go to Satkhira (District Headquarters) to see the specialist doctor?
Patient: Yes, I went last Wednesday. He prescribed me some medicine. (Showing the prescription) Look, everything is there. He gave me medicine but nothing worked. It (*ghaa*) is very itchy and painful and I cannot sleep at night.
Doctor: Are you taking these medications?
Patient: Yes, for a week. But none is working. I spent a lot of money to go to Satkhira to see the doctor, but nothing is effective.
Doctor: Move close, let me see the *ghaa*.
Patient: What kind of doctor are you that you cannot cure the *ghaa*?
Doctor: You better drink *endrin*.[7]
Patient: I would drink that if I don't have to think about my children.

Although it seems hilarious, this is a very common encounter between patients and the village doctor that I observed. The village doctor explained to me that the above patient had been suffering from *ghaa* for many years. Even after he had prescribed a high dose of antibiotics, her *ghaa* could not be healed. Having failed to manage the symptoms, the doctor advised the patient to consult a specialist at the district hospital in Satkhira. However, she complained that no improvement was observed in her symptoms. The village doctor appears to be bewildered what to do next.

The village doctor, who had been in this profession for the last eight years, runs his chamber cum pharmacy in one corner of the village bazaar. The amenities in his chamber are quite basic, consisting of a wooden table and a couple of chairs for patients to sit on. A wooden cot has been placed in one corner of the room for examining patients. There is no curtain to maintain their privacy. There are two dusty shelves in the chamber that display some basic medications. The doctor's motorcycle, which he uses to visit patients, is usually parked in front of the chamber. The chamber generally remains open in the afternoon until evening. The morning schedule of the doctor is reserved for visiting patients in their homes.

When asked about his professional training, the village doctor informed me that hands-on training through apprenticeship (*haate-kolome kaj shekha*) and obtaining a professional degree are two different things. He said that he had a formal education up to secondary school, but later he had to quit school to ease the financial burden of the family. He joined the pharmacy of one of his relatives at Kalaroa bazaar as a sales assistant, where he worked for seven years before setting up his own pharmacy. Later on, he underwent rural medical practitioner training. He claimed that he knows medicine better than many doctors and has had practical

Arsenicosis and health-seeking behaviour 81

experience on how to deal with patients. Thus, he stresses that accumulation of experience in successfully healing patients is much preferred over professional training of biomedicine. From the patient's point of view, professional degrees are redundant, irrelevant or even considered unnecessary as long as the doctor is capable of treating diseases. Effectively treating diseases is perceived to be more important than professional degrees.

When I asked the villagers if they knew anything about the degrees or qualifications of the village doctor, most respondents replied that they were not worried about it because they had known him for a long time. One villager said: "He has been running this pharmacy for many years. Many patients go to see him and he also cures many diseases." Another villager told me: "We have seen many patients visiting his chamber. Some patients also come from other villages. If his medicine does not work, why do people come to consult him?" Thus, the most important consideration for patients is whether the doctor can cure disease and his medicine is effective; rather than his certificates. The certificates and professional training are considered to be of secondary importance or of no value at all if the diseases are not cured. One *ghaa* patient, who was dissatisfied with biomedical treatment, said:

> What is the benefit of knowing what degrees the doctors have? I went to many reputed doctors, even to Kolkata. But nothing happened. *Ghaa* remains as *ghaa*. I spent a lot of money, but none can give me any effective medicine. So what are these degrees for, if they cannot cure the disease?

The village doctor is proud of his long years of practical experience in handling patients and prescribing medicine. His services range from managing everyday minor illnesses such as fever, headache, cough, cold, general weaknesses and regulating blood pressure to various minor surgical procedures such as tooth extraction, removal of pus from blisters and setting bones. Although he is unsure of how allopathic medicine works for a particular disease, he was quite prompt in citing which medicine works for what sort of diseases. Another very essential feature of his profession was to provide services on credit, as many patients are unable to pay their medical bill at the point of service. The village doctor maintained a register where he noted down the patient's name and the due amount. It was usually during the harvesting period when the amount was fully paid. Such flexibility in paying medical bills is highly convenient for poor villagers, who may not be able to pay the full amount at the time of consultation.

As far as *ghaa* treatment is concerned, the village doctor first came to know about this disease from NGO workers. Although he believes that arsenic is a poison and the *ghaa* is a result of drinking contaminated groundwater, he had a very vague idea of how it affects the human body and the long-term consequences of exposure to arsenic. When asked how the *ghaa* is different from other skin diseases, he explained thus:

> If it is not arsenicosis, why do powerful antibiotics fail to cure it? Such antibiotics work well when used to cure other skin diseases such as scabies, ringworm, etc. It works well for other *ghaa* but not for arsenic *ghaa*. Can arsenic

82 *Arsenicosis and health-seeking behaviour*

not be destroyed in any way? Sometimes temporary relief is achieved, but not the complete cure.

Thus, the failure of antibiotics appears to be a crucial point by which he distinguishes arsenicosis *ghaa* from other skin diseases. On many occasions while I was visiting his chamber, he shared his frustrations and embarrassment due to failure of allopathic medicine to cure *ghaa*. He referred many *ghaa* patients to specialist doctors, but all of these patients returned without much improvement in their condition. His chamber, then, became a place of last resort for these returnee *ghaa* patients. The failure of antibiotics to achieve desired results compelled him to prescribe overdosages of antibiotics for patients who were not suitable for such drugs, particularly children and youth. One day he explained to me the situation:

> I have administered antibiotics such as cepdoxim, flucloxociline, penicillin, pen-V, Avil.[8] I have also given many vitamins, like vitamins E and C, but the *ghaa* did not heal. During the monsoon it takes a very serious form. Many young kids are not suitable for such strong antibiotics. But as a doctor, I am under pressure. Every time I visit this patient, his parents ask why I cannot cure this *ghaa*. They often blame me and ask what kind of doctor I am that cannot cure the *ghaa*. That is why I have to give stronger antibiotics which are not good for children. What else can I do?

The above statement, which reflects the life and work of a village doctor, brings up several issues. The first and most obvious concern is the irrational (ab)use of antibiotics, particularly in the hands of non-professionals, which has already been documented elsewhere in India (Kamat and Nichter 1998; Minocha 1980; Saradamma, Higginbotham, and Nichter 2000) as well as in Vietnam (Craig 2002). It is not that the village doctor is unaware of the side effects of such high dosages of antibiotics; he prescribes them consciously knowing that it may result in heart or kidney failures. From the village doctor's point of view, it is the social pressure and expectations that demand immediate relief of a particular disease by any means; otherwise, his authority as a doctor would be questioned. Such a challenge to his medical competency puts him under pressure to administer high dosages of antibiotics, despite the known side effects. The statement above shows that the doctor is faced with many disappointing situations if the prescribed medicine does not produce effective outcomes. The village doctor is positioned at the edge of a knife; as a doctor he is expected to produce substantial positive improvements of symptoms, or his medical competency is challenged. On the other hand, from an ethical point of view, he cannot prescribe high dosages of antibiotics because of their known side effects. In fact, on many occasions when I met the village doctor, he informed me that he did not feel good visiting *ghaa* patients again, since there is no medication that is able to cure the *ghaa*.

Many patients I met were also aware of the fact that allopathic medicine can only ensure temporary relief from the symptoms. Thus, when asked if allopathic medicine works for the *ghaa*, most respondents replied that it works for some time, but when the medicine is stopped, the condition comes back to what it was before. One patient told me: "When I take allopathic medicine, the discharge and itching stop and the *ghaa* dries up. But the *ghaa* comes back when I stop taking medicines." When asked why they went to see the village doctor when the medicine was not curing the *ghaa*, most of the patients informed me that the village doctor was the only accessible person in the village that was available at most times. As one patient stated: "Where can I go except to him? He is the only doctor in our village. When my *ghaa* appears I go to consult him, although his medicine only provides temporary relief." Another patient was very pragmatic in saying: "I do not want to go to the Kalaroa hospital because we have a doctor in our village. Will the doctor in the Kalaroa hospital give different medications? The medicines are the same, so why should I go to the Kalaroa hospital and spend time and money?" Yet others brought up their personal relationship with the village doctor as a positive factor for visiting him. One patient thus said:

> I have been visiting him for many years. If there is any minor matter, I go to him. He treats me well, as he knows me well. He is very caring to me and gives me special attention. If I go to the doctor at the Kalaroa hospital, I would not feel free to talk to him the way I talk to the village doctor.

Many patients were also worried about the failure of biomedicine to cure *ghaa*. They repeatedly asked me if I knew of any medicine invented to cure it. Not just the village doctor, but also the patients became frustrated and pessimistic having seen the reappearance of *ghaa*, despite the fact that they had been consuming expensive drugs. Having not achieved any lasting cure, many patients discontinued taking the medication and became hopeless and pessimistic about their *ghaa* being healed. One patient commented: "We have to live with this. We have to live with this *ghaa*. The medicine will perhaps be invented after we die."

The failure of allopathic medicine to completely cure *ghaa* pushes the village doctor to incorporate several other healing techniques, such as Unani herbal medicine called Safi,[9] which is believed to be effective in purifying blood and increasing general body resistance to various illnesses. When prescribing Safi, however, the doctor introduces it to patients as a blood purifier. He uses this medicine on a trial basis to see if it works for *ghaa*. He explained to me:

> I am not quite sure what happens when Safi is taken, because herbal medicine works slowly. I think it can work, but it takes time to produce results because it works from within the body. Let's see what happens. If it works, it is fine. If it does not work, no problem, at least it does not have side effects like antibiotics.

Thus, the village doctor deliberately crosses his therapeutic boundary to incorporate herbal medications in order to experiment to see if it works to heal *ghaa*. Although he is unsure about the curative properties of herbal medicines, he believes that they are at least free from side effects such as antibiotics. Therefore, he uses herbal medicines on a test and trial basis to complement biomedicine.

Thus far, it has been quite evident that the failure of biomedicine to cure *ghaa* has frustrated and dissatisfied both patients and the village doctor. The village doctor is particularly despondent, as his medicine has failed to achieve desired outcomes, which challenges his medical authority. Additionally, since biomedicine does not work well enough to cure *ghaa*, the village doctor deliberately engages with syncretic medical practices by borrowing healing modalities from other medical systems, such as herbal medicine. Patients, on the other hand, become pessimistic after experiencing the failure of biomedicine and end up accepting that *ghaa* is their destiny.

The village homeopathic doctor

Homeopaths are probably one of the most accessible and popular health service providers in rural Bangladesh. Almost all villages in rural Bangladesh have homeopaths with their consultation chambers. Although most homeopathic doctors do not have any formal training, they are either self-taught or apprenticed under experienced homeopaths to render extensive health care services in rural Bangladesh. All *ghaa* patients I interviewed had tried homeopathic medicine at some point in their treatment-seeking process. Many of them consulted homeopathic doctors in sequence with other healing practitioners, such as the *kobiraj* and the village doctor. Homeopathic medicine, as developed by the German physician Samuel Hahnemann in the early nineteenth century, is based on the principle of *similia similibus curentur*, or "let like be treated by like" (Vithoulkas 1986). Homeopathic diagnosis of the disease and treatment thereof are based on the symptoms experienced and guided by the belief that the germ that causes the disease can also cure the same if administered in a very small quantity. Another very crucial aspect of homeopathic treatment is its holistic approach, where disease itself is neither treated nor deemed important; but rather, it is the human body as an integrated system of physical, mental and emotional aspects that are taken care of (Cant and Sharma 1996; Frank 2002; Frank and Ecks 2004; Scott 1998; Vithoulkas 1986; Whiteford 1999).

In my studied village, *ghaa* patients sought homeopathic treatment from two places: the village homeopathic doctor, who ran his pharmacy in the village bazaar, and the Kalaroa Upazilla headquarters, where there were a number of doctors who practiced homeopathy. From the patient's point of view, the health-seeking behaviour of homeopathic medicine is guided by the search for a reputed doctor (*valo daktar*) who will successfully heal illnesses. Patients usually came to know about a *valo daktar* through their social networks or through a therapy managing group. Once a reputed doctor is found, patients would usually attempt to seek his services depending on the time, their financial condition and the distance from their village.

The homeopathic doctor in the village was a 50-year-old man who had been practicing homeopathy for the last twenty years. He had learned homeopathic medicine through an apprenticeship as an assistant to a renowned homeopathic doctor at Kalaroa bazaar and received hands-on experience from him. When asked if he knew about the *ghaa*, he informed me that in homeopathic treatment the name of the disease and its causes are of little or no significance. As a homeopath, he is not worried about the labeling of a particular disease; rather, the most important considerations for him are behavioural, psychological and physical symptoms experienced by patients. He explained to me:

> We do not treat the disease but we treat the patient. Whether it is arsenic *ghaa* or not is not the matter for us. What matters are the symptoms (*lokkhon*). We look for symptoms. Our medications are based on symptoms. If the symptom matches, whatever the disease may be, it will be cured by the medicine.

Thus, in homeopathic treatment, minute and detailed observation of the symptoms is a prerequisite for the treatment to be successful. The doctor often told me that the selection of the right medicine is crucial in homeopathic treatment. When asked about the effectiveness of homeopathic medicine in treating *ghaa*, the doctor informed me that there are particular medicines that can cure *ghaa*. In my interviews with the patients, it became quite clear that the popularity of and interest in homeopathic medicine has been increasing. All *ghaa* patients I interviewed informed me that they had consulted homeopathic doctors not just for the *ghaa* but for many other illnesses. As far as their *ghaa* treatment is concerned, each individual had visited the homeopathic doctor between two and five times a year. Besides visiting homeopathic doctors, patients also informed me that they concurrently consulted other health care professionals. The failure of one medicine to achieve the desired results drives patients to move on to another health care service. However, this kind of oscillating behaviour often creates tension between patients and their health service providers. For example, the concurrent use of allopathic and homeopathic medicine is particularly discouraged by the village homeopaths. When asked why arsenic *ghaa* reappeared, the homeopathic doctor told me that the failure of homeopathic medicine is because of the patient's concurrent use of other medications.

Allopathic doctors, on the other hand, blame the patients in that they are often too late to seek biomedical services, as they often waste time seeking *kobiraji* and homeopathic treatment. On the other hand, homeopathic doctors consistently argue that *ghaa* patients do not keep their patience in homeopathic treatment. The homeopathic doctor informed me that the "patients come here today and go there tomorrow; can the disease be cured in this way? If treated by homeopathic medicine, they need to keep patience because homeopathic medicine works slowly. But none listens to me, as they go to allopathic doctors after some days of treatment."

There is a consistent belief among the patients that homeopathic medicine works well for chronic diseases (*jotil rog*) like dysentery, gastrointestinal problems, asthma, allergies and other chronic pain conditions such as arthritis and back pain. In contrast, allopathic medicine is believed to be more effective in treating acute or life-threatening diseases such as a heart attack, cancer and other diseases that require immediate, effective and emergency medical attention. Such a categorization of homeopathic medicine has already been documented by Frank (2002) in the context of Berlin, Germany, where patients believe that homeopathic medicine is best suited to treating chronic and non-life-threatening diseases. My informants also believe that homeopathy is effective but slow medicine that works gently to provide long-lasting result, as opposed to allopathic medicine, which is believed to provide immediate and temporary results. Since *ghaa* often reappears and no medicine seems to effectively cure it, many patients consider *ghaa* as chronic (*kothin ghaa*). Such understanding pushes them to try homeopathic medicine, which is categorized as strong medicine to be effective against chronic *ghaa* conditions. One patient thus explained to me:

> I have been suffering from *ghaa* for nearly two years. I have tried many medicines but they did not cure it. This is a *kothin ghaa*. It needs strong medicine like homeopathy to cure it because homeopathic medicine cures chronic diseases. I think this *ghaa* could be cured if a good homeopathic doctor (*valo daktar*) is consulted.

Another patient, who had been treated with homeopathic medicine for his *ghaa*, explained to me: "If strong medicine is not administered, the germ of the *ghaa* cannot be killed. It needs a strong medicine like homeopathy to cure *ghaa*; otherwise it will remain and come back again and again." Thus, the popular categorization of homeopathy as strong medicine shapes patients' utilization of this healing service, as one patient stated that homeopathic medicine is more powerful than other medicines because it cures chronic diseases (*jotil rog*). Another very important factor that popularizes homeopathy is the understanding that this medicine is gentle, tolerable, mild and free from side effects, unlike antibiotics and many other allopathic medicines. Such an understanding often motivates people to seek homeopathic medicine over other types of medications. One patient said: "Homeopathic medicine is good because it does not have any side effects. If diseases are cured using homeopathic medicine, why should we go for allopathic medicine which has side effects and costly?" A mother of a 12-year-old *ghaa* patient prefers that her daughter be treated with homeopathic medicine, which she believes is gentle and particularly suitable for young children.

During my fieldwork, I routinely heard patients saying: "We are poor and cannot afford to buy expensive medicines on a long-term basis. How much money should we spend on medicine?" Affordability thus appears to be a crucial factor in patients' decision making on which health care services to seek. Inexpensive homeopathic medicine is thus a very popular option for many in poverty-ridden rural Bangladesh. I found many *ghaa* patients who discontinued allopathic treatment and went back to homeopathic medicine because they were unable to afford expensive allopathic antibiotics. One patient informed me: "What can we do if we cannot afford allopathic medicine? We go to the homeopathic doctor because the medicine is inexpensive." Another patient stated: "Allopathic treatment is not for us, this is for the rich people who have money. We cannot afford it. So, we go to homeopathic doctor."

The failure of biomedicine to ensure effective outcome is another reason patients discontinue allopathic treatment and seek homeopathic medicine instead. On many occasions, patients told me that there was no point in taking expensive antibiotics if the *ghaa* reappears; homeopathic medicine, instead, is cheap and affordable and could be worth a try. One patient commented:

> I have been taking allopathic medicine for so long, but do not see any improvement. The *ghaa* remains as usual. I gave all my money to the doctor, but no improvement is seen. What is the point in spending money for allopathic medicine? Homeopathic medicine is cheap, and if taken for a long time, it may cure the *ghaa*.

In terms of accessibility, I got mixed reactions from patients. Some patients informed me that they would not mind a reasonable amount of travelling if a good homeopathic doctor were found. By 'reasonable time', they mean two or three hours of walking or one or two hours by bus. Some patients are quite pragmatic and say that accessibility is an issue for them, since homeopathy is a long-term treatment process that requires many visits to the doctor, making it impractical for them to travel a long distance regularly. As one patient said: "I cannot go to see a homeopathic doctor, even though I want to. It requires money and time to go there regularly. I do not have enough time and money to go there over and over again." Another patient said: "I have some other things to do, so I cannot go, although I want to. If the doctor lives far away, we cannot go because he will ask us to see him again and again. How can we visit him so many times and ignore our other activities?"

Thus, it is quite evident that local people's decision making on homeopathic treatment is guided by the understanding that *ghaa* is a chronic disease that requires strong medicine such as homeopathy to completely cure it. Homeopathic treatment is also preferred as it is believed to be mild, free from side effects and inexpensive. However, discontinuation of homeopathic medicine is also very high. Many patients either simultaneously use homeopathy and other medicines or give homeopathy a try before seeking other healing options.

Biomedical health care services

The UHC is the nearest referral public hospital that provides professional biomedical health care services to the population of this region. The UHC was established in 1982 as a 30-bed hospital with modern pathological and diagnostic facilities. There are seven medical officers, who hold at least an MBBS degree, posted to this hospital. It has recently been upgraded to a 100-bed hospital with specialized physicians and some additional facilities such as electrocardiogram and X-ray machines. Health care services are provided at a very nominal charge at the point of delivery, and some basic medications are also free subject to availability. Most of the time, however, these drugs are out of stock and patients are asked to buy medications from the market. Pathological and diagnostic facilities are also offered free of charge, although many pieces of equipment remain non-functional due to technical faults. Patients are often asked to undergo pathological and diagnostic

88 *Arsenicosis and health-seeking behaviour*

examinations in private clinics outside the UHC. Although the UHC is situated nearly 5 kilometers from the village, it is fairly accessible, nearly an hour's walk from the village. Male villagers who wish to seek health care services usually cycle there, whereas female patients travel by trishaw, which requires about half an hour travelling time.

Since there are only seven medical officers to render health care services to a huge population, patients have to wait a long time before they can consult a doctor. The waiting time ranges between one and two hours for the consultation, excluding travelling time to and from the village. The long waiting time is further exacerbated by a lack of waiting rooms. Women and children are often seen sitting on the floor. Most of the medical officers in the UHC are also affiliated with private clinics where they conduct their private practice. Those who can afford the consultation fees often try to avoid the long queues at the UHC by going to these private clinics to consult the doctor. Thus, the UHC remains the only option for poor people.

The doctor in charge of this health complex is the UHO, who looks after the overall management of the hospital. When asked about arsenicosis, its causes and health consequences, the UHO explained to me:

> The first stage of arsenicosis is called melanosis, which is manifested as spots on the skin, like brown or reddish raindrop spots. At the same time, we ask patients if they drink water from red- or green-coloured tubewells. If someone is found to have melanosis with a history of drinking water from red-coloured tubewells, we confirm that this might be a case of arsenicosis. The second stage of arsenicosis is called hyperkeratosis, meaning *ghaa* on the hands and feet. We see corns or warts on the skin and rough skin (*gota gota hoy*). Hyperkeratosis may lead to gangrene and cancer, which is the third stage of arsenicosis. We do not have any laboratory tests in this hospital to diagnose arsenicosis. We diagnose arsenicosis based on observable symptoms.

It is clear that arsenicosis is medically explained to be a physiological change that occurs because of drinking arsenic-contaminated groundwater. The diagnosis is symptomatic and based on changes in the skin colour and appearance of skin lesions. From a biomedical perspective, arsenicosis is explained to be a disease that develops slowly through different stages, including melanosis, hyperkeratosis, gangrene and cancer. Besides skin lesions as external manifestations of arsenicosis, various internal organs like the heart, liver and kidney can also be affected if arsenic-contaminated water is consumed over long periods of time. The consequences of arsenic toxicity for human physiology remain unexplored in biomedical science. The UHO mentioned that the long-term consequences of drinking arsenic-contaminated water could be far-reaching, and more human organs may be affected by arsenic toxicity. He urged further medical research on this issue.

One doctor at the UHC suspects that the increasing rate of hypertension among the population may be because of exposure to arsenic toxicity. He mentioned that the consequences of arsenic toxicity can be illustrated in both non-cancer health effects and cancerous health effects. By "non-cancer health effects" he refers to the stages of melanosis, keratosis and hyperkeratosis, whereas by "cancerous health effect" he refers to the later stages of gangrene and cancer of the extremities. He further mentioned that the hematological impact of arsenic toxicity is often manifested in anemic conditions due to deficiency of hemoglobin in red blood cells. It is believed that hepatological and gastrointestinal disorders might be associated with arsenic toxicity, as most of the arsenicosis patients present complaints of vomiting, pain in the stomach and diarrhea.

Such biomedical understandings of arsenicosis on the basis of physiology, hematology or hepatology are in direct contrast to the popular perceptions of arsenicosis as *ghaa*. As demonstrated previously, arsenicosis is socially constructed as *ghaa* primarily due to poisoning from snakebites. There is a clear gap between biomedical and social constructions of arsenicosis. One obvious implication of this gap is observed in the tension between patients and biomedical doctors in a clinical encounter. As one *ghaa* patient explained to me:

> I told the doctor that I have *ghaa* on my leg which is very itchy and painful, with pus. He checked my blood pressure and asked me which colored tubewell I drank water from. He asked me to do a blood test and advised me not to drink water from the red-marked tubewell. I thought he could give me ointment to apply on the *ghaa* so that the *ghaa* would dry up and I would get some relief from the itching. When I asked why I had to do the blood test, the doctor said I might have anemia and that I also have hypertension. I expected ointment for the *ghaa*, not to have to go for a blood test.

It is quite evident in this statement that the clinical diagnosis and treatment of arsenicosis are beyond the knowledge of the patient. He did not expect his blood to be tested just because of the *ghaa*, which he thought could simply be treated by prescribing ointments. In contrast, the doctor suspected that the patient might be suffering from anemia and hypertension due to chronic arsenicosis. In such a clinical encounter, biomedical procedures of diagnosing and treating arsenicosis sharply depart from what the actual patient perceives and experiences as the illness. The ways in which clinical frameworks offer diagnosis and treatment of arsenicosis seems unfamiliar and inappropriate by the patient. Such a mismatch between biomedicine and popular perceptions is not unique in the context of rural Bangladesh. It has been reported by Kleinman (1986: 1975) in China and Taiwan that doctors and patients have different perceptions of psychiatry and mental disorders.

Many *ghaa* patients who consulted the physician at the UHC informed me that the doctor did not explain what had happened to them; rather, they simply ordered blood tests and other clinical investigations that the patient perceived as redundant. One patient was thus quite annoyed and reacted in the following way:

> Whenever I go to see the doctor, he tells me to do unnecessary blood and other tests. Can you tell me why a blood test is needed for *ghaa* treatment? I

went to get medicine for *ghaa*, but the doctor asked me to go for a blood test. Is there no medicine for *ghaa*? Why does he tell me to go for an unnecessary blood test?

Clearly, patients' visits to the hospital is guided by the expectation of medication that will relieve their symptoms. The doctors, however, prefer clinical investigations to ascertain the disease condition. Thus, patient's expectations mostly remain unsatisfied. The pathological examinations, which are required from a biomedical point of view to diagnose arsenicosis, are often perceived as being unnecessary by the patients. On top of that, biomedical explanations of arsenicosis are based on physiological and clinical manifestations that make no sense to the lay people who handle the illness in everyday life.

A mismatch is clearly observed between the biomedical definition of arsenicosis and its social construction as *ghaa*. One immediate impact of such a mismatch is that patients tend to prefer alternative healing services over biomedical ones, and the reason they do so is quite obvious – popular understandings of *ghaa* match cultural knowledge and disease etiology of the alternative healers. Such shared cultural knowledge is one of the crucial motivating factors for burgeoning alternative healings in rural Bangladesh (Bhardwaj and Paul 1986; Feldman 1983; Green et al. 2006; Wilce 1995). In typical health-seeking encounters, patients and alternative healers share similar interpretations of the illness and its etiologies, which helps avoid any ambiguity or conflicting understanding of the problem between these two parties. One patient who was dissatisfied with biomedicine explained to me:

> When I go to the *kobiraj* or *hujur*, he clarifies everything that has happened to me. He tells me the causes of the disease – whether it is a result of weather, contaminated food or past bad deeds. But the doctors never clarify things. They just ask what happened and then write a prescription for medicine or ask for tests to be done. They never explain to us what has happened. So, how do we know about the problem?

Another patient said that he does not like allopathic doctors because they are not friendly but behave rudely (*khit-khite mejaj*). Thus, patients feel more comfortable in sharing their ailments with someone who has the same mindset and attitude to disease etiologies and therapeutic procedures. When patients visit the village *kobiraj*, homeopaths or religious healers, both actors are in a comfortable position to share their worries and concerns in a friendlier environment.

Yet, in a clinical encounter, patients' expectations are guided by the idea of getting medicine that could immediately and effectively alleviate the sufferings of *ghaa*. However, biomedicine is still constrained by limited therapeutic success in curing arsenicosis. Drinking arsenic-safe water is considered to be the only preventive measure against arsenicosis. Thus, biomedical doctors often advise patients to drink arsenic-safe water. Patients' expectation of getting medicine thus remains unfulfilled. Moreover, the biomedical construction of arsenicosis causation as a result of drinking arsenic-contaminated water does not make cultural sense on the ground. It is hard for people to believe that water, which saves and nurtures life, can be a killer. Likewise, not everyone is affected by *ghaa*, even though they drink water from the same sources. Such a mismatch in perceptions and expectations between the biomedical and popular domains creates tension between doctors and patients. Patients are skeptical about the doctors' advice on preventive measures such as drinking arsenic-safe water, as they are unsure whether the *ghaa* is really a result of drinking arsenic-contaminated water or whether their water sources are really contaminated by arsenic. They continue to drink contaminated water, despite clear biomedical disapproval of it.

There is also a predominant practice among the *ghaa* patients that they discontinue allopathic treatment midway. When asked why they do so, all of them said that they could not afford the expensive allopathic medications. As one patient said:

> How can I afford such expensive medicine? I thought I would get free medicine from the hospital, but the doctor asked me to buy it from outside. One tablet costs 20 taka, and I have to take it every day for seven days. How can I buy it? I managed to buy it for three days then gave up.

Another patient said, "I do not have that much money to buy expensive medicine. I may be able to afford it for a couple of days but not for a week." Another reason why patients do not go to the UHC is that allopathic medicine is available in the village market through the village doctor. As one patient explained to me that: "We get allopathic medicine from the bazaar, so why spend time and money to go to hospital? Medicine from the hospital and village pharmacy are the same."

Patients who visited the UHC were also dissatisfied with the long queues and waiting times. And then the doctor spends only a few minutes to consult with the patient. One patient told me that he had spent five hours waiting for just a five-minute consultation. Some other patients expressed their discontent with the fact that the doctor prescribed medication without listening properly to their complaints. One patient hilariously said: "The hospital doctors write prescriptions before listening to the problems properly." Such statements are not entirely implausible; it is part of the bigger picture of inadequate public health care services in Bangladesh (Andaleeb 2001, 2000; Zaman 2004).

Another significant characteristic of health-seeking behaviour of *ghaa* patients is the tendency to cross national borders in order to access health care services from neighbouring India. Two arsenicosis patients from the village went to Kolkata, India, to seek allopathic treatment. It was possible for them to cross the border not just because of the geographical proximity of the village to the Indian border, but also because of their cultural networks across the border. One *ghaa* patient who visited India told me how he had managed to go there:

> I contacted my cousin in Kolkata and told him that I want to give it a last try (*sesh chesta*) in Kolkata. I neither had a passport nor had been to Kolkata before. I heard that if I bribe the middleman (*dalal*), he could help me cross the

border. So I did that and went to see a skin specialist, who examined me and prescribed me some medicine. After taking the medicine, the *ghaa* became dry and the itching was also reduced. After a few days, when the medicine was finished, the *ghaa* reappeared.

It appears from the statement that distance and inaccessibility are not impeding factors if one is desperate to seek particular health care services. In fact, this patient is quite poor and belongs to quite a low economic class, so money is a major concern for him. However, financial constraints did not prevent him from searching for a specialist doctor abroad. Social networks, which Janzen (1978) calls a "therapy managing group", play a crucial role in determining how far a patient can go to seek health care services. However, Janzen's conceptualization of a therapy managing group appears to be limited when applied in a contemporary globalized context. In a global village today, a social network can be extended across national borders. Thus, the concepts of medical pluralism and the therapy managing group need to be re-conceptualized to incorporate the larger processes of the global medical marketplace that is available to any individual in these days. Obviously, the more extended social network one has, the higher the possibility of exploring these resources in the global marketplace. Therefore, health-seeking behaviour is no longer limited to an immediate geographical boundary of a village; rather, it has become part of a global medical marketplace, what Churchill (1989: 179) calls the medical supermarket, where varieties of remedies are bought and sold within everyone's reach.

Conclusion

This chapter has primarily demonstrated that arsenicosis patients predominantly use alternative healing services because of their understanding that *ghaa* is a result of snakebites, blood poisoning and fate, which can only be effectively managed by the *kobiraj* and religious *hujur*. Alternative healers are believed to have possessed the most appropriate modalities to remove poison from the body and abolish past transgressions. Biomedical explanations of arsenicosis, on the other hand, do not make much cultural sense on the ground. Water is culturally believed to be lifegiving, which can hardly contain poison to result into such deadly *ghaa*. Moreover, not all are afflicted by *ghaa* despite drinking water from the same contaminated water sources. Patients are, thus, doubtful about the biomedical explanations of arsenicosis. Biomedical professionals hold scientific and objective analyses of arsenicosis, whereas lay villagers are guided by their everyday knowledge and experiences of *ghaa*. One immediate implication of such differential understandings on health-seeking behaviour is that many patients prefer alternative healing services to biomedicine. My ethnographic evidence presented here suggests that *ghaa* patients mostly seek alternative healing services because of the fact that patients and alternative healers share similar cultural knowledge and approaches to disease etiologies. Both actors are able to comfortably share cultural knowledge about *ghaa* and discomforts, which facilitates an environment of trust and coziness between patients

Arsenicosis and health-seeking behaviour 93

and healers. Moreover, easy accessibility and inexpensiveness of alternative healing services make it popular in Bangladesh. The next chapter continues to demonstrate the implications of lay understandings of arsenicosis as *ghaa* on participation in mitigation strategies with particular reference to water supply projects that failed to ensure arsenic-safe water for the community people.

Notes

1 The local term *gasra oshud* refers to medicines that originate from plants. Different parts of the plant are locally used as *gasra oshud*, such as the leaves, skins, roots and so on.
2 Potash is the local term for potassium permanganate ($KMnO_4$) which patients use as a diluted form to paste on their *ghaa*. It is believed to have anti-inflammatory properties.
3 Taka is the Bangladeshi currency. One US dollar is equivalent to roughly 75 taka.
4 In the context of rural Bangladesh, a madrasah is a religious institution where the curriculum is generally based on courses that include Arabic, tafsir (interpretation of the Qur'an), shariah (Islamic law), hadith (the word of the Prophet Muhammad) and so on. Teachers in the madrasah are popularly known as *hujur*, as opposed to "sir" in general education.
5 The Libra astrological sign is locally referred to as *tula rashi*. It is believed that the people who belong to *tula rasi* have special divine power to perform many supernatural activities. Usually the shaman chants a mantra and blows on the body of a *tula rashi* person, who then loses sense and becomes possessed by a divine power to accomplish many things as directed by the shaman. After becoming possessed by a supernatural power, the *tula rashi* person drives a cup all over the body of the *ghaa* patient to expel poison from inside the body.
6 In the Bangladeshi Islamic religious context, *paper-fol* refers to the consequences of transgressions or a result of past bad deeds. It is popularly believed that bad deeds conducted in the past are abolished either through diseases or other forms of sufferings. Arsenicosis is thus justified as a *paper-fol* of past bad deeds.
7 Pesticides and poisons are locally called endrin. Committing suicide by ingesting endrin is quite frequent in rural Bangladesh. Since no other medicine is effective in curing *ghaa*, the village doctor jokingly suggests that she should drink endrin to get rid of this *ghaa*.
8 All of these drugs are generic versions of the penicillin, cephalosporin or fluroquinolones group of drugs, with anti-bacterial, anti-fungal or anti-histamine properties.
9 According to the leaflet attached to the bottle, Safi is a Unani herbal medicine that claims to purify and cleanse the body system. The medicine is further claimed to be effective in protecting various bodily organs, maintaining vital bodily functions, and preventing different diseases. It claims to purify blood and has anti-microbial, anti-allergic and anti-pyretic properties.

6 Arsenic mitigation strategies
Why do they fail?

Introduction

While I was conducting fieldwork in rural Bangladesh, one particular advertisement on local television became very popular. The advertisement was about electronic topping-up (e-top up) of prepaid mobile phones. Briefly, this advertisement shows a man requesting a mobile card seller to top-up his mobile phone with a certain amount of money. Since the subscriber has been spending much money on phone bills, the vendor jokingly comments, "How much you talk re?"[1] (*koto kotha bole re?*). Thus, the comment "*koto kotha bole re*" became very popular in common usage to refer to someone who is talkative. Having witnessed the failure of water supply development projects, which were implemented to provide arsenic-safe water in the village and the amount of money that had been wasted on this, one respondent, mimicking the advertisement, commented, "How much money do they waste re?" (*koto taka nosto kore re?*). Thus, from the local people's point of view, these water supply projects are just failures and simply a waste of money.

Drawing upon ethnographic data on two development projects that have been designed and implemented for providing arsenic-safe water but are rejected by the community, this chapter attempts to unpack the puzzle of why villagers who were suffering from deadly *ghaa* reject these options that could save their lives by providing arsenic-safe water. While exploring this issue, I critically examine the ways in which the local villagers, the state, NGOs and international development organizations understand and evaluate the problem and offer solutions. A critical reexamination of the issues of power, politics, ideologies and governance of these two development projects would answer the question of how most essential and lifesaving arsenic mitigation water supply projects turn into despair and failure.

This section further examines how social construction of arsenicosis as *ghaa* shapes villagers' participation in mitigation strategies offered by various development organizations. As has been demonstrated previously, official and popular understandings of arsenicosis are often in conflict with each other, resulting in very different sets of knowledge and outcomes. It is thus examined how differential perceptions about arsenicosis held by development planners and local villagers end up with unintended consequences and failure of development projects. It shows how a major health issue eventually becomes a matter of politics on the ground (Scheper-Huges 1990; Singer and Baer 1995; Singer 1985). This chapter thus concludes that culture and local knowledge are crucial in ensuring the success of development projects, which are often ignored and neglected by development planners, leading essential development projects into failure (Escobar 1991, 1995; Ferguson 1990; Friedman 2006; Hobart 1993).

Although NGO interventions in Bangladesh have generally been understood as remarkable and credited as the "agents of development par excellence" (White 1999), their involvement has increasingly come under critical scrutiny. Many development projects in Bangladesh have "failed" and brought unintended consequences to the intended beneficiaries (Adnan 2004; Karim 2008; Rahman 1999). NGOs have been charged as "political chameleons" that mobilize poor people for political intentions (Chowdhury 2001: 22). Although promoted as apolitical, it is suspected that NGOs have become influential enough to establish a parallel government or act as a "shadow state in Bangladesh" (Karim 2008: 7). It is further argued that NGOs have given up their benevolent ideologies and emerged as profit-generating, business-oriented and shadow capitalist organizations (Chowdhury 2001). After almost three decades of intervention, many rural Bangladeshis view NGOs as hybrids of the state or market, and a kind of "officer class", or simply a type of lucrative business (White 1999: 321).

My ethnographic analysis of the BAMWSP and GSK water supply projects corroborate the above findings and demonstrate that arsenic mitigation strategies do not bring any benefit to the villagers and thereby fail to achieve their goals and objectives. It is argued that the failure of these projects is an outcome of a combination of several factors, including but not limited to ignorance of local priorities and preferences and failure of the development planners to address many political, cultural and environmental considerations within which these projects were to be implemented. The following discussion analyzes these two projects with their aims, objectives and outcomes. The analysis is based on two sources: (1) the BAMWSP final project evaluation, "Implementation Completion and Results Report (ICR)", published by the World Bank, and (2) primary sources of information that I collected from the community during my fieldwork. My objective here is not just to (re)evaluate these two very essential, high-profile and lifesaving water supply projects, but to explore why they failed.

While examining their failures, I try to understand the disconnections between what the development planners and officials construct as arsenicosis and what the lay people understand as *ghaa* in their everyday life. It is hypothesized that the failure of these projects might be due to differential perceptions in understanding the problem and prioritizing solution for it. It is also important to explore why villagers who suffer from deadly *ghaa* reject options that might provide them with arsenic-safe water and save their lives. Focusing on particular cultural, political and technical faults that have been overlooked and ignored by the project planners, this study brings back the issue of "development as imposition", which fails to achieve desired outcomes. Based on ethnographic evidence, this study shows that arsenic mitigation water supply projects are not just a waste of money, which fail to achieve their goals and objectives, but also bring unintended consequences, such as conflict and distrust among different social actors on the ground.

BAMWSP: background, objectives and outcomes

In August 1997, a high-profile meeting was held between the WB and the SDC with the aim of reviewing the possibility of supporting the GoB in fighting against arsenic calamities. The meeting approved a plan for the US$44.4 million Bangladesh Arsenic Mitigation Water Supply Project. On August 28, 1998, the executive committee of the National Economic Council approved the proposal for the project. BAMWSP was then designed as one of the largest and longest development projects in Bangladesh, to be implemented in collaboration with the WB, SDC, GoB and the community. Of the US$44.4 million, the WB pledged $32.4M as credit, the SDC co-financed $3M and the rest of the cost was agreed to be shared by GoB ($4.9M) and the community ($4.1M). At the end of the project in 2007, however, the actual amount that had been spent stood at US$28.4 million and the rest of the money, US$16 million, remained unspent. The breakdown of the financing of the project is shown in Table 6.1.

Table 6.1 Financing BAMWSP

Sources of Funding	Appraisal Amount (USD million)	Actual Amount Spent (USD million)
GoB	4.90	3.66
Community	4.10	1.51
WB	32.40	23.16
SDC	3.00	0.207
Total funds	44.4	28.537

Source: World Bank 2007: 28

The World Bank rationalized the project as follows (World Bank 2007: 1):

> At that time, there was little scientific knowledge about how, why, or where arsenic occurred in drinking water sources. Doctors and health workers did not have much knowledge of the epidemiology, symptoms, or treatment methods, nor were there any records of the number of patients suffering from arsenic-related illnesses. This new development also risked rolling back the significant progress made over two decades in both the provision of safe drinking water under the shallow tubewell program and the complementary improved sanitation in the country, which had contributed to a reduction in mortality and morbidity, especially among children. Arsenic contamination of the main source of drinking water emerged as a national crisis, and action was urgently required. The Government of Bangladesh sought international assistance to address this emerging crisis. These conditions provided the rationale for the World Bank and other donors to assist Bangladesh in its efforts to tackle the arsenic problem in a coordinated manner.

Thus, the involvement of the WB in this project is justified on compassionate and ethical grounds that urgent "assistance" and "intervention" are required to save arsenic-affected people in Bangladesh. Bangladesh is thus constructed as an "object" that requires immediate intervention through development projects. A broad objective was set: "to reduce morbidity and mortality in both the rural and urban population caused by arsenic contamination of Bangladesh's groundwater within sustainable water supply, health, and water management strategies" (World Bank 2007: 1). The Bank adopted "learning-by-doing" and "flexible" approaches, as there were several uncertainties in the situation due to limited knowledge about arsenic and the lack of prior experience in implementing such a project by the WB (World Bank 2007: 5). Thus, Bangladesh was set as a "laboratory case" for intensive learning by the development organizations. Three components of the project were identified: (1) on-site mitigation, (2) an improved understanding of the arsenic problem and (3) strengthening the implementation capacity of the organizations involved. Under these three broad components, a number of specific targets were set:

- Screening tubewells to concretely establish the spatial extent of arsenic contamination, the level of arsenic concentration and labeling unsafe sources.
- Creating mass awareness about the effects of arsenic ingestion.
- Developing and providing affordable and appropriate mitigation options on a cost-sharing basis.
- Ensuring a decentralized and participatory implementation modality among the various stakeholders.
- Use of NGOs for mobilizing the community, forming community-based organizations and preparing community action plans.
- Setting up a comprehensive database under the National Arsenic Mitigation Information Centre (NAMIC) comprising information on the spatial distribution of arsenic contamination, the level of arsenic concentration, patient information, details of the mitigation options implemented, and hydrogeological data from groundwater investigations.

Although the project prioritized preventive strategies for arsenic poisoning, there was no provision of health care services for existing arsenicosis patients. It was argued that the provision of health care services is the responsibility of the Ministry of Health and Family Welfare through its existing health posts (World Bank 2007: 6). Initially, the project envisaged covering 4,000 villages; however, the plan was later revised for a manageable 1,800 villages.

Project structure and implementation process

Three levels of stakeholders were identified to implement the project activities. At the top, there were donor organizations and the state apparatus; the intermediary level was made up of the DPHE, local government authorities and NGOs; while at the micro level the communities would be involved to implement the project. Clearly defined responsibilities were drawn up for each of these stakeholders. The Project Management Unit (PMU) was responsible for the overall management of the project, while DPHE provided technical support. One local NGO was hired

98 *Arsenic mitigation strategies*

for each of the villages to provide support for awareness creation, community mobilization, screening tubewells, patient identification and the promotion of mitigation options. Although the project was supposed to be implemented through partnerships among these stakeholders, maintaining coordination among them appeared to be a major challenge, and the progress was extremely slow during the first two and a half years of operation. The donors blamed the government for its bureaucratic, slow processes and threatened to cancel funding or even completely withdraw from the project (World Bank 2007: 4). There was a clear contradiction between the DPHE and the PMU. The World Bank (2007: 8) reported:

> A number of directors did not share the project concept, were unable to break away from the working practices of the DPHE, or were not sufficiently motivated to move the project forward. Over a 2½-year period (December 1999 to December 2000; June 2002 to December 2003), the project was rated "unsatisfactory" for implementation.

As part of the objective to strengthen the local government bodies, the UP was fully incorporated into the project. The main responsibility of the UP was to implement project activities at the village level, particularly maintaining coordination between the appointed local NGO and the community. According to the project proposal, the community was considered to be the core implementer of the project activities and was expected to take part in a "fully participatory" manner. It was envisaged that the involvement of the community would ensure participatory decision making regarding the installation and maintenance of arsenic mitigation options. It was also expected that the community would be mobilized and empowered to form community-based organizations called WAMWUGs, which would be responsible for preparing and implementing a CAP as well as be responsible for maintaining these mitigation options after handover. Major responsibilities of the various stakeholders are shown in Figure 6.1.

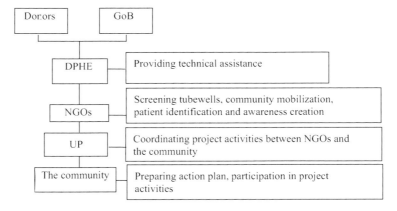

Figure 6.1 BAMWSP project structure, stakeholders and their responsibilities

Project outcomes

At the end of the project in 2007, the WB evaluated the overall activities of the project and rated it as "moderately satisfactory", although the rating was not clarified any further (World Bank 2007: 11). The WB also identified the project as a "complex project", as several different stakeholders were involved in the process. The donors were particularly dissatisfied with the bureaucratic and lengthy decision-making process of the government, which they believe impeded the overall project implementation process. Project activities moved really slowly in the first four years, and development experts began to consider BAMWSP as just one more failed project (World Bank 2007: 44). The WB, however, defended the project by stating that its performance improved rapidly after the project planning was restructured and a new project director was recruited, replacing the earlier one. The WB evaluated the project on three key activities: (1) on-site mitigation (2) an improved understanding of the arsenic problem, and (3) strengthening the implementation capacity of the government.

As part of the provision of on-site mitigation, a total of 9,272 deep tubewells, 300 rainwater harvesting systems, 393 dug-wells and 1 piped water supply system were installed in 1,800 villages. These were expected to provide arsenic-safe water to an estimated 2.5 million people of the rural population. All of these on-site mitigation options were claimed to have been implemented by the community in collaboration with the NGOs and UP in a fully participatory manner. The final project evaluation report claims that the installation of these arsenic mitigation options would significantly reduce arsenic ingestion by the population at risk. These mitigation options were claimed to be "sustainable" for the following reasons (World Bank 2007: 15):

> . . . use of a decentralized participatory approach with a key role for local government and communities that have planned, organized, and supervised construction; use of technologies that were not complex, were capable of construction by small contractors, and were easily maintained by community artisans; and community contribution of at least 10 percent of capital costs and assumption of responsibility for operation and maintenance.

Another outcome of this project was the training of health care professionals so that arsenicosis patients could be identified and effectively treated. By the end of the project, a total of 2,300 doctors had been trained to manage arsenicosis. It is claimed that the knowledge about the extent of arsenic contamination in Bangladesh and its medical management have been improved. The WB reported:

> There was little scientific knowledge about how, why, or where arsenic occurred in drinking water sources. Doctors and health workers did not have much knowledge of the epidemiology, symptoms, or treatment methods, nor were there any records of the number of patients suffering from arsenic-related illnesses.

100 Arsenic mitigation strategies

Thus, from the WB's point of view, Bangladesh was constructed as a place of "little scientific knowledge about arsenic", which invariably shapes the rationale for the country to be a suitable target for intervention. Such a constructed image then "shapes not only the formation of reports and documents, but the construction of organizations, institutions, and programs" (Ferguson 1990: 73). The final evaluation report declared that the project intervention gained significantly improved knowledge on the extent and origins of arsenic poisoning in Bangladesh. It was revealed that arsenic contamination was far worse than it was initially thought. Underground water sources of fifty-four districts, out of a total of sixty-four, had higher concentrations of arsenic toxicity than the permissible levels. While unsafe tubewells were painted as red, a sign of danger, safe sources were coloured green so that people became aware of the safe drinking water and refrained from drinking from arsenic-contaminated tubewells.

Based on the information collected from a nationwide survey, the publicly accessible NAMIC database was established. It was envisaged that this database would provide information on the spatial distribution of arsenic contamination, patient information, water quality test results, geohydrological information and technical reports, which would be accessible to all for further research (World Bank 2007: 16). Although the database became available during the lifetime of the project, it disappeared soon after the project ended.

The WB constructed Bangladesh as a "weak" state with "low capacity of the communities, local and central government in participatory planning and design and in [operation and management] of water supply systems" (World Bank 2007: v). Such an image creation of inefficient state apparatus was necessary for the WB to rationalize intervention as well as to justify the need for the state to be strengthened so that development activities could be efficiently promoted. The context is the same as Hobart rightly argues: "In order for them [people] to be able to progress, these peoples have first to be constituted as 'underdeveloped' and ignorant" (Hobart 1993: 2). Once the "object of intervention" was rationalized, the next step was to justify the project outcomes. The World Bank (2007: 16) reported that the project has significantly improved the capacities of the various stakeholders to implement development activities:

> A highly effective and successful model, trusted by communities, for delivery of safe water to a large number of villages, with explicit cost sharing criteria, has evolved. Union Parishads and communities have been empowered to plan and construct facilities for safe water through an approach that includes capital cost sharing and responsibility for operation and maintenance.

It is claimed that the community was empowered, since 4,331 CAPs had been prepared with a demand-driven and participatory approach. It further claims that the capacity of the local government body was strengthened and that it had become more responsive and accountable to the villagers. Table 6.2 illustrates the WB's final assessment of various components of the project.

Table 6.2 The World Bank's evaluation of the project

Indicators	Ratings of the Outcome
Relevance of objectives	Satisfactory
Relevance of design and implementation	Satisfactory
Achievement of project development objectives	Moderately satisfactory
Overall outcome rating	Moderately satisfactory
World Bank's performance	Satisfactory
Borrowers' performance	Moderately satisfactory
Implementing agencies or agencies' performance	Moderately satisfactory

Source: World Bank 2007: 12

Although the WB's final assessment report rated the project as "moderately satisfactory", my ethnographic findings reveal a total failure in achieving the goals and objectives of this project. Interestingly, the Bank's performance has been rated as satisfactory while the borrowers' and other stakeholders' performances are evaluated as moderately satisfactory.

Drawing upon ethnographic data, the following discussion illustrates how and why local villagers evaluate this project as a failure and a total waste of money. It is demonstrated how villagers express their discontent as their hard-earned money was being wasted in the name of cost-sharing and participation. As an unintended consequences of this project, it is shown how the relationships among villagers, local government institutions and NGOs have deteriorated as a result of this unsuccessful development project.

The reality behind the rhetoric: an ethnographic analysis of the project

Drawing upon primary ethnographic data, findings of this study reveal a completely different picture from what was claimed by the WB's final evaluation report. The village that was selected for this study is one of the highly arsenic-contaminated areas, with 97.88 percent of the tubewells tainted with arsenic toxicity. For this reason, BAMWSP paid special attention to this village (NAMIC 2006). As part of the on-site mitigation option of this project, one dug-well, one deep tubewell and two pond-sand filters (PSFs)[2] were installed in this village. During my fieldwork, however, I found all of these options abandoned by the villagers. A number of daily national newspapers reported that BAMWSP mitigation options implemented in other parts of the country were also rejected by the local users. For example, The daily *Prothom Alo* reported on August 12, 2008 that dug-wells and other options offered by BAMWSP had already been rejected in most parts of the country, resulting in millions of dollars of wastage. The same newspaper reported on April 6, 2008 that DPHE and UP officials at Dumki Upazilla of Patuakhali District in southern Bangladesh demanded bribes for providing arsenic mitigation options to the villagers.

While understanding the failure of this project, a number of problems were identified. One of the most remarkable mistakes was that the project planners quickly assumed that providing arsenic-safe water to the villagers could be the easy solution to the problem. They were wrong. They grossly failed to take into account how local people understand, explain and experience arsenic poisoning and its resultant health impacts. Actual expectations and priorities of the villagers were grossly ignored. This study has revealed that arsenicosis is culturally understood as *ghaa*, which is shaped by the particular sociocultural, religious and ecological constraints under which the local population live. Many villagers perceive *ghaa* as a result of blood poisoning from snakebites, which makes sense in a specific environmental context where snakebites are a frequent occurrence. Water is culturally understood as a lifegiver, and the villagers do not realize that *ghaa* could be a result of drinking contaminated water. Such understanding has been reinforced by the fact that many villagers drink water from the same water sources but not all of them are affected by *ghaa*. Thus, *ghaa* is predominantly perceived to be preordained and an examination from Allah because of an individual's past transgressions.

In contrast, BAMWSP officials presumed that arsenicosis is a waterborne disease and that the provision of arsenic-safe water is the only solution. They are perhaps right in their own way; however, they grossly failed to realize that villagers might have a different understanding of the problem. Clearly, the ways in which arsenicosis is perceived by development planners are in direct contrast to the lay understandings of this matter. BAMWSP officials offered solutions based on how they defined the problem without taking into consideration the local knowledge and cultural system that might impact on the outcomes. Thus, popular understandings of *ghaa* are not only ignored but also dismissed as the "word of the illiterate villagers", as one DPHE official mentions:

> They are the illiterate people. They do not know much about arsenic. How can they explain arsenicosis to you? They call it *ghaa* because it looks like that . . . but it is not *ghaa*. These are the words of the *illiterate villagers* (emphasis added). They do not know where it is coming from or the consequences of it.

This type of dismissal of local knowledge as superstitious raises a very fundamental question: if project planners fail to understand or ignore local priorities, expectations and understandings, how can they conceptualize an agenda that would create awareness and strategize a sustainable development program that would bring greater benefits to the community people? Why should villagers who have long been conveniently accessing water from the nearby tubewell move to dugwells or other water sources supplied by the project? My ethnographic findings suggest that the project failed to produce any such motivational force that could overwrite the popular understandings of arsenicosis as *ghaa* so that villagers are motivated to use arsenic-safe water sources. The motivational and awareness creation required to change behaviour are totally absent in this project. The local villagers simply become another "object" and passive recipients of the development project, as Hobart (1993: 5) rightly mentions:

> Local knowledges often constitute people as potential agents. For instance in healing, the patient is widely expected to participate actively in the diagnosis and cure. By contrast, scientific knowledge as observed in development practice generally represents the superior knowing expert as agent and the people being developed as ignorant passive recipients of objects of this knowledge.

My point here is that one of the main reasons these arsenic mitigation strategies fail is primarily because of ignoring local expectations and priorities. The ways in which development planners understand arsenicosis as a waterborne disease and a solution to this by providing arsenic-safe water do not make cultural sense on the ground. Local people did not respond to the call for changing their water consumption behaviour. Therefore, a high-profile water supply project ultimately failed. The village headmaster summarized the overall BAMWSP activity as follows:

> Villagers became really happy that there is some kind of solution at least. But the water that came out of the deep tubewells was reddish, salty and bad-smelling. They started to drink this water, since there was no other option. But how many days can they drink such water? They lost interest and nobody went there to collect water. The tubewells were also destroyed and none repaired it. That is the end of the deep tubewell. Public health officials again said that there is another project that would be very good and suitable. And we saw the arrival of the dug-well project. One dug-well was installed near the village market. People were happy but the problem started during summer when the well dried up. People became dissatisfied again. During the monsoon, spoilt water from outside entered into the well. People stopped drinking the water from there. The well is there but none goes there to collect water and the tubewell has been stolen.

A number of cultural and technical problems can be gleaned from the statement above. One of the first problems is the water quality of the wells provided by the project, which is salty, reddish, smelly and undrinkable. Project officials neither explained why the water quality was such nor took any action to fix it. Villagers asked for the deep tubewell to be reinstalled at a deeper layer, which might have better water quality, but the project personnel refused to do so because they did not have enough funds for this purpose. The project personnel stated that if any reinstallation is required, funds must be mobilized by the water users. Thus, a technically faulty mitigation option was imposed on the villagers. The same technically faulty dug-well was installed. The project personnel did not realize that water levels of this region sharply fall during summer. The shallow dug-wells that were provided failed to retain water during the summer when there is a high demand for drinking water. The villagers again asked the DPHE engineers to fix the problem, but they refused to do so. The dug-wells were also badly designed, as contaminated water from the outside entered into the well during the monsoon. In addition, the villagers found frogs and snakes in the water, which discouraged them from drinking from that well. Such badly designed and technically faulty water options dissatisfied the villagers and they refrained from using them, as one villager said:

> They [the project people] were all deceptive people (*fakibaaz*). They did not put enough ring-wells, and also did not cover up properly so that frogs and spoilt water from outside could not enter into the well. Will people drink water from there having seen this?

For quite a long time, villagers have had easy and convenient access to water from tubewells, which are just around the courtyard of every household. They have gotten used to it. Project officials and NGOs now advise the villagers to leave such convenient water sources and fetch water from dug-wells, which is considered age-old and traditional. The amount of motivation and effort required to change water consumption behaviour was glaringly inadequate in these projects. Although one NGO was appointed to mobilize the villagers, it spent only three months for this purpose, which was completely inadequate by any measure for creating awareness. The implication is obvious that the project failed to sufficiently mobilize villagers so that they changed their water consumption behaviour and were attracted to the project-provided arsenic-safe water. As one older villager hilariously put it: "I heard my forefathers used to drink water from dug-wells, now we are modern and we have tubewells. But these people are telling us to drink water from the dug-well. Are we becoming modern or going back?" (See Figure 6.2)

There were also some problems in making the project participatory. Although project officials wanted to implement the project through a process of participatory governance, in reality they misunderstood community participation as apolitical, fast and easy. They failed to realize that community mobilization and spontaneous participation can be a really slow, painful and lengthy process (Morgan 1993; Ugalde 1985; Zaidi 1999). They presumed that community participation could be easily achieved, as if villagers were ready, well-informed about arsenic and just waiting to be organized to get involved in the project. Although rhetorically the project envisioned that the community would make their own decisions, in reality the decisions were made by project officials, local elites and politically influential villagers. When asked if villagers were given the opportunity to participate in the decision-making process of installing dug-wells and deep tubewells, many villagers informed me that it was the influential members of the village and the officials of the UP who decided everything for them. The younger generations, who were

Arsenic mitigation strategies 105

Figure 6.2 Abandoned dug-well

more enthusiastic about getting involved in the project, were excluded. One college student said:

> If there is any committee, the headmaster and Khan Morol are always there. The headmaster is very busy in his school but he is always on the committee, as if no committee can be formed without him. We respect them as senior members of the village, but they should also take some younger people like us. We want to be involved in the project but they never think of us. Since they are senior members (*murubbi*), we cannot say anything in front of them.

Another villager also expressed his unhappiness thus:

> Whenever anyone comes to visit the village, he first looks for the headmaster or Khan Morol. They never come to talk with us. Are we not part of the village? Don't we live in this village? We may not be well educated like them, but we live in the village and we know many things about the village.

It is quite evident from the above statements that the committees formed to implement project activities were not representative, but dominated by the village elites. It can be said that there was no adequate representation from different age, sex and class groups of the village. The claim in the World Bank's final evaluation report that "the participatory process adopted under the implementation modality was highly satisfactory" (World Bank 2007: 7) appears to be illusory and rhetorical to the actual local villagers. Under the mask of "participatory process", a top-down and authoritative development project has been implemented where the village elites and politically influential UP officials played key roles in the name of "community representation". Far from being demand driven, the BAMWSP project has just appeared to be another example of a "supply-driven" project without adequate participation and ownership on the part of the villagers.

There are also some problems associated with the post-handover operation and maintenance of the water sources. Although the project facilitated the formation of WAMWUGs to take care of these resources, in reality no such group existed when I conducted fieldwork. When asked if there existed such a committee, many respondents either replied negatively or remained silent. One older person suggested that I ask the headmaster if he knew anything about this. The headmaster informed me that he had helped to form many committees on many occasions and could not remember exactly which committee I was referring to. He informed me that they formed committees as they were asked to do so. Clearly, these committees exist only in the development reports and not on the ground. Although the project rhetorically considered the local community as an active partner and owner of the development project, in reality a top-down development program has been implemented without adequate participation by the villagers. One college student thus said:

> They have money, so they will spend it anyway. They have to spend the money. They do not consider whether we want it or not. They will implement it anyway. How much money do they waste re!

Thus, the BAMWSP project is considered to be a waste of money. People did not have any ownership and control of the project. No serious attempts were made to mobilize people and facilitate them to form into a representative CBO that could take care of these resources. No training, orientation or guidelines have been provided for the post-handover operation and maintenance of resources, since it is simply assumed to be a responsibility of the villagers. The project is also gender biased. In rural Bangladesh, it is considered the responsibility of the women to fetch water; however, their representation and participation were neither ensured nor encouraged at any stage of the project implementation process. The project reinforced the existing patriarchal norms in the village by excluding women from the process.

The project of installing a PSF was another disappointment. Although people were initially enthusiastic about the PSF system, they soon lost interest in it due to technological problems. As one owner of a PSF system explained to me:

> The project people persuaded me to install a PSF. I shared 10 thousand taka and they contributed the rest. The system initially functioned well. Women used to fetch water in the morning and afternoon. The water quality was also

good. But the problem started when there was no water in the pond during summer. The DPHE engineer suggested to re-excavate the pond at a deeper layer. I asked if it was the responsibility of the DPHE to re-excavate the pond. They said that the policy had been changed and it was the responsibility of the owner. I could not afford to re-excavate the pond and the system was abandoned. Had I been informed earlier that they would not re-excavate the pond later on, I would not have taken it. I wasted the money I shared . . . a lot of money. I could have used that money to reconstruct my house, which was badly needed as the monsoon was setting in. They [DPHE] just cheated me.

Clearly, the owner of the PSF was quite unhappy after installing the system. He considers it as a form of cheating that the DPHE refused to re-excavate the pond, which it had promised earlier. There is clearly a tension between the two parties. DPHE did not properly inform the receiver about the PSF proposal, terms and conditions, particularly its post-construction operation and maintenance. The project officials wrongly assumed that the villagers would be able to operate and maintain the system, which did not happen and the system became non-functional due to a lack of re-excavation. The amount of money that was cost-shared by the owner was just wasted (Figure 6.3). Thus, the PSF owner is highly dissatisfied with this and engaged in a direct confrontation with the DPHE authority. Villagers also accused the UP officials and NGOs that promoted deep tubewells and dug-wells which ended up in failure to provide safe drinking water. Thus, an environment of distrust and hostility has been created among the stakeholders, which was completely unimagined during planning of the project. Rather than providing arsenic-safe water and promoting the health and well-being of the community, the project ended up in creating hostility among the community people, local government and NGOs. One villager thus explained the situation:

> They [NGO and UP] are very clever. They come to the village and speak convincingly to persuade us to do what they want. They provide these arsenic mitigation options. But look at these dug-wells, deep tubewells and PSF which are non-functional, but no one comes to fix them. They just install them and that's all. Why don't they come to see this problem now? They are all like this. They are all deceptive people. So, it is better to stay away from them.

In another interview, a PSF owner said:

> They [DPHE] persuaded me to go for this PSF by saying that it is good and the water is arsenic safe. They said that they would share the cost and I have to give only a small amount. I was convinced to install a PSF and now this is non-functional and has become a burden for me. Will they return my money? The money is lost and we also don't have water.

Thus, villagers were clearly disappointed and had lost faith and trust in the NGOs and local government bodies. The people considered them fraudulent and

Figure 6.3 Unused pond-sand filter

deceptive. Rather than strengthening the relationship among different stakeholders, the project further weakened it by provoking confrontational and hostile relations. These unintended consequences of the failed development project were unimagined by the planners. Findings of this study thus corroborate the post-structuralist critique of development that these water supply projects do not just fail in providing arsenic-safe water, but also bring unfortunate miseries to the villagers, whose hard-earned money has been wasted in the name of cost-sharing. The people on the ground deeply regret that these monies were used to such futility. Thus, these villagers have not only become the target of development projects but have also become the victims of development disasters.

The GSK water treatment plants

It was in 2003 when the first *ghaa* patient died in the village, an occurrence which was widely published in the daily national newspapers. This news drew instant attention to many national and international organizations working in Bangladesh. GSK, a multinational pharmaceutical company, also came to know about the sad news and the acute problem of arsenic contamination in the village. The communications manager of GSK-Bangladesh visited the village in 2004 and met with the local high school headmaster and other members of the community. As part of GSK's non-profit community involvement project, he expressed his interest to install water treatment plants in the village. Villagers enthusiastically committed all sorts of support. GSK then pledged to install two community-based water treatment plants in the village.

Formation of the AAM

A series of meetings were held during the first quarter of 2004 between the villagers and the GSK representative on how to implement the overall project activities. GSK suggested that an association be formed by the community members to supervise the implementation of project-related activities. On July 14, 2004, a meeting was held at the local high school where representatives of the community agreed to establish the Association for Arsenic Mitigation. A seven-member executive committee was formed, with the local high school headmaster as the president. Other members were selected from the village, including one male and one female UP member, three senior members of the community and one representative from GSK. The committee then wrote a letter to the GSK-Dhaka office informing it about the formation of this association. In a reply to that letter on July 18, 2004, GSK appreciated this initiative and wrote:

> This is the beginning of a great journey to rescue villagers from the arsenic contamination in their drinking water. We are happy to find you out as our partner. We believe with your dynamic leadership, the committee would be able to implement the project.

Following the formation of AAM, several meetings were organized to confirm the constitution, aims and objectives of this association. Since the association did not have any formal office, the high school classrooms were used as meeting venues. Most of the committee members of the AAM were previously members of the BAMWSP project and were therefore aware of the challenges the project faced. The committee identified that lack of sufficient knowledge about arsenic contamination is one of the main constraints of implementing the project. It then prioritized awareness creation among the villagers as its top agenda. The committee also realized that awareness creation would not be successful unless alternative safe options of drinking water were ensured. Thus, besides awareness creation, the AAM also prioritized the provision of arsenic-safe water as its agenda.

In August 2004, a team from GSK visited the village to examine the feasibility of installing an arsenic treatment plant. The first dilemma was to select a strategic site on which to install the system that would be easily accessible to most of the villagers. The headmaster proposed that the plant be installed at the high school playground so that students would get priority in accessing the arsenic-safe water. The geographical location of the high school was such that women from the other part of the village would have to travel a long distance to collect water. Considering this case and the large population of the village, GSK promised to install two systems so that all villagers could have access to safe water within a minimum walking distance.

An MOU was signed between the two parties, where AAM was given the full authority and responsibility to implement the overall project-related activities. With full financial assistance from GSK, two systems were installed under the direct supervision of the AAM. The systems were technically sophisticated. Using an electric motor, the groundwater was pumped into an overhead tank and then flowed down through an iron removal filter to remove iron and an arsenic removal filter to remove arsenic from the water before accumulating it in a lower storage tank. A number of taps were attached to the lower storage tank so that treated water could be collected. One arsenic removal filter could treat about one million liters of water or last about two years. After this, the filter needs to be replaced, which costs about US$300. The iron removal filter also needs to be changed whenever necessary.

On August 17, 2004, two water treatment plants were officially inaugurated and handed over to the AAM. Since the systems were technologically sophisticated and required expert maintenance, the association decided to recruit one caretaker to look after the system. A couple of young people from the village expressed their interest in being caretakers of the plant. Following an interview, the committee selected two caretakers for the plants and decided to pay them 1,500 taka (US$20) each as a monthly allowance. The caretakers were appointed for the overall management of the system, including pumping water twice daily into the overhead tank, distributing water twice a day, cleaning the iron and arsenic removal filters and collecting monthly payments from subscribers. The caretakers were provided with basic training on how to operate the system.

Once the system had been installed and the two caretakers were recruited, the next step was to decide how to distribute the water. There were initial disagreements between the UP officials and the AAM. The UP chairman insisted that the water should be distributed freely. The committee disagreed and argued that the system would not be financially sustainable and ownership could not be developed if water were provided free. The UP chairman counter-argued that the UP would bear the costs of maintaining the system. The committee then realized that the chairman was politically motivated and intended to provide free water in order to accumulate votes in the next election. A special meeting was called to resolve the matter, where it was decided that 10 taka (US$0.15) would be levied as a monthly water bill per household. The caretaker was given the responsibility of maintaining a ledger book with all the relevant details of the subscribers.

It was estimated that if an average of 500 households paid 10 taka per month, a total of 5,000 taka would be accumulated monthly, which would be enough to pay the electricity bill and salary of the caretakers. However, this calculation soon led to disappointment, as the number of water users fell below 100 households. The amount of money generated from the water bill was not enough to pay the electricity bill, let alone pay the salary of the caretakers and other maintenance costs. The caretakers then began to serve on a voluntary basis without any salary. GSK suggested that the mobilization needed to be enhanced so that villagers would be motivated to subscribe to arsenic-safe water from the treatment plant. The AAM failed to do so, since it did not have enough manpower, and the unpaid caretakers were not motivated enough to engage in such extensive community mobilization.

The emergence of Unnoyon and conflict with the AAM

GSK was unhappy with the failure of the AAM to increase the number of subscribers to arsenic-safe water. In several meetings with the AAM, GSK repeatedly raised its concern regarding the low participation of villagers in the water supply systems. As the AAM failed to take any quick initiatives to mobilize villagers to use water from the plant, GSK decided to hire a third party to provide assistance in creating awareness among the villagers. GSK contracted Unnoyon, a local NGO, to look after the plants and mobilize villagers. On March 25, 2006, an MOU was signed between GSK and Unnoyon whereby the latter was given the responsibility of the overall management of the two water treatment plants. After nearly two years of operation by the AAM, the plants were handed over to Unnoyon. GSK envisaged that Unnoyon and AAM would work together to make the water supply system successful.

Such a change in handover had a number of implications. AAM became inactive and thought that it was the responsibility of Unnoyon to look after the plants. The earlier close collaboration between GSK and AAM became weaker as GSK began to rely more on Unnoyon to operate the plants. Unnoyon appointed one female worker for this village with responsibilities such as creating awareness among villagers about arsenic, taking care of the water treatment plants and organizing monthly meetings with the AAM so that close cooperation between Unnoyon and AAM could be maintained. During my fieldwork, however, I found that neither the number of water users increased nor was the treatment plants properly maintained. No meetings were held between Unnoyon and AAM, and the female staffer of Unnoyon infrequently visited the village. Since the plants were not properly maintained, an examination of the water quality revealed high concentrations of arsenic and iron. There were no significant differences in water quality between the contaminated tubewells and the water treatment plants. The plants were sitting idly without maintenance and operation, reflecting failure of another water supply project. The villagers were again dissatisfied and frustrated as their long desire to have arsenic-safe water remained unfulfilled (see Figure 6.4).

Explaining the failure of the GSK water treatment plants

At this point it is worth exploring why such a well-intentioned and well-planned development project failed. Why did only 20 percent of households subscribe to arsenic-safe water from the treatment plants? Why did patients who suffered from deadly *ghaa* continue to reject safe water sources? My ethnographic findings reveal a number of cultural, political and technological issues that were neither fully understood nor adequately addressed by GSK, AAM and Unnoyon.

112 *Arsenic mitigation strategies*

Figure 6.4 Rejected water treatment plant

The following discussion highlights why such an important water supply program failed on the ground.

Differential perceptions and "the growth of ignorance"

In his edited volume *An Anthropological Critique of Development: The Growth of Ignorance*, Mark Hobart argues that development planners not only ignore local knowledge but also consider it as an obstacle to rational progress and development (Hobart 1993: 2). In order for development projects to be successful, "scientific" knowledge of the "experts" must be implanted, ousting local traditional knowledge. Such evidence is clearly present in the cases described above, where GSK officials ethnocentrically assumed that villagers were ready to receive arsenic-safe water without taking into consideration whether villagers really valued arsenic-safe water as their priority. GSK authorities expected that the water supply project would be successful, as if the villagers were already fully aware of the risks associated with drinking arsenic-contaminated water. The project officials neither understood the ways in which villagers perceived *ghaa* nor prioritized any extensive community mobilization programs before implanting sophisticated technology so that people were made aware of the consequences of drinking arsenic-contaminated water. Before installing a sophisticated water treatment plant, no significant effort was made to understand the actual expectations and priorities of the villagers. Sufficient attention was not paid to understand whether villagers really valued arsenic-safe water or if they even wanted these mitigation technologies. No doubt that GSK had good intentions to serve the community; however, it wrongly presumed that the community would readily accept any program that provided them with arsenic-safe water.

The ways in which GSK understood arsenicosis, its detrimental health effects and preventive measures did not make cultural sense on the ground. As discussed previously, the biomedical construction of arsenicosis, which approaches it as a disease that occurs because of drinking arsenic-contaminated water, is in direct contrast with the popular understandings of arsenicosis as *ghaa*. There is clearly a disconnection between what GSK understands as arsenicosis and what the villagers perceive as *ghaa*. GSK endorses the value of biomedical knowledge by ignoring the local notions of *ghaa* as an illness which is predominantly believed to be caused by ill fate or snakebites. GSK did not really make any significant effort to understand how the problem was locally perceived and dealt with in practice. Following Hobart (1993) and Nichter (2008), I argue that cultural perceptions and local knowledge significantly matter if health development interventions are to be successful. In my studied village, local knowledge of *ghaa* was not only ignored by the development planners but also perceived to be the "word of illiterate villagers". My findings corroborate a study by Ahmad, Goldar and Misra, who demonstrate that a strong correlation exists between people's perception of risk and the promotion of mitigation technologies. As they rightly point out:

> The value of arsenic-free drinking water to rural people is influenced by their risk perceptions, and has important implications for social acceptability of arsenic mitigation technologies being promoted. Evidently, if rural people do not have much concern for arsenic contamination despite its known dangers, and place a low value on arsenic-free drinking water, then the cost of mitigation technologies may turn out to be a major hindrance to their promotion among the rural households.
>
> (Ahmad, Goldar, and Misra 2005: 174)

This discussion thus links to an earlier chapter where I demonstrate how popular perceptions of arsenicosis as *ghaa* are shaped by specific cultural, religious and environmental contexts under which local people live. Many villagers believe that *ghaa* is not caused by contaminated water, since many of them drink water from the same contaminated tubewells but are unaffected by *ghaa*. Villagers thus place a very low value on arsenic-safe water. Development planners, on the other hand, are guided by the biomedical and scientific assumptions which disprove any cultural knowledge of *ghaa* and place a high value on providing arsenic-safe water as the solution to this problem. This study thus firmly exemplifies how differential perceptions between development planners and the intended beneficiaries in assessing the risk and strategizing solutions might turn a well-intentioned and well-planned project into a failure.

There are also some other cultural misunderstandings on the ground regarding subscription for water. Villagers did not welcome the idea of subscription, as it goes against the cultural norm that everyone has the right to obtain water free of charge. Culturally, water is believed to be synonymous with life itself, to be provided free, unlike other commodities that are bought and sold in the market. Many villagers perceived subscription as a way of selling water and as a type of business that offended them. As one older villager stated: "My fourteen generations never bought water and now we have to pay for the water. We have to buy water to drink. Who will buy water from them?" Another villager said: "Water is free everywhere. We never buy water. They have set up a machine and are charging money to buy water. I better use tubewell water." The committee was aware of this issue and informed GSK about the concern. In reply, GSK wrote:

> Apparently it may seem that we are selling water. This is not true, however. We want to come out of such misconception. We want villagers, irrespective of rich and poor, to get the benefit of arsenic-free water. Everyone should drink arsenic-free water. If everyone gets involved, the amount of subscription would also be nominal.

GSK realizes that some amount of financial contribution by the users would create ownership of the project and make it sustainable. However, in reality, villagers did not accept the idea of subscription. From the part of GSK, no assessment was done during the project planning phase to evaluate whether villagers would be willing to pay for water. Surprisingly, the level of community mobilization and awareness creation required to minimize this gap was virtually absent in this project. Neither GSK nor Unnoyon took any initiative that could accommodate different knowledge systems, create awareness and achieve a broader understanding of arsenicosis which might foster possibilities for greater success and the sustainability of the project.

The politics of participation

There were also some problems in making the project participatory. Although GSK envisioned that the formation of the AAM would ensure community participation, it failed to take into consideration the internal politics and class hierarchies within the community. The committee that was formed can in no way be said to be representative of the different age, sex and class groups in the village. Those who were on the executive committee of the AAM were mainly the village elites and politically influential UP officials. There was virtually no representation of lay villagers, young people and women on the committee. When asked if they were involved in any capacity on the committee, many villagers replied negatively, stating instead that it was the headmaster, Khan Morol and the UP chairman who knew everything about the project. One villager thus commented:

> Many times we see them meeting in the school. We do not know what they do inside. We cannot go in to see what they are doing. They make all

decisions. They tell us about the plant and ask us to get water from there. That's all.

When asked how representative the committee was, the headmaster defended it thus:

> It is not possible to take everyone onto the committee. It is always good to keep the committee small. Sometimes (the villagers) do not understand many technical things. If someone is taken onto the committee, others would be unhappy because they are not selected. There are many politics in the village. So, it is better to make a small committee. We make decisions but share with the villagers later on.

Although it was claimed that all members of the community would be involved in this project, in reality only a few politically influential village elites formed the committee and decided where the plants were to be installed, how much to charge for the water and who would take care of the systems. Lay villagers did not have any say in the decision-making process. Even within the committee, the decision-making process was not as participatory as expected by GSK. Some members were politically more powerful and were able to influence the decisions. One example of such a conflict was over the question of how to distribute water. Although the committee proposed a 10-taka subscription for the water, the UP official insisted that water should be provided free of charge. The caretaker of the plant explained to me thus:

> He (the member of the UP) does not understand the situation. He wanted the plant to be under Union Parishad. That means, he will be in power and have control over the plant. They are the nonsense people. They do not understand the reality. He thought that if water were given free, people would vote for him in the coming election. Because of his influence, water was given for free for the first two weeks. GSK was unhappy with this decision and the committee also protested against it.

Thus, politically influential UP officials wanted the water to be distributed free in order to win the upcoming election. He wanted to use the water treatment plant as a political platform to get votes. This decision was highly opposed by other committee members and created tension among them. Besides such political disagreements, disputes emerged over monetary matters that were generated through subscriptions. Many villagers informed me that the revenue generated from water subscriptions had either been misappropriated or misused in a non-transparent manner, since the committee did not disclose any of its financial matters to villagers. Thus, an environment of distrust emerged between the villagers and committee members. GSK failed to realize these internal politics and considered participation as an apolitical and voluntary matter. They wrongly presumed that any initiative of providing arsenic-safe water would be applauded by the community. In reality, however, the project ended up with unintended consequences, such as the emergence of political conflict and distrust among different stakeholders.

Conflict between AAM and Unnoyon

Another reason the project failed was because of a persistent conflict between Unnoyon and AAM. Although GSK expected that a close collaboration between Unnoyon and AAM would strengthen the smooth operation and maintenance of the water treatment plants, this did not happen on the ground. AAM was unhappy that the treatment plants were handed over to Unnoyon. This handover offended the AAM authority, which considered it as a way of discrediting them. One member of the committee thus said: "Our association installed the plants. We have been operating them for two years. Now the ownership has been transferred to Unnoyon. In a way, the plants have been taken away from us. This is a discredit to us." The local committee thus became unmotivated and disinterested in running the plants and cooperating with Unnoyon.

No precise guidelines were provided on how to maintain collaboration between AAM and Unnoyon. Instead, there was confusion about the roles that these two different stakeholders were to play in this project. As a result of this ambiguity, conflict between the staff members of Unnoyon and AAM became inevitable. The Unnoyon staff considered themselves accountable to the Unnoyon authority, whereas the AAM caretaker considered himself accountable to the local management committee. The sole Unnoyon staffer expected the AAM caretaker to follow her orders but the latter did not consider this to be the case. Rather than cooperating with each other, they became involved in antagonisms, which made the caretaker unhappy. He attempted to quit his position, as he explained to me:

> Since the beginning I have been in conflict with the Unnoyon staffer. She orders me to do this or do that. I do not do her job, why should I follow her orders? One day she threatened me that if I have to continue this job, I have to follow her orders. Do I work under her? I work for the villagers, not under her. Who is she to order me around? Several times I wanted to quit this job. But the headmaster always asked me to remain patient and continue.

The local caretaker was clearly frustrated and felt that he was not being paid enough for the work he did. The ambiguity of responsibilities and unclear chain of command created tensions among staff members of both organizations. The Unnoyon staffer blamed the local caretaker for not cooperating with her, whereas the caretaker questioned her authority. Hostilities between them created an apathetic work environment. Attempts at creating awareness among the villagers were heavily affected by this deteriorated relationship. The Unnoyon staffer became irregular in paying door-to-door visits in order to organize monthly meetings and create awareness. While I was conducting fieldwork, programs for awareness creation among the villagers were almost non-existent. Staff members of both AAM

Arsenic mitigation strategies 117

and Unnoyon appeared to be frustrated, as none of them had any idea how to improve the situation. As the headmaster said:

> We obviously want the treatment plant to continue, because we need arsenic-safe water. But I do not know how to continue it. The plant is not working properly and there are many problems. Unnoyon has already informed us that they are no longer interested in this plant. I do not know what is going on here and who is going to take responsibility for the plant.

Villagers were aware of such hostile relationships. On many occasions, villagers expressed their discontent with the water treatment plants. As one villager commented, "They are more busy fighting with each other than running the plants to provide arsenic-safe water". Another villager was agitated about this and stated:

> Previously there was a problem between the UP chairman and the committee. That problem was somehow managed. But now there is another problem between the staff of Unnoyon and the village caretaker. The problems started from the beginning. How are they going to solve the problem? Will they solve the problem or run the plants for cleaning water?

Having seen such hostilities, villagers totally lost their interest in these plants. One villager hilariously mentioned: "They [GSK] came to provide arsenic-safe water but created problems. Rather than providing water, they are now quarrelling with each other. We do not need water but stop the hostility please." Clearly, antagonistic and hostile relationships among the stakeholders jeopardized the overall project activities. Villagers were also dissatisfied with the deteriorated relationships, which adversely affected the smooth operation of the plants. Thus, a well-intentioned project which was supposed to ensure arsenic-safe water ended up in frustration, disappointment and failure.

The technological burden

Besides these cultural and political drawbacks, there were some technical burdens of the GSK project that ultimately contributed to the non-functioning of the plants. One major constraint was the meagre supply of electricity in the village, especially during the summer months, when it remained turned off most of the time. The water treatment plant was operated by electricity and the scarcity of electricity severely hampered the operation of the machines. Most of the time the overhead tanks remained unfilled, as the pump could not be operated. As a result of inadequate water supply in the overhead tanks, the plants failed to produce enough treated water to meet the demands of the users. Those who subscribed to the plant water were unhappy and could no longer justify why they subscribed to arsenic-safe water. One subscriber thus said:

> During summer months when the demand for water is very high, the plant cannot provide enough water. The caretaker always says that there is no electricity

to run the machine. We are then bound to drink water from the contaminated tubewells. If we have to drink arsenic-contaminated water from the tubewells, what is the point of subscribing to the plant water? We do not get water but at the end of the month we have to pay the bill.

Thus, the failure of the plants to produce enough arsenic-safe water obligated subscribers to drink contaminated tubewell water. One villager angrily suggested that the plants should cease operations permanently, since they could not produce enough water to meet the demand. He said: "We do not just want to see these machines, we want water. If these machines do not work, if we do not get water from there, what is the value of this machine?" Sometimes subscribers quarreled with the caretaker if they did not get water from the plant. The caretaker seemed to be helpless and frustrated. He explained to me that:

> I do not know in what inauspicious moment I took this responsibility. Villagers comment badly. How can I give them water if there is no supply? Is this in my hands? If I cannot run the pump machine, how can water be supplied? The villagers do not understand this. They just want water.

Besides irregular supply of electricity, the situation was further exacerbated by the falling water levels during summer months when the shallow tubewell attached to the pump machine could not reach the water level. While the machine was being installed, some villagers did inform the technician that the water levels fell sharply during the summer months and requested a deep tubewell. The plant technician, however, did not realize the local geological formation and thought that a shallow tubewell would be sufficient to reach water levels all the year round. This did not happen, and it became very difficult to obtain water during summer months. The technician was called in to fix the problem but he failed to do so. Thus, ignoring the villagers' request, the technician installed a shallow tubewell that failed to access water levels during the summer months. In addition to that, a technically sophisticated water treatment plant was installed which was to be operated by electricity. It was completely beyond the realization of the implementers that scanty electricity supply might affect the operation of this plant. This consequently led to the non-functioning of the system. Thus, in the name of providing arsenic-safe water, a badly designed and technically faulty system had been implanted which the community people did not like.

Water quality: fear, suspicion and taste

In a letter dated August 24, 2004, the AAM expressed its concerns to GSK about the water quality of the two treatment plants. The AAM informed GSK that the water appeared to be reddish, and a layer of sediment was observed in the water. Many subscribers suspected that the system was not functioning well enough to effectively remove arsenic from the water. They also noticed that the taste of the plant water had changed and feared that the plants had failed to remove iron from the water. As a result of these suspicions and the degraded water quality, many villagers withdrew from the water subscription. The headmaster explained to me why the number of subscribers had declined suddenly:

> It is mostly because of the water quality. Previously the water was light and clean but now has become reddish and dirty. People think that there may be arsenic in the water. We sent the water to the laboratory, and high concentrations of arsenic were found. In fact, there is no difference between the water from the tubewell and the water from the plant. When people came to know about this, they stopped collecting water from the plant.

One reason the plants failed to produce clean water was because of their poor maintenance. The arsenic and iron removal filters of the plants needed to be changed after a certain period of use. Because of financial constraints, however, these filters could not be purchased and replaced as required, which resulted in poor-quality water being dispensed from the plants. During my fieldwork, I found the water treatment plant sitting idly on the school grounds, waiting to be repaired by someone. The AAM committee members were bewildered and did not know anything about when the plant was to be fixed. The Unnoyon staff had stopped visiting the village and taking care of the plant. No one took the responsibility to repair the plant, which was left unsupervised and stood idly. The community was frustrated and sometimes annoyed to have witnessed such a waste of money. I found that villagers continue to drink water from the highly contaminated tubewells, as they did before the arrival of these projects. The goals and objectives of BAMWSP and GSK to provide arsenic-safe water to the villagers remained completely unfulfilled.

Conclusion

I began this chapter by referring to a local TV commercial that is relevant to development projects implemented in this village. Villagers, upon witnessing these failed development projects, began to mimic the advertisement and say: "how much money do they waste re?" (*koto taka nosto kore re?*) to refer to the ways in which money had been wasted in the name of these arsenic mitigation water supply projects. This chapter has demonstrated that their failures were primarily due to a mismatch in understandings of arsenicosis by the local villagers and the development experts. Development planners, being guided by the biomedical assumptions, realized that the solution to the problem was to ensure delivery of arsenic-safe water to the villagers and thought that any such water supply project would be welcomed by the villagers. However, they grossly failed to understand how villagers make sense of arsenicosis and whether they really prioritize or value arsenic-safe water as the solution to the problem. No attempt was made to understand whether villagers were really aware of the detrimental health impacts of drinking arsenic-contaminated water. The amount of mobilization and awareness creation required to motivate villagers to change their water-consumption behaviour from tubewells to newly installed systems was grossly inadequate. The mitigation strategies implanted, such as dug-wells, PSFs and water treatment plants, had a number of malfunctions that the villagers did not like. Far from being able to ensure clean water, these projects resulted in weakening relationships among the different stakeholders. The villagers were highly discontented that their hard-earned money had been wasted in the name of cost-sharing. My ethnographic evidence therefore led me to conclude that the ways in which development experts perceive arsenicosis and prioritize solutions to this problem do not match local perceptions, expectations and prioritizations, leading highly desirable and well-planned water supply projects into failure.

Notes

1 The Bengali word "re" is a suffix that is casually used in informal and friendly conversations.
2 A pond-sand filter is a technical system that purifies surface water, usually from a pond, using sand, brick-rocks and other indigenous elements. The system is usually installed at the bank of a pond. The water is usually collected from the pond to be accumulated in the system to be purified for consumption.

7 Conclusion
The primacy of culture in health and development

I went to southwestern Bangladesh to explore two specific aspects of arsenic poisoning: firstly, why do arsenicosis patients, despite having fairly easy access to biomedicine, predominantly utilize alternative healing services? and secondly, why do individuals who are suffering from deadly arsenicosis reject options of arsenic-safe water that could save them from this disease? To answer these questions, I find it crucial to examine how arsenicosis is understood, experienced and responded to by different social actors. It is important to see how arsenicosis is medically and officially constructed and the ways in which such constructions depart from the lay understandings of arsenicosis as *ghaa*. It then enables me to explain the implications of such disjuncture in terms of health-seeking behaviour of subjects and their participation in mitigation strategies. This study is thus an ethnographic analysis of a particular disease, which is medically labeled as arsenicosis but understood and experienced by lay villagers using a very different cultural logic and worldview. It shows how arsenicosis has been vernacularized as *ghaa* in everyday life. The discussion that follows briefly summarizes some of the main points of my enquiries with particular reference to their theoretical and practical implications.

One key objective of this study is to examine how arsenicosis is variously understood and explained by different social actors, such as medical doctors, development planners and lay villagers. From a biomedical point of view, arsenicosis is approached through particular pathophysiological and clinical manifestations, such as melanosis, keratosis, hyperkeratosis, gangrene and carcinogenic consequences. Arsenicosis is medically defined as a disease that affects biological functioning of almost all internal organs of the affected individuals. Drinking arsenic-contaminated water is believed to be the primary cause of this disease so defined. There is no cure for arsenicosis at this moment, and treatment is limited to mostly preventive measures, such as refraining from drinking arsenic-contaminated water and management of physical symptoms. This is a dominant mode of understanding the disease and one that is accepted by many other development and official agencies in Bangladesh.

Beyond such biomedical and scientific explanations of arsenicosis, ethnographic data suggest that local villagers have a very different set of explanations of this disease. Throughout the fieldwork process, one most important guiding question was to examine whether lay villagers understood about arsenicosis or the English word arsenicosis and it scientific explanations made any sense to a predominantly Bengali-speaking rural community. My ethnographic evidence suggests that local villagers possess a different set of knowledge and use different language when they talk about what biomedicine labels as arsenicosis. In their everyday language, arsenicosis is culturally understood, explained and experienced as *ghaa*. As has been discussed in Chapter 4, perceptions of health and illness in general and *ghaa* in particular are shaped by specific sociocultural, religious and environmental contexts under which the rural Bangladeshis live. Thus, although I went to study arsenicosis, I found the description of *ghaa* in practice. Given that *ghaa* is a kind of general skin disease in rural Bangladesh, the question remains how arsenicosis *ghaa* is different from other skin lesions. This study found a well-developed ethno-taxonomy that villagers use to categorize and explain *ghaa*. It is a predominant belief among the villagers that *ghaa* is a result of blood poisoning due to snakebites, which makes sense in an ecological context where snakebites are frequent occurrences. Villagers also categorize poison based on its potency and severity. The poison that causes *ghaa* is believed to be a strong poison (*kothin bish*), which cannot be cured even with biomedical treatment. Unlike other skin ailments, *ghaa* is understood to be chronic and persistent, flaring up (*bare*) sometimes and diminishing (*kome*) at others but never going away permanently. Such a recurrent characteristic is considered to be a major point of departure between arsenicosis *ghaa* and other skin ailments.

Yet, many others strongly believe that fate (*kopal*) is an indispensable factor in determining who will be affected by *ghaa*. Such a belief is strongly grounded in fatalistic explanations and the logic of divine agency. To answer the question "Why me?", many villagers believe that *ghaa* is fated and as such entirely beyond human control. Such argument has been substantiated by the evidence that not all are affected by *ghaa*, even though they drink water from the same contaminated sources. Thus, it is a predominant understanding amongst villagers that *ghaa* is a curse of Allah (*allar gojob*) inflicted on humans due to past transgressions and disobedience of divine rules. Many villagers, therefore, rationalize *ghaa* by saying that this disease and its sufferings are inevitable and a mechanism through which past transgressions and bad deeds would be pardoned.

Clearly, biomedical and social construction of arsenicosis are based on entirely different logics and worldviews. The former is grounded in scientific and objective facts, whereas the latter is based on subjective understandings of handling the illness in everyday life and living under a specific sociocultural and ecological system that shapes the knowledge base of arsenicosis. In rural Bangladesh, water is culturally valued as life-affirming, thus making it difficult to think of as containing poison which can kill humans. Moreover, it is believed that many people have been drinking water from the same contaminated water sources but remain unaffected. Therefore, the biomedical argument that arsenicosis originates from poisoned water does not make cultural sense on the ground. This reflects how lay knowledge of *ghaa* departs significantly from scientific and biomedical constructions of arsenicosis. Built on this argument, one core concern of this study has been to demonstrate the implications of such differential understandings on the health-seeking behaviour of subjects and their participation in mitigation strategies.

To answer the question of why arsenicosis patients rely extensively on alternative healing services, despite reasonably easy access to biomedicine at the UHC, my ethnographic evidence suggests a strong correlation between the social construction of *ghaa* and the ways such understandings shape the health-seeking behaviour of the subjects. Since *ghaa* is predominantly believed to be an illness caused by snakebites and blood poisoning, it is perceived that such poisons must be removed from the body in order for it to be completely healed. It is argued that such removal of poison from the body can best be performed by either the religious *hujur* with his blowing water or by the village *kobiraj* with his herbal medications. Therefore, after noticing the appearance of *ghaa*, patients prefer visiting a *hujur* or *kobiraj* who they consider possesses the expertise to drive out poison from the body, something that biomedicine does not claim to treat. Moreover, my ethnographic evidence further suggests that *ghaa* is believed to be preordained, fated and a divine curse. To get rid of such *ghaa*, patients thus approach a religious *hujur*, who is believed to have the capacity to solve the problem through chanting (*jhar-fuk*), blowing water (*pani-pora*) and prescribing amulets (*tabiz*). Many patients further believe that only solemn prayers and apologies to Allah for previous transgressions might save them from such a devastating misfortune.

My ethnographic evidence further reveals that visits to the UHC for allopathic treatment of *ghaa* often end up in dissatisfaction and frustration. Biomedical doctors do not adequately explain the causes of *ghaa*; rather, they suggest blood tests and other expensive clinical investigations which lay patients consider redundant or unnecessary. Patients go to the hospital with an expectation of necessary medication which will cure *ghaa*. Biomedical doctors, however, prescribe preventive measures such as drinking arsenic-safe water, which makes patients dissatisfied, since their expectation of getting medication remains unfulfilled. Thus, patients find it pointless to seek treatment from biomedical practitioners and continue to drink contaminated water despite clear biomedical disapproval of it. Biomedical knowledge and authority are thus ignored, challenged and not acted upon by patients on the ground. Instead, patients prefer seeking alternative healing services, since the lay cultural notions of *ghaa* match with the understandings of alternative healers. Both parties share similar cultural knowledge about arsenicosis as *ghaa* and mutually negotiate a congenial healing route. Unlike biomedical treatment, alternative healings are easily accessible, not to mention inexpensive, rendering them very popular and affordable options for many poor patients in rural Bangladesh.

To answer the other crucial question of why high-profile arsenic mitigation strategies fail requires a revisit to the ways in which arsenicosis has been variously understood and responded to. As has been demonstrated previously, arsenicosis has been socially constructed as *ghaa* and is explained through specific sociocultural and religious perspectives, with little or no relationship to the consumption of arsenic-contaminated water. Development planners, on the other hand, conforming to the biomedical and scientific explanations of arsenicosis, realize that providing arsenic-safe water is the only solution to this problem. A clear mismatch is evident here between cultural understandings of *ghaa* and the development planners' construction of arsenicosis. Development agencies presume that any project of an arsenic mitigation strategy would be welcomed by the villagers as if they were well informed about the health impacts of consuming arsenic-contaminated water and would be ready to participate in these projects. Without adequately understanding local needs and priorities or whether villagers really value arsenic-safe water as the solution to the problem, development planners impose these water supply projects on the community. Local people who have long been used to drinking water from tubewells are now asked by the development experts to drink water from the project-provided dug-wells, PSFs and water treatment plants, which are perceived by the villagers as inconvenient, traditional and backward. These options are thereby rejected and abandoned.

These projects have further created technological burdens for the community. Ignoring the local geographical reality, the project officials provided shallow dug-wells and PSFs which dried up during summer months when demand for drinking water is very high. The water that came out of these sources was salty, reddish and undrinkable. The sophisticated water treatment plants that were provided by GSK were also of no use, since there was inadequate supply of electricity in the village to run the systems. Villagers also did not welcome the system of water subscription, since water is culturally valued as lifesaving and something that is not to be bought and sold like other commodities in the market. Thus, culturally inappropriate, technically faulty and ecologically impractical mitigation options were imposed on the villagers, which they did not like.

There were also some problems in making these projects participatory. Although these projects were expected to be implemented through participatory governance, community involvement and participatory decision making, in reality village elites, influential UP officials and local political leaders represented the community. By keeping aside lay villagers, young and enthusiastic individuals, these influential persons became members of the implementation committee. Lay people did not have any ownership and control over these projects. Although collecting water and water-related household activities are mostly tasks for the women in rural Bangladesh, their priorities, expectations and representations in the project were grossly overlooked. In the name of participatory development, top-down, authoritative and gender-biased development projects were implemented.

The matter of supplying arsenic-safe water has been politicized, variously taken up and strategized by various interest groups. The UP officials insisted that arsenic-safe water be supplied free of charge, thereby using the water supply scheme as a political platform for accumulating votes for the next round of elections. Local villagers, on the other hand, were dissatisfied that their hard-earned money had been wasted in the name of cost-sharing. The local management committee and Unnoyon staffer were engaged in conflicts over the issues of control, power and authority of the water treatment plants. An apparently non-political matter of water supply preeminently emerged as a political phenomenon on the ground. As unintended consequences of development (Ferguson 1990), these projects, which

Conclusion: the primacy of culture 125

were supposed to provide arsenic-safe water for reducing morbidity and mortality, in fact ended up with political tension and conflict among different stakeholders, leading potentially useful and desirable water supply projects into failure.

Having outlined the main findings and arguments of this study, this book further highlights specific theoretical and policy recommendations. It is argued that at least two theoretical frameworks would be necessary to holistically examine arsenic poisoning and its associated health and development consequences. It is clearly demonstrated that arsenicosis is not just a disease manifested in biological dysfunctions of bodily systems; rather, it is experienced as an illness by patients who live in a specific sociocultural, political and ecological context. Social constructionism (Berger and Luckmann 1966; Schutz and Luckmann 1973) provides a powerful theoretical framework to understand how such illness is understood and experienced by the lay subjects. Drawing upon lay terminologies, languages and categorizations, social constructionism helps to better understand the mundane nature of this illness. Besides such a micro perspective, a post-structuralist development discourse (Escobar 1995; Esteva 1992; Ferguson 1990; Mohan 1997; Nederveen-pieterse 2000; Rahnema and Bawtree 1997) would be helpful to understand how arsenicosis as a health matter is shaped by and linked with the global capitalist enterprises through various water supply development projects. By critically reexamining orthodox development and its processes, this perspective further helps to examine why arsenic mitigation water supply projects fail in rural Bangladesh. This study thus argues that it requires a combination of both social constructionism and post-structuralist critique of development to have a holistic understanding of arsenic poisoning.

While examining the medical systems in rural Bangladesh, this book further argues that the concept of medical pluralism needs to be reconsidered – it appears to be much more complex and problematic than exemplified in the social sciences literature. The ways in which medical pluralism has been defined as the 'coexistence of different medical systems' simply discount many monolithic and dynamic characteristics of the medical diversity in practice. My ethnographic findings suggest that practitioners of different medical systems borrow modalities or therapeutic procedures from each other. The local *kobiraj* uses biomedical ointments, whereas the village allopathic doctor prescribes blood-purifying herbal tonic for remedying *ghaa*. Such syncretic practices of borrowing therapeutic modalities add new directions in the study of medical pluralism in rural Bangladesh. The notion of medical pluralism needs to be reconceptualized to appreciate assorted internal dynamics and syncretic medical practices within it. Different medical systems within a pluralistic setting are no longer considered to be isolated or discrete entities; rather, medical pluralism can now be studied as a "multiplicity of healing techniques, rather than of medical systems" (Stoner 1986: 46).

Findings of this study further challenge the notion of health-seeking behaviour in a medically plural setting. As evident in this study, in search of a "good doctor" (*valo daktar*), rural Bangladeshi patients do not mind travelling reasonable distance and even crossing the national boundary to partake of global health care services. This challenges the boundary of health-seeking behaviour, since the advent of globalization and the spread of technology such as the Internet have opened up new opportunities for patients to take part in the global medical marketplace. Following Nichter (2002), it is argued that the boundary of the "therapy managing group" needs to be reconceptualized to incorporate extended social networks across national boundaries. This study suggests that rural Bangladeshis, with assistance from their relatives living abroad, cross the national border to participate in global health care services. Thus, the initial formulation of a "therapy managing group" (Janzen 1978) appears to be narrow in the context of rural Bangladesh.

Besides these theoretical considerations, this study suggests specific policy recommendations for public health and development interventions. One key finding of this study is that the modes in which development projects are conceptualized and implemented are critical. It has been demonstrated that development projects are grounded in biomedical conceptions of arsenicosis, whereas lay constructions are rooted in a very different understanding of how and why arsenicosis occurs. No synchronization between these two sets of explanations is observed. How this lay knowledge can be incorporated into development projects is a key question. In light of failed water supply projects launched by BAMWSP and GSK, this study reinforces the idea that local sociocultural and politico-ecological contexts are crucial in making development projects successful and sustainable (Ferguson 1990; Friedman 2006). NGOs and development practitioners need to appreciate how people on the ground understand, define and prioritize their problems. It would be useful for the project planners to listen to villagers who are handling the situation on a day-to-day basis. A bottom-up approach with more meaningful community participation would be helpful in sustaining mitigation strategies. A fair representation from all walks of life would ensure meaningful community participation in the development projects. Diversity of viewpoints is important as a mechanism that checks and balances domination and monopoly by agendas and political interests of the powerful.

Awareness creation on the ground could be a rigorous and persistent component of any development and public health projects. Ethnographic findings of this study suggest that the languages to be used for awareness creation and message dissemination must conform to local vocabularies and knowledge systems. For example, instead of using the English word arsenicosis, the local term *ghaa* could be used in the billboards, leaflets and awareness campaigns so that villagers could relate these messages to their everyday lived experiences. An information booth could be opened in each village where villagers may obtain relevant information about arsenic poisoning, its health impacts and treatment procedures. Appropriate health promotion and educational programs could be designed so that the link between drinking arsenic-contaminated water and the causation of arsenicosis disease may be conveyed more effectively. A culturally appropriate health education program is important in bridging the gaps among public health practitioners, development planners and lay individuals. Examples of such concerted health education efforts are many – for example, AIDS and hypertension management in Africa (Airhihenbuwa 1989; Gwede and McDermott 1992; Walker 2000) and mental health education in Canada (Cumming and Cumming 1955). This study, which is rich in first-hand ethnographic data, could be useful in this direction to formulate more culturally appropriate health education and awareness programs about arsenicosis.

To make awareness creation and information dissemination more rigorous and effective, discussions of arsenicosis could be incorporated into school textbooks so that students could be exposed to the issues and disseminate the information to family members. Since many villagers have access to radio and television, mass media could also play an important role in disseminating information about arsenicosis. The government might consider employing the existing HAs at the village level to disseminate information about arsenicosis to the villagers. These HAs might pay door-to-door visits in order to make villagers aware of arsenic contamination in water and its detrimental health effects. Last, but not the least, this study suggests that a culturally acceptable strategy of disseminating information about arsenicosis might include alternative healers, the village imams and religious leaders, who could be trained with basic information about the dangers of drinking arsenic-contaminated water and its resultant health impacts. They could serve as important mediators between health planners and lay communities.

Finally, anthropologists alone cannot solve this pervasive health crisis faced by rural Bangladeshis. Although this ethnography of arsenicosis is rich in first-hand and sociocultural data, the approach only unveils one dimension of this complex phenomenon. A more effective approach that addresses the complexity of arsenicosis would necessarily have to be multidisciplinary, incorporating insights from public health discussions, development policy formulations, participatory governance, biomedical logic and lay discourse. The rich sociocultural data generated by this study are meaningful to the end that it highlights the contrasting perceptions of the disease amongst different categories of social actors. Fighting this pervasive public health disaster in rural Bangladesh requires these varied actors – biomedical practitioners, development planners and lay villagers – to come to some common understandings about the disease in order to combat it successfully.

Bibliography

Acharyya, S. K. (et al.) (1999) Arsenic poisoning in the Ganges Delta. *Nature*, Vol. 401: 545.

Adib, S. M. (2004) From the biomedical model to the Islamic alternative: A brief overview of medical practices in the contemporary Arab world. *Social Science and Medicine*, Vol. 58: 697–702.

Adnan, S. (2004) *Migration, land alienation and ethnic conflict: Causes of poverty in the Chittagong hill tracts in Bangladesh*. Dhaka: Research and Advisory Services.

Ahmad, J.; Goldar, B.; and Misra, S. (2005) Value of arsenic-free drinking water to rural households in Bangladesh. *Journal of Environmental Management*, Vol. 74: 173–185.

Ahmad, M. (2002) *Governance, structural adjustment and the state of corruption in Bangladesh*. Dhaka: Transparency International Bangladesh.

Ahmed, S. M. (et al.) (2000) Gender, socioeconomic development and health-seeking behavior in Bangladesh. *Social Science and Medicine*, Vol. 51: 361–371.

Ahmed, S. M. (2008) Taking healthcare where the community is: The story of the shasthya sebikas of BRAC in Bangladesh. *BRAC University Journal*, Vol. V(1): 39–45.

Airhihenbuwa, C. O. (1989) Perspectives on AIDS in Africa: Strategies for prevention and control. *AIDS Education and Prevention*, Vol. 1(1): 57–69.

Alamgir, F.; Mahmud, T.; and Iftekharuzzaman. (2004) "Corruption and parliamentary oversight: Primacy of the political will." Paper presented at the Transparency International Bangladesh (TIB), Dhaka, 9 December 2006.

Aldana, Mendoza J.; Piechulek, H.; and Al-Sabir, A. (2001) Client satisfaction and quality of health care in rural Bangladesh. *Bulletin of the World Health Organization*, Vol. 79: 512–517.

Allen, N. J. (1976) "Shamanism among the Thlung Rai." In John T. Hitchcock and Rex L. Jones (eds.), *Spirit possession in the Nepal Himalayas*, pp. 124–140. New Delhi: Vikas.

Amin, Z. (et al.) (2008) Medical education in Bangladesh. *Medical Teacher*, Vol. 30(3): 243–247.

Andaleeb, S. S. (2000) Public and private hospitals in Bangladesh: Service quality and predictors of hospital choice. *Health Policy and Planning*, Vol. 15(1): 95–102.

Andaleeb, S. S. (2001) Service quality perceptions and patient satisfaction: A study of hospitals in a developing country. *Social Science and Medicine*, Vol. 52: 1359–1370.

Andersson, K. P.; Gibson, C. C.; and Lehoucq, F. (2006) Municipal politics and forest governance: Comparative analysis of decentralization in Bolivia and Guatemala. *World Development*, Vol. 34(3): 576–595.

Andersson, K. P. and van Laerhoven, F. (2007) From local strongman to facilitator: Institutional incentives for participatory municipal governance in Latin America. *Comparative Political Studies*, Vol. 40(9): 1085–1111.

Bibliography

Ashraf, A.; Chowdhury, S.; and Streefland, P. (1982) Health, disease and health care in rural Bangladesh. *Social Science and Medicine*, Vol. 16: 2041–2054.

Bala, P. (1991) *Imperialism and medicine in Bengal: A socio-historical perspective*. New Delhi: Sage Publications.

Bala, P. (2007) *Medicine and medical policies in India: Social and historical perspectives*. Lanham: Lexington Books.

Bangladesh Health Watch (BHW). (2007) *Challenges of achieving equity in health*. Dhaka: James P. Grant School of Public Health, BRAC University.

Barth, F. (1993) *Balinese worlds*. Chicago: The University of Chicago Press.

BBS. (2001) *Statistical pocket book of Bangladesh 2001*. Dhaka: Bangladesh Bureau of Statistics, Ministry of Planning, Government of the People's Republic of Bangladesh.

Beckerleg, S. (1994) Medical pluralism and Islam in Swahili communities in Kenya. *Medical Anthropology Quarterly*, New Series, Vol. 8(3): 299–313.

Berger, P. L. and Luckmann, T. (1966) *The social construction of reality: A treatise in the sociology of knowledge*. New York: Anchor Books.

Bernard, R. H. (2002) *Research methods in anthropology*. Walnut Creek: Alta Mira Press.

Berreman, G. D. (1972) *Hindus of the Himalayas: Ethnography and change*. Berkeley: University of California Press.

BGS. (1999) *Ground water studies for arsenic contamination in Bangladesh: Final report*. London: British Geological Survey.

Bhardwaj, S. M. and Paul, B. K. (1986) Medical pluralism and infant mortality in a rural area of Bangladesh. *Social Science and Medicine*, Vol. 23(10): 1003–1010.

Bhattacharya, P.; Chatterjee, D.; and Jacks, G. (1997) Occurrence of arsenic-contaminated groundwater in alluvial aquifers from Delta Plains, eastern India: Options for safe drinking water supply. *Water Resources Development*, Vol. 13(1): 79–92.

Bishop, P. and Davis, G. (2002) Mapping public participation in policy choices. *Australian Journal of Public Administration*, Vol. 61(1): 14–29.

Biswas, B. K. (et al.) (1998) Detailed study report of Samta, one of the arsenic-affected villages of Jessore district, Bangladesh. *Current Science*, Vol. 74(2): 134–145.

Black, M. and Talbot, R. (2005) *Water: A matter of life and health*. New Delhi: Oxford University Press.

Blair, H. (2000) Participation and accountability at the periphery: Democratic local governance in six countries. *World Development*, Vol. 28(1): 21–39.

Blaxter, M. (1995) "What is health?" In Basiro Davey, Alastair Gray and Clive Scale (eds.), *Health and disease: A reader*, pp. 26–32. Philadelphia: Open University Press.

Borré, K. (1991) Seal blood, Inuit blood, and diet: A biocultural model of physiology and cultural identity. *Medical Anthropology Quarterly*, Vol. 5(1): 48–62.

Boswell, D. M. (1969) "Personal crises and the mobilization of the social networks." In Clyde J. Mitchell (ed.), *Social networks in urban situations: Analysis of personal relationships in central African towns*, pp. 245–296. Manchester: Manchester University Press.

Brammer, H. and Ravenscroft, P. (2009) Arsenic in ground water: A threat to sustainable agriculture in South and South-east Asia. *Environment International*, Vol. 35: 647–654.

Bräutigam, D. (2004) The people's budget? Politics, participation and pro-poor policy. *Development Policy Review*, Vol. 22(6): 653–668.

Brown, P. (1995) Naming and framing: The social construction of diagnosis and illness. *Journal of Health and Social Behavior*, Vol. 35: 34–52.

Buckingham, J. (2002) *Leprosy in colonial south India: Medicine and confinement*. New York: Palgrave.

Bury, M. R. (1986) Social construction and the development of medical sociology. *Sociology of Health and Illness*, Vol. 8(2): 137–169.
Bury, M. R. (1991) The sociology of chronic illness: A review of research and prospects. *Sociology of Health and Illness*, Vol. 13(4): 451–468.
Caldwell, D. (et al.) (2003) Searching for an optimum solution to the Bangladesh arsenic crisis. *Social Science and Medicine*, Vol. (56): 2089–2096.
Cant, S. and Sharma, U. (1996) Demarcation and transformation within homoeopathic knowledge: A strategy of professionalization. *Social Science and Medicine*, Vol. 42(4): 579–588.
Cassel, J. (1977) "Social and cultural implication of food and food habits." In David Landy (ed.), *Culture, disease and dealing: Studies in medical anthropology*, pp. 236–242. New York: Macmillan Publishing.
Chakraborti, D. (et al.) (2002) Arsenic calamity in the Indian subcontinent: What lessons have been learned? *Talanta*, Vol. 58(2002): 3–22.
Chatterjee, M. (1991) "Indian women their health and economic productivity." World Bank Discussion Paper 109. Washington, DC: World Bank.
Chatterji, J. (2007) *The spoils of partition: Bengal and India, 1947–1967*. Cambridge: Cambridge University Press.
Chen, C. (et al.) (1994) "Ischemic heart disease induced by ingested inorganic arsenic." In Willard R. Chappel, Charles O. Abernathy and C. Richard Cothern (eds.), *Arsenic: Exposure and health*, pp. 83–90. Northwood: Science and Technology Letters.
Chen, C. and Wang, C. (1990) Ecological correlation between arsenic level in well water and age-adjusted mortality from malignant neoplasms. *Cancer Research*, Vol. 50: 5470–5474.
Chen, Y. (et al.) (2003) Arsenic methylation and bladder cancer risk in Taiwan. *Cancer Causes and Control*, Vol. 14(4): 303–310.
Chowdhury, A. (2001) Local heroes. *New Internationalist*, Vol. 332: 22–24.
Chowdhury, M.A.R. and Alam, A. M. (1997) "BRAC's poverty alleviation efforts: A quarter century of experiences and learning." In Geoffrey D. Wood and Iffath A. Sharif (eds.), *Who needs credit? Poverty and finance in Bangladesh*, pp. 171–192. London: Zed Books.
Chowdhury, T. R. (et al.) (1999) Arsenic poisoning in the Ganges Delta. *Nature*, Vol. 401: 545–546.
Churchill, L. R. (1989) Trust, autonomy, and advance directives. *Journal of Religion and Health*, Vol. 28(3): 175–183.
Clammer, J. (1984) "Approaches to ethnographic research." In R. F. Ellen (ed.), *Ethnographic research: A guide to general conduct*, pp. 62–85. London: Academic Press.
Connor, L. H. (2004) Relief, risk and renewal: Mixed therapy regimens in an Australian suburb. *Social Science and Medicine*, Vol. 59: 1695–1705.
Corbridge, S. (ed.) (1995) *Development studies: A reader*. London: E. Arnold.
Cosminsky, S. and Scrimshaw, M. (1980) Medical pluralism on a Guatemalan plantation. *Social Science and Medicine*, Vol. 14B: 267–278.
Craig, D. (2002) *Familiar medicine: Everyday health knowledge and practice in today's Vietnam*. Honolulu: University of Hawai'i Press.
Crook, R. C. and Manor, J. (1998) *Democracy and decentralization in South East Asia and West Africa: Participation, accountability, and performance*. Cambridge, MA: Cambridge University Press.
Cullen, W. R. (2008) *Is arsenic an aphrodisiac? The sociochemistry of an element*. Cambridge: RSC Publishing.

Bibliography

Cumming, J. and Cumming, E. (1955) "Mental health education in a Canadian community." In B. Paul (ed.), *Health, culture and community: Case studies of public reactions to health programs*, pp. 43–70. London: Russell Sage Foundation.

Das, D. (et al.) (1996) Arsenic in groundwater in six districts of West Bengal, India. *Environmental Geochemistry and Health*, Vol. 18(2): 5–15.

Devine, J. (2003) The paradox of sustainability: Reflections of NGOs in Bangladesh. *Annals of the American Academy of Political and Social Science*, Vol. 590: 227–242.

Donohoe, M. (2003) Causes and health consequences of environmental degradation and social injustice. *Social Science and Medicine*, Vol. 56: 573–587.

Douglas, M. (1966) *Purity and danger: An analysis of the concepts of pollution and taboo*. London: ARK Paperbacks.

Drugs (Control) Ordinance. (1982) Ministry of law and land reforms, Government of the People's Republic of Bangladesh.

Du Bois, C. (1986) "Studies in an Indian town." In Peggy Golde (ed.), *Women in the field: Anthropological experiences*, pp. 221–236. Berkeley: University of California Press.

Dubos, R. (1995) "Mirage of health." In Basiro Davey, Alastair Gray and Clive Scale (eds.), *Health and disease: A reader*, pp. 4–10. Philadelphia: Open University Press.

Dunn, F. L. (1976) "Traditional Asian medicine and cosmopolitan medicine as adaptive systems." In Charles Leslie (ed.), *Asian medical systems: A comparative study*, pp. 133–158. Berkeley: University of California Press.

Ehrenreich, B. and English, D. (1978) *For her own good: 150 years of the experts' advice to women*. New York: Anchor Books.

Ellen, R. F. (ed.) (1984) *Ethnographic research: A guide to general conduct*. London: Academic Press.

Engel, R. R. (et al.) (1994) Vascular effects of chronic arsenic exposure: A review. *Epidemiologic Review*, Vol. 16: 184–209.

Ernst, W. (1999) "Introduction: Historical and contemporary perspective on race, science and medicine." In Waltraud Ernst and Bernard Harris (eds.), *Race, science and medicine, 1700–1960*, pp. 1–28. London: Routledge.

Escobar, A. (1988) Power and visibility: Development and the invention and management of the Third World. *Cultural Anthropology*, Vol. 3(4): 428–443.

Escobar, A. (1991) Anthropology and the development encounter: The making and marketing of development anthropology. *American Ethnologist*, Vol. 18(4): 658–682.

Escobar, A. (1995) *Encountering development: The making and unmaking of the Third World*. Princeton: Princeton University Press.

Escobar, A. (2000) Beyond the search for a paradigm? Post-development and beyond. *Development*, 43(4): 421–436.

Escobar, A. (2004) Beyond the Third World: Imperial globality, global coloniality and anti-globalisation social movements. *Third World Quarterly*, Vol. 25(1): 207–230.

Esteva, G. (1992) "Development." In Wolfgang Sachs (ed.), *The development dictionary: A guide to knowledge as power*, pp. 6–26. London: Zed Books.

Evans-Pritchard, E. E. (1937) *Witchcraft, oracles, and magic among the Azande*. Oxford: Oxford University Press.

Fabrega, H. Jr. and Manning, P. K. (1979) Illness episodes, illness severity and treatment options in a pluralistic setting. *Social Science and Medicine*, Vol. 13B: 41–51.

Fabrega, H. and Nutini, H. (1993) Witchcraft-explained childhood tragedies in Tlaxcala, and their medical squeal. *Social Science and Medicine*, Vol. 36(6): 793–805.

FAO. (1999) *Nutrition country profile – Bangladesh*. Rome: Food and Agriculture Organization of the United Nations.

Farquhar, J. (1994) Eating Chinese medicine. *Cultural Anthropology*, Vol. 9(4): 471–497.
Feldman, S. (1983) The use of private health care providers in rural Bangladesh: A response to Claquin. *Social Science and Medicine*, Vol. 17(23): 1887–1896.
Ferguson, J. (1990) *The anti-politics machine: "Development", depoliticization, and bureaucratic power in Lesotho*. Minneapolis: University of Minnesota Press.
Ferguson, J. (1997) "Anthropology and its evil twin: 'Development' in the constitution of a discipline." In Frederick Cooper and Randall Packard (eds.), *International development and the social sciences: Essays on the history and politics of knowledge*, pp. 150–175. Berkeley: University of California Press.
Ferreccio, C. (et al.) (2000) Lung cancer and arsenic concentrations in drinking water in Chile. *Epidemiology*, Vol. 11(6): 673–679.
Ferreccio, C. and Sancha, M. A. (2006) Arsenic exposure and its impact on health in Chile. *Journal of Health, Population and Nutrition*, Vol. 24(2): 164–175.
Field, M. J. (1937) *Religion and medicine of the Gā People*. London: Oxford University Press.
Forsey, M. (2004) "He is not a spy; he's one of us": Ethnographic positioning in a middle-class setting." In Lynne Hume and Jane Mulcock (eds.), *Anthropologists in the field: Cases in participant observation*, pp. 59–70. New York: Columbia University Press.
Foster, G. M. (1976) Disease etiologies in non-western medical systems. *American Anthropologist*, Vol. 78(4): 773–782.
Foucault, M. (1972) *The archaeology of knowledge*. London: Tavistock Publications.
Francis, P. and James, R. (2003) Balancing rural poverty reduction and citizen participation: The contradictions of Uganda's decentralization program. *World Development*, Vol. 31(2): 325–337.
Frank, R. (2002) Homeopath and patient – a dyad of harmony? *Social Science and Medicine*, Vol. 55: 1285–1296.
Frank, R. and Ecks, S. (2004) Towards an ethnography of Indian homeopathy. *Anthropology and Medicine*, Vol. 11(3): 307–326.
Friedman, J. T. (2006) Beyond the post-structural impasse in the anthropology of development. *Dialectical Anthropology*, Vol. 30: 201–225.
Gardner, K. and Lewis, D. (1996) *Anthropology, development and the post-modern challenge*. London: Pluto Press.
Gaventa, J. (2004) "Towards participatory governance: Assessing the transformative possibilities." In S. Hickey and G. Mohan (eds.), *Participation: From tyranny to transformation? Exploring new approaches to participation in development*, pp. 25–41. London and New York: Zed Books.
Geertz, C. (1973) *The interpretation of cultures: Selected essays*. New York: Basic Books.
Glick, L. B. (1967) Medicine as an ethnographic category: The Gimi of the New Guinea highlands. *Ethnology*, Vol. 6(1): 31–56.
Glick, L. B. (1977) "Medicine as an ethnographic category: The Gimi of the New Guinea highlands." In David Landy (ed.), *Culture, disease and healing: Studies in medical anthropology*, pp. 58–70. New York: Macmillan Publishing.
Golomb, L. (1988) The interplay of traditional therapies in South Thailand. *Social Science and Medicine*, Vol. 27(8): 761–768.
Good, B. J. (1994) *Medicine, rationality, and experience: An anthropological perspective*. Cambridge: Cambridge University Press.
Green, H. (et al.) (2006) "We are not completely westernized": Dual medical systems and pathways to health care among Chinese migrant women in England. *Social Science and Medicine*, Vol. 62: 1498–1509.

134 Bibliography

Gupta, B. (1976) "Indigenous medicine in nineteenth and twentieth century Bengal." In Charles Leslie (ed.), *Asian medical systems: A comparative study*, pp. 368–378. Berkeley: University of California Press.

Gwede, C. and McDermott, R. J. (1992) AIDS in sub-Saharan Africa: Implications of health education. *AIDS Education and Prevention*, Vol. 4(4): 350–361.

Hammersley, M. and Atkinson, P. (1995) *Ethnography: Principles in practice*. London: Routledge.

Haque, S. M. (2001) Recent transition in governance in South Asia: Contexts, dimensions, and implications. *International Journal of Public Administration*, Vol. 24(12): 1405–1436.

Harvey, D. (et al.) (2005) Groundwater arsenic contamination on the Ganges Delta: Biogeochemistry, hydrology, human perturbations, and human suffering on a large scale. *Comptes Rendus Geoscience*, Vol. 337(2005): 285–296.

Hashemi, S. M. and Morshed, L. (1997) "Grameen bank: A case study." In Geoffrey D. Wood and Iffath Sharif (eds.), *Who needs credit: Poverty and finance in Bangladesh*. London and New York: Zed Books.

Hashima-e-Nasreen (et al.) (2007) Maternal, neonatal and child health programmes in Bangladesh: Review of good practices and lessons learned. Research Monograph Series No. 32. BRAC: Research and Evaluation Division.

Heggenhougen, H. K. (1980) Bomohs, doctors and sinsehs: Medical pluralism in Malaysia. *Social Science and Medicine*, Vol. 14B: 235–244.

Henke, K. R. (2009) "Arsenic in natural environments." In Kevin R. Henke (ed.), *Arsenic: Environmental chemistry, health threats, and waste treatment*, pp. 69–236. Hoboken: Wiley.

Hobart, M. (1993) "Introduction: The growth of ignorance?" In Mark Hobart (ed.), *An anthropological critique of development: The growth of ignorance*, pp. 1–30. London: Routledge.

Hopenhayn-Rich, C. (et al.) (1996) Bladder cancer mortality associated with arsenic in drinking water in Argentina. *Epidemiology*, Vol. 7: 117–124.

Hopenhayn-Rich, C. (et al.) (2000) Chronic arsenic exposure and risk of infant mortality in two areas of Chile. *Environmental Health Perspectives*, Vol. 108(7): 667–673.

Horowitz, R. (1996) "Getting in." In Carolyn D. Smith and William Kornblum (eds.), *In the field: Readings on the field research experience*, pp. 41–50. London: Praeger.

Hossain, M. F. (2006) Arsenic contamination in Bangladesh – an overview. *Agriculture, Ecosystems and Environment*, Vol. 113(1): 1–16.

Hulme, D. and Edwards, M. (1997) *NGOs, states and donors: Too close for comfort?* London: Macmillan.

Islam, S. M. (2004) Who benefits, how benefits: The political economy of Grameen Bank's microcredit programme in rural Bangladesh. *Oriental Anthropologists*, Vol. 4(1): 1–17.

Islam, S. M. (2005) Oscillating between marginality and modernity: Transitional Oraon cultural milieu of Northwest Bangladesh. *South Asian Anthropologist*, Vol. 5(2): 179–185.

Islam, S. M. (2010) Indigenous people, NGOs and the politics of alternative development discourse in Bangladesh. *Dhaka University Journal of Development Studies*, Vol. 1: 17–28.

Islam, S. M. (2012) Health for all or health for some? Healthcare provisions and financing in Bangladesh and India: A comparative analysis. *Harvard Asia Quarterly*, Vol. 14(4): 74–83.

Islam, S. M. (2014) On anthropological fieldwork: Does fieldwork experience matter in writing postmodern ethnography? *The Anthropologist*, 17(2): 327–332.

Islam, K. and Bachman, S. (1983) PHC in Bangladesh: Too much to ask. *Social Science and Medicine*, Vol. 17(19): 1463–1466.

Jackson, C. J. and Jackson-Carroll, L. (1994) The social significance of routine health behavior in Tamang daily life. *Social Science and Medicine*, Vol. 38(7): 999–1010.

Janes, C. R. (1999) The health transition, global modernity and the crisis of traditional medicine: The Tibetan case. *Social Science and Medicine*, Vol. 48: 1803–1820.

Janzen, J. M. (1978) *The quest for therapy: Medical pluralism in Lower Zaire*. Berkeley: University of California Press.

Jeffery, R. and Jeffery, P. M. (1993) "Traditional birth attendants in rural north India: The social organization of childbearing." In Shirley Lindenbaum and Margaret Lock (eds.), *Knowledge, power and practice: The anthropology of medicine and everyday life*, pp. 7–31. Berkeley: University of California Press.

Jewkes, R. and Murcott, A. (1998) Community representatives: Representing the "community"? *Social Science and Medicine*, Vol. 46(7): 843–858.

Jike, V. T. (2004) Environmental degradation, social disequilibrium, and the dilemma of sustainable development in the Niger-Delta of Nigeria. *Journal of Black Studies*, Vol. 34(5): 686–701.

Kamat, V. R. and Nichter, M. (1998) Pharmacies, self-medication and pharmaceutical marketing in Bombay, India. *Social Science and Medicine*, Vol. 47(6): 779–794.

Kaosar, A. (2004) The tremendous cost of seeking hospital obstetric care in Bangladesh. *Reproductive Health Matters*, Vol. 12(24): 171–180.

Karim, A. (1988) Shamanism in Bangladesh. *Asian Folklore Studies*, Vol. 47: 277–309.

Karim, L. (2008) Demystifying micro-credit: The Grameen bank, NGOs, and neoliberalism in Bangladesh. *Cultural Dynamics*, Vol. 20(1): 5–29.

Kaufert, P. A. and O'Neil, J. (1993) "Analysis of a dialogue on risks in childbirth: Clinicians, epidemiologists, and Inuit women." In Shirley Lindenbaum and Margaret Lock (eds.), *Knowledge, power and practice: The anthropology of medicine and everyday life*, pp. 32–54. Berkeley: University of California Press.

Kettel, B. (1996) Women, health and the environment. *Social Science and Medicine*, Vol. 42(10): 1367–1379.

Khagram, S. (2004) *Dams and development: Transnational struggles for water and power*. Ithaca: Cornell University Press.

Khan, W. A. (et al.) (1997) Arsenic contamination in the ground water and its effect on human health with particular reference to Bangladesh. *Journal of Preventive and Social Medicine*, Vol. 16(1): 65–73.

Khan, Y. (2007) *The great partition: The making of India and Pakistan*. New Haven: Yale University Press.

Khandker, S. R. (1993) "Poverty reduction strategy: The Grameen Bank experience." In Shahidur R. Khandker, Baqui Khalily and Zahir Khan (eds.), *Grameen Bank: What do we know?* Washington, DC: Education and Social Policy Department, World Bank.

Khandker, S. R. and Khalily, B. (1996) "The Bangladesh Rural Advancement Committee's credit programmes: Performance and sustainability." The World Bank Discussion Paper no. 324. Washington, DC: The World Bank.

Kinniburgh, D. G. (et al.) (2003) "The scale and causes of the groundwater arsenic problem in Bangladesh." In Alan H. Welch and Kenneth G. Stollenwerk (eds.), *Arsenic in ground water*, pp. 211–257. Boston: Kluwer Academic Publishers.

Kleinman, A. (1978) What kind of model for the anthropology of medical systems? *American Anthropologist*, Vol. 80(3): 661–665.

Kleinman, A. (1980) *Patients and healers in the context of culture: An exploration of the borderland between anthropology, medicine and psychiatry.* Berkeley: University of California Press.

Kleinman, A. (1986) *Social origins of distress and disease: Depression, neurasthenia, and pain in modern China.* New Haven: Yale University Press.

Kleinman, A. (1988) *The illness narratives: Suffering, healing, and the human condition.* New York: Basic Books.

Koblinsky, M.; Campbell, Oona M. R.; and Harlow, S. D. (1993) "Mother and more: A broader perspective on women's health." In Marge Koblinsky, Judith Timyan and Jill Gay (eds.), *The health of women: A global perspective*, pp. 33–62. Oxford: Westview Press.

Kothari, A. and Bhartari, R. (1984) Narmada valley project: Development or destruction? *Economic and Political Weekly*, Vol. 19(22): 907–920.

Kothari, R. (1988) *Rethinking development: In search of humane alternatives.* Delhi: Ajanta.

Kumar, A. (1998) *Medicine and the Raj: British medical policy in India, 1835–1911.* New Delhi: Sage Publications.

Kumar, D. (2002) "Health and medicine in British India and Dutch Indies: A comparative study." Paper presented in the Conference of Asian Medicine: Nationalism, Transnationalism and the Politics of Culture held at the Asian Studies Center, University of Pittsburgh, 14–16 November.

Laderman, C. (1981) Symbolic and empirical reality: A new approach to the analysis of food avoidances. *American Ethnologist*, Vol. 8(3): 468–493.

Laderman, C. (1987) Destructive heat and cooling prayer: Malay humoralism in pregnancy, childbirth and postpartum period. *Social Science and Medicine*, Vol. 25(4): 357–365.

Lamm, S. H. (et al.) (2006) Arsenic cancer risk confounder in Southwest Taiwan data set. *Environmental Health Perspectives*, Vol. 114(7): 1077–1082.

Leslie, C. and Young, A. (1992) *Paths to Asian medical knowledge.* Berkeley: University of California Press.

Liebeskind, C. (2002) "Arguing science: Unani tibb, hakims and biomedicine in India, 1900–50." In Waltraud Ernst (ed.), *Plural medicine, tradition and modernity, 1800–2000*, pp. 58–75. London: Routledge.

Lindenbaum, S. and Lock, M. (eds.) (1993) *Knowledge, power and practice: The anthropology of medicine and everyday life.* Berkeley: University of California Press.

Lindquist, G. (2002) Healing efficacy and the construction of charisma: A family's journey through the multiple medical field in Russia. *Anthropology and Medicine*, Vol. 9(3): 337–358.

Lock, M. (1980) *East Asian medicine in urban Japan.* Berkeley: University of California Press.

Lu, H. C. (1986) *Chinese system of food cures: Prevention and remedies.* New York: Sterling.

Lupton, D. (1996) *Food, the body and the self.* London: Sage Publications.

Lupton, D. (1997) *Medicine as culture: Illness, disease and the body in Western societies.* London: Sage Publications.

MacLean, C. M. (1969) Traditional healers and their female clients: An aspect of Nigerian sickness behavior. *Journal of Health and Social Behavior*, Vol. 10(3): 172–186.

Madan, T. N. (1987) Community involvement in health policy; Socio-structural and dynamic aspects of health beliefs. *Social Science and Medicine*, Vol. 25(6): 615–620.

Manderson, L. (1987) Hot-cold food and medical theories: Overview and introduction. *Social Science and Medicine*, Vol. 25(4): 329–330.

Marcus, G. E. (1998) *Ethnography through thick and thin*. Princeton: Princeton University Press.
Marcus, G. E. and Fischer, M. J. (1986) *Anthropology as cultural critique: An experimental moment in the human sciences*. Chicago: University of Chicago Press.
Mattingly, C. and Garro, L. C. (eds.) (2000) *Narrative and the cultural construction of illness and healing*. Berkeley: University of California Press.
Mayfield, J. B. (1997) *One can make difference: The challenges and opportunities of dealing with world poverty*. New York: University Press of America.
Mazumder, Guha D. N. (2005) Effect of chronic intake of arsenic-contaminated water on liver. *Toxicology and Applied Pharmacology*, Vol. 206: 169–175.
Mckay, D. A. (1980) "Food, illness, and folk medicine: Insights from Ulu Trengganu, West Malaysia." In J.R.K. Robson (ed.), *Food, ecology and culture: Readings in the anthropology of dietary practices*, pp. 61–66. New York: Gordon and Breach Science Publishers.
Meharg, A. A. (2005) *Venomous earth: How arsenic caused the world's worst mass poisoning*. New York: Macmillan.
Messer, E. (1987) The hot and cold in mesoamerican indigenous and hispanicized thought. *Social Science and Medicine*, Vol. 25(4): 339–346.
Minocha, A. A. (1980) Medical pluralism and health services in India. *Social Science and Medicine*, Vol. 14B: 217–223.
Mohan, G. (1997) Developing differences: Post-structuralism and political economy in contemporary development studies. *Review of African Political Economy*, Vol. 73: 311–328.
Morgan, L. F. (1993) *Community participation in health: The politics of primary care in Costa Rica*. Cambridge: Cambridge University Press.
Mukherjee, A.; Fryar, A. E.; and O'Shea, B. M. (2009) "Major occurrences of elevated arsenic in groundwater and other natural waters." In Kevin R. Henke (ed.), *Arsenic: Environmental chemistry, health threats and waste treatment*, pp. 303–350. Malden: Wiley.
Naemiratch, B. and Manderson, L. (2007) Lay explanations of type 2 diabetes in Bangkok, Thailand. *Anthropology and Medicine*, Vol. 14(1): 83–94.
NAMIC. (2006) National screening program: Union wise summary results. Accessed from www.bamwsp.org on 22 July 2008.
Nandy, A. (ed.) (1988) *Science, hegemony and violence: A requiem for modernity*. New Delhi: Oxford University Press.
Nederveen-pieterse, J. (2000) After post-development. *Third World Quarterly*, Vol. 21(2): 175–191.
Nguyen, Van A. (et al.) (2009) Contamination of groundwater and risk assessment for arsenic exposure in Ha Nam province, Vietnam. *Environment International*, Vol. 35: 466–472.
Nichter, M. (1980) The layperson's perception of medicine as perspective into the utilization of multiple therapy systems in the Indian context. *Social Science and Medicine*, Vol. 14B: 225–239.
Nichter, M. (1984) Project community diagnosis: Participatory research as a first step toward community involvement in primary health care. *Social Science and Medicine*, Vol. 19(3): 237–252.
Nichter, M. (1986) Modes of food classification and the diet-health contingency: A south Indian case study. In R. S. Khare and M.S.A. Rao (eds.), *Food, society, and culture: Aspects in South Asian food systems*, pp. 185–222. Durham: Carolina Academic Press.

Bibliography

Nichter, M. (1987) Cultural dimensions of hot, cold and sema in Sinhalese health culture. *Social Science and Medicine*, Vol. 25(4): 377–387.

Nichter, M. (2002) "The social relations of therapy management." In Mark Nichter and Margaret Lock (eds.), *New horizons in medical anthropology: Essays in honour of Charles Leslie*, pp. 81–110. London: Routledge.

Nichter, M. (2008) *Global health: Why cultural perceptions, social representations, and biopolitics matter*. Tucson: The University of Arizona Press.

Nickson, R. (et al.) (1998) Arsenic poisoning of Bangladesh groundwater. *Nature*, Vol. 395: 338.

Nordstrom, C. R. (1988) Exploring pluralism: The many faces of ayurveda. *Social Science and Medicine*, Vol. 27(5): 479–489.

Nustad, K. G. (2001) Development: The devil we know? *Third World Quarterly*, Vol. 22(4): 479–489.

Ohnuki-Tierney, E. (1984) *Illness and culture in contemporary Japan: An anthropological view*. Cambridge: Cambridge University Press.

Palriwala, R. (2005) Fieldwork in a post-colonial anthropology: Experience and the comparative. *Social Anthropology*, Vol. 13(2): 151–170.

Pandey, G. (2001) *Remembering partition: Violence, nationalism, and history in India*. New York: Cambridge University Press.

Parsons, T. (1951) *The social system*. Chicago: Free Press.

Patkar, M. (1998) The people's policy on development, displacement and resettlement: Need to link displacement and development. *Economic and Political Weekly*, Vol. 33(38): 2432–2433.

Patterson, T.J.S. (2001) "The relationship of Indian and European practitioners of medicine from the sixteenth century." In G. Jan Meulenbeld and Dominik Wujastyk (eds.), *Studies on Indian medical history*, pp. 111–120. Delhi: Motilal Banarsidass Publishers.

Paul, B. K. (1983) A note on the hierarchy of health facilities in Bangladesh. *Social Science and Medicine*, Vol. 17(3): 189–191.

Paul, B. K. (1999) National health care "by-passing" in Bangladesh: A comparative study. *Social Science and Medicine*, Vol. 49: 679–689.

Paul, B. K. (2004) Arsenic contamination awareness among the rural residents in Bangladesh. *Social Science and Medicine*, Vol. 59: 1741–1755.

Paul, B. K. and Rumsey, D. J. (2002) Utilization of health facilities and trained birth attendants for childbirth in rural Bangladesh: An empirical study. *Social Science and Medicine*, Vol. 54: 1755–1765.

Pelto, P. J. and Pelto, G. H. (1978) *Anthropological research: The structure of inquiry*. Cambridge: Cambridge University Press.

Pelto, P. J. and Pelto, G. H. (1990) "Field methods in medical anthropology." In T. M. Johnson and C. F. Sargent (ed.), *Medical anthropology: Contemporary theory and method*. New York: Praeger Publishers.

Pfaffenberger, B. (1990) The harsh facts of hydraulics: Technology and society in Sri Lanka's colonization schemes. *Technology and Culture*, Vol. 31(3): 361–397.

Pigg, S. L. (1990) "Disenchanting shamans: Representations of modernity and the transformation of healing in Nepal." Unpublished doctoral dissertation. Cornell University.

Pigg, S. L. (1995) The social symbolism of healing in Nepal. *Ethnology*, Vol. 34(1): 17–36.

Pool, R. (1987) Hot and cold as an explanatory model: The example of Bharuch district in Gujarat, India. *Social Science and Medicine*, Vol. 25(4): 389–399.

Press, I. (1980) Problems in the definition and classification of medical systems. *Social Science and Medicine*, Vol. 14B: 45–57.

Quah, S. R. (1989) "Confirming the triumph of practicality." In Stella R. Quah (ed.), *The triumph of practicality: Tradition and modernity in healthcare utilization in selected Asian countries*, pp. 180–195. Singapore: Institute of Southeast Asian Studies.

Quah, S. R. (2003) Traditional healing systems and the ethos of science. *Social Science and Medicine*, Vol. 57: 1997–2012.

Radin, P. (1957) *Primitive religion: Its nature and origin*. New York: Dover Publications.

Rahman, A. (1999) *Women and microcredit in rural Bangladesh: Anthropological study of the rhetoric and realities of Grameen bank lending*. Boulder: Westview Press.

Rahman, A. (et al.) (2005) *Bangladesh health and injury survey: Report on children*. Dhaka: MOHFW, ICMH, UNICEF and TASC.

Rahnema, M. and Bawtree, V. (eds.) (1997) *The post-development reader*. London: Zed Books.

Ravenscroft, P.; Brammer, H.; and Richards, K. (2009) *Arsenic pollution: A global synthesis*. Malden: Wiley-Blackwell.

Reeve, M. (2000) Concepts of illness and treatment practice in a Caboclo community of the Lower Amazon. *Medical Anthropology Quarterly*, Vol. 14(1): 96–108.

Rifkin, S. B.; Muller, F.; and Bichmann, W. (1988) Primary health care: On measuring participation. *Social Science and Medicine*, Vol. 26(9): 931–940.

Rivers, W.H.R. (1924) *Medicine, magic and religion*. New York. Harcourt Brace.

Robinson, K. M. (1986) *Stepchildren of progress: The political economy of development in an Indonesian mining town*. Albany: State University of New York Press.

Rousham, E. K. (1994) Perceptions and treatment of intestinal worms in rural Bangladesh: Local differences in knowledge and behaviour. *Social Science and Medicine*, Vol. 39(8): 1063–1068.

Sangvai, S. (2002) Narmada displacement: Continuing outrage. *Economic and Political Weekly*, Vol. 37(22) 2132–2134.

Saradamma, R. D.; Higginbotham, N.; and Nichter, M. (2000) Social factors influencing the acquisition of antibiotics without prescription in Kerala State, South India. *Social Science and Medicine*, Vol. 50: 891–903.

Scheper-Hughes, N. (1990) Three propositions for a critically applied medical anthropology. *Social Science and Medicine*, Vol. 30(2): 189–197.

Schutz, A. (1962) *Collected papers, vol. 1: The problem of social reality*. The Hague: Martinus Nijhoff.

Schutz, A. (1967) *The phenomenology of the social world*. London: Heineman Educational Books.

Schutz, A. and Luckmann, T. (1973) *The structures of the life-world*. Evanston: Northwestern University Press.

Scott, A. (1998) Homoeopathy as a feminist form of medicine. *Sociology of Health and Illness*, Vol. 20(2): 191–214.

Sen, A. (1999) *Development as freedom*. New York: Norton.

Shatkin, G. (2000) Obstacles to empowerment: Local politics and civil society in metropolitan Manila, the Philippines. *Urban Studies*, Vol. 37(12): 2357–2375.

Shawyer, R. J. (et al.) (1996) The role of clinical vignettes in rapid ethnographic research: A folk taxonomy of diarrhoea in Thailand. *Social Science and Medicine*, Vol. 42(1): 111–12.

Singer, M. (1985) Developing critical perspective in medical anthropology. *Medical Anthropology Quarterly*, Vol. 17(5): 128–129.

Singer, M. and Baer, H. (1995) *Critical medical anthropology*. New York: Baywood Publishing Company.

140 Bibliography

Smedley, P. L. and Kinniburgh, D. G. (2002) A review of the source, behaviour and distribution of arsenic in natural waters. *Applied Geochemistry*, Vol. 17(5): 517–568.

Smith, A. H. (et al.) (1994) "Epidemiological study designs to address potential high bladder cancer risks from arsenic in drinking water." In Willard R. Chappel, Charles O. Abernathy and C. Richard Cothern (eds.), *Arsenic: Exposure and health*, pp. 109–118. Northwood: Science and Technology Letters.

Smith, A. H.; Lingas, E.; and Rahman, M. (2000) Contamination of drinking-water by arsenic in Bangladesh: A public health emergency. *Bulletin of the World Health Organization*, Vol. 78(9): 1093–1103.

Sobhan, R. (1993) *Bangladesh: Problems of governance*. New Delhi: Konark Press.

Sperber, D. (1985) *On anthropological knowledge: Three essays*. Cambridge: Cambridge University Press.

Stanton, B. and Clemens, J. (1989) User fees for healthcare in developing countries: A case study of Bangladesh. *Social Science and Medicine*, Vol. 29(10): 1199–1205.

Stone, L. (1976) Concepts of illness and curing in a central Nepal village. *Contributions to Nepalese Studies*, Vol. 3: 55–80.

Stone, L. (1983) Hierarchy and food in Nepalese healing rituals. *Social Science and Medicine*, Vol. 17(14): 971–978.

Stoner, B. P. (1986) Understanding medical systems: Traditional, modern, and syncretic health care alternatives in medically pluralistic societies. *Medical Anthropology Newsletter*, Vol. 17(2): 44–48.

Tan, T. Y. and Kudaisya, G. (2000) *The aftermath of partition in South Asia*. London: Routledge.

Tennekoon, S. 1988. Rituals of development: The accelerated Mahaväli development program of Sri Lanka. *American Ethnologist*, Vol. 15(2): 294–310.

Tondel, M. (et al.) (1999) The relationship of arsenic levels in drinking water and the prevalence rate of skin lesions in Bangladesh. *Environmental Health Perspectives*, Vol. 107(9): 727–729.

Tsuda, T. (1998) Ethnicity and the anthropologist: Negotiating identities in the field. *Anthropological Quarterly*, Vol. 71(3): 107–124.

Turner, B. S. (1995) *Medical power and social knowledge*. London: Sage Publications.

Turner, B. S. (2000) "The history of the changing concepts of health and illness: Outline of a general model of illness categories." In Gary L. Albrecht, Ray Fitzpatrick and Susan C. Scrimshaw (eds.), *The handbook of social studies in health and medicine*, pp. 9–23. London: Sage Publications.

Turner, V. W. (1968) *The drums of affliction: A study of religious processes among the Ndembu of Zambia*. London: Oxford University Press.

Ugalde, A. (1985) Ideological dimensions of community participation in Latin American health programs. *Social Science and Medicine*, Vol. 21(1): 41–53.

UNICEF. (2006) *The state of the world's children 2007: Women and children the double dividend of gender equality*. New York: UNICEF.

Vithoulkas, G. (1986) *The science of homoeopathy*. Wellingborough: Thorsons Publishers.

Walker, C. (2000) An educational intervention of hypertension management in older African Americans. *Ethnicity and Diseases*, Vol. 10: 165–174.

Waxler-Morrison, Nancy E. (1988) Plural medicine in Sri Lanka: Do Ayurvedic and Western medical practices differ? *Social Science and Medicine*, Vol. 27(5): 531–544.

Weeks, E. C. (2000) The practice of deliberative democracy: Results from four large scale trials. *Public Administration Review*, Vol. 60(4): 360–372.

Weidman, H. H. (1986) "On ambivalence and the field." In Peggy Golde (ed.), *Women in the field: Anthropological experiences*, pp. 239–263. Berkeley: University of California Press.

Weinberg, D. (2009) "Social constructionism." In Bryan S. Turner (ed.), *The new Blackwell companion to social theory*, pp. 281–299. Chichester: Wiley-Blackwell.

Weisberg, D. H. (1984) The practice of Dr Paep: Continuity and change in indigenous healing in Northern Thailand. *Social Science and Medicine*, Vol. 18(2): 117–128.

White, S. (1999) NGOs, civil society, and the state in Bangladesh: The politics of representing the poor. *Development and Change*, Vol. 30: 307–326.

Whiteford, M. B. (1999) Homoeopathic medicine in the city of Oaxaca, Mexico: Patients' perspectives and observations. *Medical Anthropology Quarterly*, New Series, Vol. 13(1): 69–78.

WHO. (1979) *Formulating strategies for health for all by the year 2000: Guiding principles and essential issues*. Geneva: World Health Organization.

WHO. (2000) *Bangladesh national nutrition project*. Health, nutrition and population sector unit: South Asia region. Geneva: World Health Organization.

WHO. (2006a) *The world health report 2006: Working together for health*. Geneva: World Health Organization.

WHO. (2006b) *Guidelines for drinking-water quality*. Geneva: World Health Organization.

Wilce, J. M. (1995) "I can't tell you all my troubles": Conflict, resistance, and metacommunication in Bangladeshi illness interactions. *American Ethnologist*, Vol. 22(4): 927–952.

Wilce, J. M. (1997) Discourse, power and the diagnosis of weakness: Encountering practitioners in Bangladesh. *Medical Anthropology Quarterly*, Vol. 11(3): 352–374.

Wolffers, I. (1989) Traditional practitioners' behavioural adaptations to changing patients' demands in Sri Lanka. *Social Science and Medicine*, Vol. 29: 1111–1119.

World Bank (2003) *Making services work for poor people. World development report 2004*. Washington, DC: World Bank and Oxford University Press.

World Bank. (2007) Implementation completion and results report on a credit in the amount of SDR 24.2 Million (US $ 44.4 million equivalent) to Bangladesh for arsenic mitigation water supply. The World Bank, South Asia Region: Environment and Water Resources Unit.

Wooding, C. J. (1979) Traditional healing and medicine in Winti: A sociological interpretation. *Issue: A Journal of Opinion*, Vol. 9(3): 35–40.

Yan, Y. Y. (2000) The influence of weather on human mortality in Hong Kong. *Social Science and Medicine*, Vol. 50: 419–427.

Young, A. (1982) The anthropologies of illness and sickness. *Annual Review of Anthropology*, Vol. 11: 257–285.

Young, A. (1983) The relevance of traditional medical cultures to modern primary health care. *Social Science and Medicine*, Vol. 17: 1205–1211.

Young, T. J. (2004) Illness behaviour: A selective review and synthesis. *Sociology of Health and Illness*, Vol. 26(1): 1–31.

Yu, Ming-Ho. (2001) *Environmental toxicology: Impacts of environmental toxicants on living systems*. London: Lewis Publishers.

Yunus, M. (1997) "The Grameen Bank story: Rural credit in Bangladesh." In Anirudh Krishna, Norman Uphoff and Milton J. Esman (eds.), *Reasons for hope: Instructive experiences in rural development*, pp. 9–24. West Hartford: Kumarian Press.

Yunus, M. (1998) *Banker to the poor: The autobiography of Muhammad Yunus, founder of the Grameen Bank*. London: Aurum Press.

Yunus, M. (1999) *Banker to the poor: Micro-lending and the battle against world poverty*. New York: Public Affairs.
Zaidi, A. S. (1999) *The new development paradigm: Papers on institutions, NGOs, gender and local government*. Oxford: Oxford University Press.
Zaman, S. (2004) Poverty and violence, frustration and inventiveness: Hospital ward life in Bangladesh. *Social Science and Medicine*, Vol. 59: 2025–2036.
Zvosec, D. L. (1996) "Perceptions and experiences of tuberculosis in Nepal: A biobehavioural perspective." Unpublished doctoral dissertation. University of Hawaii.
Zysk, K. G. (1991) *Asceticism and healing in ancient India: Medicine in the Buddhist monastery*. Delhi: Oxford University Press.

Index

abdominal 32
abhawa 54–6
abhorred 63
ability 45–6, 69
abolish 64–5, 92–3
abolishment 52
abolition 65
abundant 20
accessibility 26, 39, 74, 78, 87, 93
accountability iv, viii, 22, 36, 130–1
acculturation 26
actors 2, 4, 7, 10, 12–13, 16–17, 19, 25–6, 90, 92, 95, 121, 127
acute 32, 85, 108
adaptations 132, 141
Adib 53, 129
Adivasi iv
adultery 54
advancement xvi, 135
advantageous 26
advent 125
adverse 54, 117
advice 41, 50, 91, 132
affluent 35, 39
affordability 78, 79, 86
afterlife 52–3
agency xvii, 4, 7, 10, 19, 22, 64, 101, 121–2, 124
agenda 8, 19, 21–2, 37, 102, 109, 126
agents 8, 34, 37, 51, 95, 103
agricultural 7, 9, 20, 30–1, 36–7, 44–5, 47, 71, 36, 132, 134
ailments 58, 60, 90, 122
allah 44, 52–4, 62–5, 71, 73–4, 77, 102, 122–3
allergic 48, 85, 93
allopathic 8, 10, 12, 25, 39–40, 48–9, 71, 73–9, 81–3, 85–7, 90–1, 123, 125
alluvial 30–1, 130

alternatives 136, 140
ambiguity 90, 116
ambivalence 141
ambulatory 13, 38
amlodipine 66
amputated 58, 34, 65
amulets 13, 40–1, 72, 123
anatomical 12, 40, 46
anemia 89
anga 47
antagonism 36, 116, 117
anthropological i, 2, 4–6, 12–13, 17, 43, 56, 75, 133–4, 138, 140
antibiotics 8, 24, 68, 79–84, 86–7, 139
anticolonial 41
antiglobalisation 132
antipyretic 93
antiseptic 69
apolitical 22, 95, 104, 115
apprenticeship 76, 80, 84
arsenate 28
arsenicosis i, xi, xiv, 1–19, 23, 25–7, 29, 32–4, 40–68, 76, 81–2, 88–95, 97, 99, 102–3, 113–14, 119–27
arsenite 28
arsenopyrite 30, 31
arteries 33, 60
arthritis 85
asthma 55–6, 85
atherosclerosis 33
Ayurveda 24, 34–5, 36, 38, 47, 140
azan 50, 66

bacteria 2, 93
bahir 60
baki 78
BAMWSP xii–xiii, xvi, 5, 10, 12, 19, 23, 56, 66, 95–6, 98–9, 101–3, 106, 109, 119, 126

144 *Index*

barefoot 39
barir 68–9, 71
Bengali iv, vi, viii, 4, 13, 66, 120, 122
bigrayo 52
biomedicine 5, 10, 12, 23–6, 28, 33, 35–6, 38, 65, 67, 72, 74, 77, 79, 81, 83–4, 86, 89–90, 92, 121–3, 136
biopolitics 138
bish 46, 58–60, 72, 122
Blackfoot xvi, 29
bomohs 134
BRAC xvi, 37, 129–31, 134
bronchitis 54–5
bureaucratic 10, 19, 22, 98–9, 133

cancer 1, 4, 29, 32–4, 40, 77, 85, 88–9, 131, 133–4, 136, 140
carcinogenic 32, 33, 121
carcinogenic 33
cardiovascular 32–3, 54
chacha 75
chelation 34
chemotherapies 68
chikitisa 71
chikitsa 68–71
chikitshok xvi, 39
chronic 14, 32–4, 37, 53–4, 60, 62–3, 85–7, 89, 122, 131–2, 137
chulkani 48, 57, 69
clinical 12–14, 32–3, 40, 43, 51, 89–90, 121, 123, 139
colonial 11, 34–5, 130, 138
communicable 76
consciousness 16
constellations 19
constructionism 11, 14–18, 27, 125, 141
contamination i, 3–4, 12, 28–32, 40, 96–7, 99–100, 108–9, 113, 127, 130, 134–5, 138
corruption 22–3, 36, 129
culture xi, 41–2, 48–9, 53, 95, 121–7, 132, 136–8
curative 37, 78, 83

daktar 84, 86, 125
dawa 49
delta 29–30, 32, 129–31, 134–5
democracy iii, vi, 130–1, 140
democratization ii, vi
depoliticization 133
dermatological 32–3
desertification 41
destiny 52–3, 84
development i, iii, vi, viii, xi, xiv, 2, 4–8, 10–14, 16–22, 27, 33, 35, 37, 64, 94–7, 99–103, 106, 108, 111–13, 119–21, 124–7, 129, 131–42
diabetes 33, 52, 137
diagnosis 9–10, 40, 67, 84, 88–9, 103, 130, 137, 141
diarrhea 2, 32, 54, 56, 139
dimethyl 28
discharge 57, 61, 63, 69–70, 80, 83
discourse v, 11, 18–19, 22, 27, 125, 127, 134
divine 93, 122–3
dokan 79
donors 22, 96, 98–9, 134
DPHE xvi, 10, 23, 57, 97–8, 102, 104, 107
dugwells 102, 104, 124
dushito 76
dysentery 85

ecological 5, 9, 12–14, 32, 41–2, 51, 56, 58, 65, 102, 122, 125–6
ecosystems 134
eczema 57, 60, 66, 70, 76
electrocardiogram 33, 87
endrin 80, 93
environmental 19–21, 41, 54, 56, 95, 102, 113, 122, 132, 141
epidemic vii, 2, 4, 96, 99, 133–4
ethnocentrically 112
ethnomedical 24
ethnomedicine 24
ethnotaxonomy 58, 62
etiology 4, 9, 12, 16, 18, 26, 42–3, 51–2, 56, 58, 90, 92, 133
eurocentric 18
experts 2, 10, 12–13, 18, 99, 112, 119–20, 124, 132

fakibaaz 104
Falgun 62, 66
farakka 32, 41
fate 52–4, 56, 63–5, 73, 92, 113, 122
fellowship xiv
fertilizer 30–1, 46, 61
feverish 45
fieldwork xiv, 6, 8, 10–11, 43–4, 56, 62, 70–2, 75, 79, 86, 94–5, 101, 106, 111, 116, 119, 121, 134
flucloxociline 82
folk 24, 54, 56, 137, 139
foodways 47
fungal 70, 93

Ganges 41, 129, 131, 134
gangrene 32–4, 40, 65, 88–9, 121
gasra 59, 69, 71–2, 93

gastrointestinal 2, 32–3, 48, 54, 85, 89
gender 21, 106, 124, 140, 142
geochemical 30–2
geographical 7, 26, 36, 91–2, 109, 124
geohydrological 100
geological xvi, 30, 118, 130
geopolitical 9
germ 51, 84, 86
ghaa xi, xiii, 12–13, 26, 42, 45, 50, 54, 56–65, 67–95, 102–3, 108, 111–13, 121–6
ghastly 1
GlaxoSmithKline xiv, xvi
globalization v, 7, 21, 25, 126
gojob 64, 74, 122
gormi 48
groom 47–8
gosol 47, 49
gota 57, 88
governance vi, 22–3, 27, 36, 94, 104, 124, 127, 129–30, 133–4, 140
Grameen 134–5, 139, 141
groundwater i, 1–3, 29–32, 40, 81, 88, 97, 110, 130, 132, 135, 137–8

hadith 71, 74, 93
hakims 35–6, 136
halud 69–71
hatpakha 48, 66
headmaster xiv, 64, 103, 105–6, 108–9, 114–17, 119
healer xiv, 10, 12–13, 25–6, 34, 40–1, 67, 69, 72, 77, 90, 92–3, 123, 127, 136
healing 10, 23, 71, 74–5, 90, 123
hearth 8
hegemonic 5, 18, 137
hematology 89
hemoglobin 89
hepatology 89
hepatopathy 33
herbalists 40
herbs 34, 69, 71, 75
Himalayas 30, 129–30
histamine 93
historical 9, 11, 14, 28, 34, 36, 130
holistic i, 4, 7, 11, 14, 27, 46, 84, 125
holud 69–70
homeopathic 8, 10, 49, 66, 84–7
homeopathy 25, 38, 84, 86–7, 133
hospitals 38–9, 129
hostile 108, 117
hostility xv, 21, 107, 117
hujur 10, 13, 40–1, 52–3, 58–9, 65–6, 71–5, 90, 92–3, 123
hydrology 30–1, 134
hyperkeratosis 1, 33, 40, 88–9, 121

ideologies vi, 19, 21, 94–5
imam 9, 41, 71, 127
imperialism 35, 130, 132
inauspicious 50, 52, 118
indigenous 20, 24, 35–6, 41, 68, 120, 137, 141
inflammatory 93
ingestion 28–9, 32, 48, 97, 99
injections 24, 75
inorganic 28, 131
institutions 18, 21, 23, 100–1, 142
intestinal 43, 60, 139
intoxicate 61
investigations 89–90, 97, 123
ischemic 33, 131
itchiness 69

jotil 54, 85–6

karma 53
kashi 54
keratosis 29, 33–4, 40, 89, 121
kobiraj 10, 25, 39, 48, 55, 57–9, 66, 70–2, 75–9, 84, 90, 92, 123, 125
kopal 51–4, 63–4, 122
kothin 58–9, 86, 122

laboratory 88, 97, 119
labourers 7, 47
Laderman 47, 54, 136
landless 7, 37
latrines 37
layperson 137
leaders 9, 124, 127
leadership 41, 109
leaflets 57, 93, 126
leafy 34
legacy 35
legitimacy 27
legitimize 22
leisure iii
lentils 34
leprosy 130
lesions 3, 32–3, 88, 122, 140
Leslie 42, 132, 134, 136, 138
Lesotho 20, 133
lessons 131, 134
Lewis 21, 133, 141
liberalization iii
liberation 36
Libra 73, 76–7, 93
library x, 9
lifegiver 102
lifegiving 92
lifesaving 94–5, 124

Index   145

146 *Index*

lifetime 100
lifeworld 15
limitations 17–18, 28, 39, 41
Lindenbaum 17, 135–6
Lingas 1, 3–4, 140
linguistic 44
liquids 48
livelihood 46
locally 13, 19, 57, 66, 71, 75, 79, 93, 113
location 109
logic 49, 52, 121–2, 127
lokkhon 85
Luckmann 11, 14–18, 125, 130, 139
lungs 1
Lupton 16, 47, 136
lymphatic 33

Maagh 62, 66
madrasah ii, 71, 93
magrib 50, 66, 72
Mahavāli 20, 140
mantra 66, 93
melanosis 33, 40, 88–9, 121
microcredit 20–1, 37, 134, 139
mitigation i, xi, 2, 4–6, 9, 12–13, 17–18, 21–2, 27, 65, 93–121, 123–6, 141
mobilization v, 25, 98, 104, 110–12, 114, 119, 130
moila 50–1
molom 61, 66
monsoon 37, 55, 59, 62–3, 82, 103–4, 107
murubbi 105

nalanda 34
nanawa 47
nandy 18, 137
Narmada 20, 136, 139
narratives 5–6, 8, 51, 60, 68, 136
nations xvi–xvii, 132
nationwide 66, 100
natives 8
naturalistic 26, 51, 56
navigation 41
Nederveen 18, 125, 137
negatively 46, 106, 114
negotiation 15
neighbors 9, 63
neonatal 37, 134
Nepalese 49, 53, 60, 140
nephropathy 33
nerves 33
neuropathy 33
Nichter 23–5, 47, 49, 82, 113, 126, 135, 137–9

Nickson 30, 138
Nigeria 20, 135
noncarcinogenic 32
nonitchy 57
nustad 18, 138
Nutini 52, 132
nutrition 33, 37, 39, 141
nutritious 49
nutrition 132–3
neoliberalism ii, vi, 135
neoliberal iii, viii, 21
nutritional 32–3
nationalism ii, v–vi, 35–6, 136, 138
neem 69–71
Nepal iii–iv, vi, 29, 43, 52, 68, 129, 138, 140, 142
NGOs i, iv, viii, 1, 6–7, 9–10, 19, 21–2, 37, 64, 94–5, 97–9, 101, 104, 107, 126, 132, 134–5, 141–2
NAMIC xvi, 7, 97, 100–1, 137

objectification 15
objectives 8, 10–12, 19–21, 95–6, 101, 109, 119
obligated 21, 118
observable 37, 88
observations 24, 141
obstacle 20, 112, 139
obstetric 135
occupation 7, 55, 71
occurrence 28, 30, 58–9, 102, 108
offended 114, 116
officer xvi, 10, 87–8, 95
officials xiv, 8, 10–11, 22–3, 57, 95, 102–4, 106–7, 110, 112, 114–15, 124
Ohnuki 49, 51, 138
ointment 34, 66, 77, 89, 125
ominous 50
oppression 18
ordinances 74
organic 28
organizations xiv, 4–5, 7, 19, 21–2, 67, 94–5, 97–8, 100, 108, 116
organochlorine 31
organs 33–4, 48, 50, 60–2, 76, 88, 93, 121
oriental iv, 134
orientalism iv
orientation 106
orthodox 125
oscillating 85, 134
oshud 59, 69, 71–2, 79, 93
oshukh 52–3
oshuvo 50–1
osila 53, 73–4

osustho 43
outbreak i, 2, 65
outcome 6, 20–1, 39, 86, 95, 99, 101
outpatient 13
overdosages 82
overhead 110, 117
ownership 106, 110, 114, 116, 124
oxen 44, 46
oxidation 30
oxide 30–1
oxidization 32
oxyhydroxides 30

paap 64
pachra 48, 57
pancreas 33
pani-pora 74
patriarchal 18, 21, 106
penicillin 82, 93
pesticides 31, 46, 58, 61, 66
pharmacology 39, 68
pharmacy 8, 10, 40, 66, 70, 79–81, 84, 91
pluralism 11, 14, 23–5, 27, 92, 125, 130–1, 134–5, 137–8
pluralistic 11, 25, 35, 40, 43, 125, 132, 140
pneumonia 55
pollution 20, 54, 132, 139
potash 70, 93
potency 58, 60, 122
prescriptions 40, 91
PSF 101, 120, 124
psychiatry 89, 136
pyrite 30

quackery 39
Quah 26, 139
quarreled 117–18
quarrelling 117
quaternary 30
quest viii, 16, 135

radicalism vi
rashi 73, 76–7, 79, 93
rationale 96, 100
rationality 17, 100, 122, 133
Ravenscroft 2, 28–9, 32, 34, 130, 139
reality 15–17, 20, 25, 57, 101, 104, 106, 114–15, 124, 130, 136, 139
recipients 19, 21, 103
reciprocity 15
reconceptualized 14, 25, 125–6
recurrence 62–3, 69
referral 13, 25, 38, 87
reflexivity 17

reform iii, v–vi, 36, 132
regionalism ii
rehabilitation iv
relationships 7, 15, 19, 21, 101, 117, 120, 130
relatives 16–17, 25–6, 80, 126
relativism 17
relief 25, 77, 82–3, 89
religiously 42
remedy 47, 49, 54, 68, 74
representation vii, 24, 105–6, 114, 126
resettlement iv, vi, 20, 138
resilient 60
resistance iii, 34, 61, 83, 141
respiratory 54–5
responsibility 21–2, 97–100, 106–7, 110–11, 117–19
resultant i, 6, 14, 27, 40, 102, 127
resuscitation 68
retail 7, 40
rhetoric 106, 101, 139
rhetorically 104, 106
rheumatism 54
ringworm 57, 60, 66, 76, 81
rogi 76
rokto 61, 76
rosh 57, 69
Rousham 43, 139
routine 7, 9, 13, 50, 54, 68–9, 73, 86, 135
rudimentary 5, 67, 69–71

Safi 83, 93
sastho 43
sebika 37, 129
sediments 30–1, 118
shakti 45
shalya 34
shamanism 93, 129, 135
shamans 51, 138
shoitan 50
shokti 45
shorbot 48–9, 66
shorir 44, 48, 57, 60
shuvo 50–1
snakebites 40, 58–62, 65, 72, 75–6, 79, 89, 92, 102, 113, 122–3
sorcerers 51
sorcery 76
sordi 45, 48, 54
spiritual 25, 72, 79
subscribe 64, 111, 117
supernatural 23, 40, 51, 93
superstition 35, 102
sustainability 13, 114, 132, 135

sustho 43
swadeshi 36, 41
symptoms i, 1, 3–4, 10, 13, 16–17, 25–6, 33, 40, 45–6, 48, 56–8, 62–3, 80, 82, 84–5, 88, 90, 96, 99, 121
syncretic 5, 24–5, 27, 41, 76, 84, 125, 140

tabiz 72–3, 123
tablet 91
taboo 132
tafsir 93
tainted 1, 101
Taiwan 29, 33, 89, 131, 136
taka 70–1, 78, 91, 93–4, 106, 110, 115, 119
Talbot vii, 2, 130
tales 50
Tamang 68, 135
taxonomy 4, 48, 54, 56, 122, 139
technically 104, 110, 118, 124
technological 41, 106, 111–12, 117, 124
tension 35, 85, 89, 91, 107, 115, 125
terminologies 42–3, 49, 56, 68, 125
thanda 47–8
therapeutic 5, 24–5, 35, 67–8, 79, 83, 90, 125
therapy 25–7, 34, 84, 92, 126, 131, 135, 137–8
Tierney 49, 51, 138
toxicants 141
toxicity 3, 32, 74, 77, 88–9, 100–1
tragedy 1, 4, 132
transgressions 64–5, 74, 77, 92–3, 102, 122–3
treatment xii, 5, 9–10, 15, 24, 26, 34–5, 37, 39, 49, 51, 54, 61, 64, 67–8, 75–9, 81, 84–7, 89, 91, 96, 99, 108–12, 115–24, 126, 132, 134, 137, 139
tricycle 65
trishaw 9, 45–6, 76, 88
tuberculosis 55, 142
tubewells 2–3, 7, 31, 64, 66, 88, 97–101, 103–4, 107, 111, 113, 118–20, 124
tula 73, 76–7, 79, 93
turmeric 69, 73
tyranny 133

ubiquitous 28
UHC 38
UHFWC xvi, 38
unaffected 122
Unani 8, 35–6, 38, 83, 93, 136
unclean 47
underdeveloped 18, 20, 100
undrinkable 103, 124
unemployment 20
unfavorable 55, 59
unforeseen 19, 21
unfortunate 3, 65, 108
UNICEF xiv, xvii, 1–3, 19, 21, 37, 139–40
unintended 5, 18–20, 94–5, 101, 108, 116, 124
unsafe 97, 100
Upazilla xvi, 6–8, 10, 13, 78, 84, 102
urinary 33
urine 48
usaid xvii, 21, 39
USEPA xvii, 4, 32
users 5, 27, 101, 103, 110–11, 114, 117

vagyo 51–3
vaids 35–6
vaidyas 34
verandah 9, 59, 72
vernacularized 4, 12, 17, 42, 56, 121
voddorlok 35

waterborne 2–3, 20, 102–3
witchcraft 132
witches 51
wives 50
Wolffers 24, 141
wolfgang 132
women ii, iv, 8, 16, 20–1, 33, 37, 48, 50–1, 54–5, 106, 109, 114, 124, 131–3, 135–6
wooding 77, 141
words 102
workers iii, 7, 38, 71, 81, 96, 99, 111
workforce 38
worlds 130
worldviews 16, 121–2
worsened 62–3
wrongly 107, 113, 115

Xinjiang 29

yielded 36, 68
yoga 36
yogurt 48
york x, 1, 130–4, 136–40, 142
youth vi, 82
Yunus 37, 141–2

Zaidi 104, 142
Zaire 25, 135
Zaman 38, 43, 91, 142
Zambia 25, 140
Zvosec 43, 52–3, 142
Zysk 34, 142